THE AGE OF THE ECONOMIC REVOLUTION 1876 – 1900

The
AGE
of the
ECONOMIC
REVOLUTION

1876
1900

CARL N. DEGLER
Vassar College

David M. Potter, Carl N. Degler, Editors
American History Series

John Sherman, University of Washington
Cartographic Consultant

Scott, Foresman and Company

To David M. Potter

Cover photo: Historical Society of Montana

Library of Congress Catalog Card No. 67-14492
Copyright © 1967 by Scott, Foresman and Company, Glenview, Illinois 60025
All rights reserved. Printed in the United States of America.

Regional offices of Scott, Foresman and Company are located in
Atlanta, Dallas, Glenview, Palo Alto, and Oakland, N.J.

PREFACE

This book, which deals with the closing decades of the nineteenth century, is the first title to be published in a series of eight (to be offered alternatively in two large volumes) that will encompass the history of the United States from the first explorations and settlements to the present. Together the series will constitute in general coverage and time span the kind of work that students usually employ as a textbook for a college survey course in American history. In that sense this volume is a part of a larger textbook, which accounts for the absence from these pages of certain aspects of foreign policy in the late 1890's; they will appear in the subsequent volume. Both this book and the series as a whole, however, are intended to be different from the material covered in the usual survey text.

Customarily, a textbook is largely filled with a chronological account of the "essential" facts of the past. Facts and chronology are, it is true, the building stones of historical knowledge, and familiarity with both is essential, but they do not provide the structure of the past by themselves. Rather, it is the framework of an era that the student must grasp if he is to retain and make sense out of the myriad facts that any book — text or other — throws in his path. By framework, however, I am not suggesting a skeleton or outline but the unity or essential thrust of the period — in short, its meaning. *The Age of the Economic Revolution* seeks to provide that framework by relating the many important events of the era to larger themes. As the title suggests, industrialization and the ways in which it transformed American society and thought are the central themes. Each chapter, in effect, addresses itself to the question: "How did the coming of the factory and the city alter the United States?"

Emphasis falls throughout upon explanation of the past. Why did events turn out as they did? What significance did these developments have for subsequent American history? What importance do they have for the present? How does the American experience compare with that of other countries in similar circumstances? How and why did American attitudes and values alter between 1876 and 1900?

The organization and some of the less important facts that are to be found in more conventional textbooks are absent from these pages. It is the conviction of the author and the editors of the series that understanding the relationship among events is more important than just memorizing customarily-agreed-upon facts. Therefore, some facts have been omitted simply because they do not contribute to an understanding of the structure of the period. Those who turn to the chapter on cultural patterns, for example, will find that it does not contain the usual large number of titles of books and names of authors. Instead, only a handful of writers, philosophers, and artists have been discussed, but each has been covered in some depth. Even these individuals have been included, not just for themselves, but because consideration of their works or lives throws light on the ways in which industrialization changed the values and aspirations of Americans. On the other hand, there are subjects included here that do not ordinarily appear in textbooks. The rise of Roman Catholicism and Judaism, for instance, is treated at some length, because the rapid growth of and changes in these two religious groups are the result of one response to the Economic Revolution: increased immigration.

This book has been written for American college students; that is, readers who have some acquaintance with the history of the United States. While the usual effort has been made to clarify and define obscure or unfamiliar terms and persons, a certain basic familiarity with the subject has been taken for granted. Thus in the chapter on politics the customary chronological survey of presidential administrations has been abandoned in favor of presenting the large political patterns and problems of those years. These patterns and issues have been related to the theme of industrialization.

No student who has passed successfully through an American high school need worry about his ability to comprehend what appears within these covers, but it is hoped that his understanding of the direction and the causes behind the movements of American history will be enhanced by reading this book.

Although I take full responsibility for any errors and shortcomings that remain, I want to acknowledge gratefully the help I have received in trying to eliminate as many as possible. My greatest debt is owed, undoubtedly, to David M. Potter, whose vision of what this volume might be has alternately inspired and discouraged me. His high standards of historical interpretation and writing and his indefatigable labors as editor, colleague, and enlightened human being have helped to shape this book more than his modesty permits him to recognize. Whatever originality of conception it now contains is as much his doing as mine. I am indebted as well to the close and perceptive reading given the manuscript by my colleagues in this series, Thomas C. Cochran and Richard Abrams, and by William I. Hair and Joseph Boskin, all of whom saved me from many errors of ignorance or misunderstanding. My gratitude is extended to John Sherman for his sage advice in developing the cartographic materials. I also wish to thank my wife, Catherine Grady Degler, and William A. Frohlich and Randy Rosner at Scott, Foresman for their willingness to struggle with my prose to ensure its clarity and conciseness. Elizabeth Churchill and Mildred Tubby have my appreciation for their expert typing of the manuscript in the course of its revisions. In addition, I am indebted to Paul G. Degler and Suzanne C. Degler for their close checking of the bibliographies, which saved their careless father from many embarrassing errors.

Carl N. Degler

CONTENTS

CHAPTER ONE

THE GREAT DIVIDE, 1876—1890

*T*HE UNITED STATES in 1876 celebrated its first century of independence. In the course of that period the American people had faced numerous issues and problems. Some of them, such as the struggle over neutral rights in the 1790's and the War of 1812, were disposed of relatively quickly, if only because they arose from temporary foreign problems. Others, like the steady peopling of a continent, continued to occupy a large part of the nation's energies throughout the century and beyond. One issue — slavery — mounted in intensity until it virtually crowded out all others and split the nation asunder. From at least 1850 until the end of Reconstruction, slavery and its corollary, the future of the Negro, dominated the politics and much of the thought of the American people. After the withdrawal of the last federal troops from the South in 1877, however, the question of the Negro, though still unresolved, swiftly passed from the national stage. Other and fresh concerns began to take its place. The centennial year, 1876, therefore marks a dividing line in the history of the United States and a suitable beginning for this book.

Appropriately, the nation celebrated its Centennial in 1876 with a mammoth exposition in the city of Philadelphia, where independence had first been declared. In the light of subsequent developments, the Philadelphia Exposition was doubly fitting, for on display were numerous American-made industrial machines, engines, and inventions, including an operating model of Alexander Graham Bell's new telephone. By 1876, the United States was already in a new phase of its history, of which the symbols would be machines and factories, and the hallmark a high rate of industrial production.

Growth of an Industrial Society

A New Industrial People. The Economic Revolution of the last half of the nineteenth century was more than a proliferation of factories and machines; it was the transformation of a society. Within a span of years no longer than a newborn infant takes to become an adult, a nation of small property owners (the majority of whom were self-employed farmers) became a nation in which most men had little or no connection with the land, were largely without property, and worked for other men. The pattern of their lives was now determined not by the rising and setting of the sun and the slow, steady cycle of the seasons, but by the sharp blast of the factory whistle and the relentless tempo of the machine. Many men no longer lived among the unchanging hills and valleys but within the crowded and ever changing confines of the city. (Actually a majority of Americans did not live in cities until 1920; yet by the end of the nineteenth century the city and the factory dominated the affairs of the nation.) Moreover, even those left behind on the land felt the transforming effects, for by the close of the nineteenth century the farm would be

Photo: The integral relationship between the railroads and steel mills enabled the mills, such as this one in Homestead, Pennsylvania, to grow to enormous size. Railroads carried raw material to the mills, and took away finished products used, among other things, in building new railroads.

Despite the innovations of the Economic Revolution, some nineteenth-century steel foundries such as this one in Pittsburgh, required large numbers of men to work with little help from machines. In such untidy and ill-lit structures men usually labored most of each day of every week.

mechanized and the farmer would be a businessman, as tightly enmeshed in the web of the market as a Pittsburgh steelworker or a Boston banker. What that Economic Revolution was, how it came about, and how it affected the lives and thought of people in the United States are the principal themes of this book.

Since the story of this revolution is as complex as it is fascinating, this introductory chapter will set forth its main outlines and call attention to some of the broader implications which cannot be discussed in the rest of the book. Subsequent chapters will fill out the story and show how the Economic Revolution affected politics, society, and thought.

America's Place in the Industrialization of the Modern World. This great transformation was not unique to America. In the eighteenth century, England had taken the same road; during the nineteenth century, Japan in Asia, and Germany and other countries in Europe followed the United States. In the twentieth century, Russia, the backward giant of Europe, also made the leap from underdevelopment to industrial maturity. Today, still other nations in Latin America, Africa, and Asia are girding themselves for a similar effort. In general, each of the industrialized nations shared a common experience, though some, like England and Russia, probably found the social and human costs higher than the United States did. In the impact of the transformation, however, each country's experience was unique.

Perhaps the distinguishing features of the American Economic Revolution were its astonishing success and the rapidity with which it was accomplished; by the 1890's, the United States had become the greatest industrial power in the world. It is always hazardous to attempt to pinpoint the exact time span of any economic and social transition. Yet the pattern of events strongly suggests that the years between 1876 and 1890 were crucial in the transition of the United States from an underdeveloped nation to a mature industrial society. Industry and cities were in a far more advanced state in the 1890's than they were in the 1860's or 1870's. Politically, socially, and industrially the 1890's were actually a part of the twentieth century; the problems and the aspirations of Americans then were already those of people in the 1900's. For example, the issues that engaged the attention of Republican leaders like Theodore Roosevelt and Robert La Follette in the 1890's were much the same as those they would wrestle with in the early twentieth century. These concerns bore little resemblance to the issues that earlier Republicans, such as Abraham Lincoln and Ulysses Grant, had dealt with. Lincoln, after all, had no occasion to handle the problems of labor unions, industrial monopolies, or farm credit—the staple concerns of Democrats and Republicans alike in the 1890's and for many years thereafter.

The Triumph of Urban Industrialism. Let us look now at some of the reasons for regarding the transition of the United States to an industrial society as substantially complete by 1890. That year the annual value of manufactured goods surpassed that of agricultural commodities for the first time in American history, even though farming was still setting production records almost annually. By then 57 per cent of the nation's labor force worked outside of agriculture, whereas only 20 years earlier farmers had comprised more than half the working population. During the decade of the 1880's alone, the number of industrial workers jumped 50 per cent, while the capital invested in manufacturing rose 137 per cent. The total value of manufactures produced in that ten-year span increased 75 per cent as compared with a 60 per cent advance in the previous decade. The number of miles of railroad track laid in the 1880's was greater than for any other decade in American history. As many miles of track were laid in those ten years as from 1828, the beginning of railroading in this country, to 1870; in fact, in 1885 and 1886 alone, over 21,000 miles were added to the nation's trackage, or over two thirds the mileage that existed in the whole country in 1860. By 1890, the railroad net of the United States, though not yet complete, was more extensive than that of all of Europe, including Russia.

Not surprisingly, the 1880's also witnessed a rapid growth of cities—the locale of factories and the terminals of railroad lines. Cities, it is true, were not new in America; some, like New York, Boston, Philadelphia, and New Orleans, had been important and flourishing ports and even centers of manufacturing for decades. But the growth of most of the great cities of the interior awaited the expansion of manufacturing and railroads in the years after the Civil War. Between 1860 and the present, no decade has registered as high a rate of urban growth as the eighties. In that crucial period, 88 cities doubled their populations. Significantly, many instances of that rapid urban growth were to be found in the Middle West, where manufacturing was leaping forward. Chicago's population rose from half a million to more than a million; St. Paul and Minneapolis doubled in size between 1880 and 1890. Milwaukee, Detroit, Columbus, and Cleveland increased at least 60 per cent. In 1880, one out of every five Middle Westerners lived in cities of 4000 or more; by 1890, one out of three did.

The Indian: Casualty of the Economic Revolution. The 1880's witnessed not only the growth of factories and the building of cities, but the termination of issues that once had loomed large in the affairs of Americans. Ever since colonial days, Americans had fought the Indians for possession of the continent; in the 1880's, the long battle came to an end. Throughout that conflict between two cultures, misunderstanding, violence, and injustice on the part of white men were common. Regardless of the good or bad intentions that may have underlain the various Indian policies of the United States, all of them seemed to have had the same result: steadily the Indians were pushed into the least desirable parts of the country. By the time of the Civil War, only the semiarid Great Plains and the dry, desolate Great Basin region west of the Rocky Mountains remained open without restriction to the Indians. But even there the Indians did not rest unmolested, for soon after the war the Economic Revolution enabled white men to exploit and settle that once-scorned region.

As we shall see in a subsequent chapter, the new technology of railroads, barbed wire, and steel plow, and the growth of urban markets permitted the first settlement of the "Great American Desert," as distinguished from its mere military occupation. In that sense, the Economic Revolution destroyed the last vestiges of the Indians' isolation and opened a new chapter in the relations between the aborigine and the white man. Miners, cattlemen, and farmers now invaded the last refuge of the Indian in the 1870's and 1880's. Sportsmen and buffalo skinners came too, and wantonly slaughtered the shaggy beasts that roamed in gigantic herds across the plains. Perhaps as many as three million bison were killed annually during the 1870's; by the middle 1880's the orgy had almost exterminated them. Since the buffalo provided the Indians of the plains with their food and clothing, the slaughtering of the great herds was as important indirectly in overcoming Indian resistance as the direct military actions by the United States Army. Gradually, always painfully, in an almost uninterrupted series of Indian skirmishes and wars during the 1870's, the Army herded the remaining Indians onto reservations. By the 1880's the struggle was over. The last significant encounter between Indian warriors and the Army took place in 1876 at the

Little Big Horn River in Montana, where General George A. Custer and over 250 men of the Seventh Cavalry were wiped out by the Sioux under Sitting Bull and Crazy Horse. During the 1880's, only the embittered Apache Chief Geronimo and a few of his braves still eluded the Army's efforts to place all Indians on reservations. In 1886, Geronimo surrendered.

The relentless warfare that was required to maintain the reservation policy in the 1870's and 1880's is one of the saddest episodes in the long and troubled history of race relations in the United States. The details of each Indian war may have been fresh, but the cruelty, treachery, and ruthlessness inflicted upon the Indians were constant factors. What was novel in the history of Indian relations was the emergence in the 1880's of a completely new attitude toward the red man. It seems that only after the Indians were thoroughly subdued could Americans shake off that mixture of fear and hatred that had always prevented their sympathetic understanding of these simple yet proud people.

In the 1880's, the American people began to treat the Indians as human beings for the first time. A landmark in the rise of the Indian rights movement was Helen Hunt Jackson's *A Century of Dishonor,* published in 1881. Because it was drawn from the records of the Indian Bureau itself, Mrs. Jack-

Buffalo Bill Cody, shown clasping the hands of two still proud chiefs, turned some Indians into harmless carnival performers, while other whites tried to make the red man conform to "American" ways by compelling him to cut his hair and abandon his native dress.

son's indictment of official government policy toward the Indians was tellingly effective. The book aroused wide popular support for better treatment of the Indians and encouraged the Indian rights organizations, which became increasingly vocal and influential during the 1880's. The agitation on behalf of the Indians culminated in 1887 when Congress passed the General Allotment (Dawes) Act; this sought to bring the Indians into the mainstream of American life by making them citizens and small land-owning farmers. The law provided that the reservation lands, then held collectively by the tribes, would be distributed among and owned by individual Indian heads of families. The aim was to end the segregation of the Indians, long fostered by the policy of maintaining reservations. Such an individualistic solution to the Indian problem was quite in keeping with the philosophy that underlay the Economic Revolution.

Time would show, however, that this approach to the Indians and their culture was anthropologically unsound and hence ultimately, if unintentionally, cruel. Unlike the Negro slaves, the Indians were simply unprepared culturally for participation in a white society. Negroes, even as slaves, had acquired much of the culture of white men; they knew how to farm, they could speak the language of the white man, they were accustomed to his ways and had adopted his values, even if their acculturation under slavery had not been perfect. The Indians, on the other hand, had never come into close cultural association with white men except in isolated instances; therefore, when forced to adopt the ways of white Americans under the policy enunciated by the Dawes Act, they lost both their lands to white men (some 90 million acres by 1930) and their own self-respect as a culture. In 1934, Congress reversed the policy introduced by the Dawes Act, thereby halting the breakup of the reservations, and protecting and encouraging, rather than destroying, what remained of Indian culture.

Subordination of the Issue of Negro Rights. The public concern for Negro rights, which had engaged the nation's attention for so long, also changed during these years, affording a striking example of how the Economic Revolution reshaped issues. Senate Republican leaders, in 1890, refused to permit a vote on a House-passed bill to protect Negro voting in the South, principally because they wanted the votes of southern senators to help pass the McKinley Tariff. In choosing to work for the tariff instead of the Negro voting bill, the Republicans, once the champions of the Negro, clearly demonstrated the powerful influence of the Economic Revolution upon politics and the eclipse of other issues that had once commanded the attention of their party and the nation.

The tariff, to be sure, was an old chestnut in political life, but unlike Negro rights it was relevant to economic growth. As industry spread throughout the country, traditional sectional attitudes toward the tariff changed. A number of southern senators, for example, urged higher rates in the tariff of 1894 now that the South was beginning to manufacture goods. Unlike Indian and

Negro rights, however, the tariff was not a dead political issue; then and later, it was either hotly denounced as an abuse of industrial power and privilege or defended as essential for economic growth. In either case, it remained a live political question because it was relevant to the Economic Revolution.

New Era, New Concerns

The Coming of Railroad Monopoly. This revolution created new problems at the same time that it superseded old ones. The extensive railroad lines and the large business enterprises of the period, for all their economic advantages, constituted aggregates of power that could not be controlled in the traditional manner. Competition among producers, which under a capitalist system had been the principal device for protecting consumers against high prices, poor quality, and inferior services, was not effective when the size of the firms became so great that no genuine economic rivalry existed. In the case of the railroads, furthermore, competition could not be used for the control of rates, since in most instances the building of parallel or otherwise competing lines would have been too expensive to be practical.

Faced with the new problem posed by industrial and railroad monopoly, Congress and the political parties in the course of the 1880's debated various solutions. In 1888 the platforms of all the parties, minor as well as major, pledged some action to control the abuses of economic power. As will be seen in the next chapter, Congress, in 1887, attempted to handle the question of railroad power through the establishment of the Interstate Commerce Commission, and in 1890 it passed the Sherman Antitrust Act to maintain competition among industrial firms. Both of these measures proved inadequate, for not all men agreed on their need or their merits as solutions to the problem. Nonetheless, their enactment bespoke the rising concern of Americans with one class of problems that arose out of a developing industrial society.

Increased Immigration: The Welcome Diminishes. During the 1880's, the Economic Revolution also caused Americans to alter their view of immigration. In previous years, this nation had welcomed all immigrants, if only because they were indispensable in peopling an empty continent and supplying labor for an expanding economy. Even during the days of the Know-Nothings in the 1850's, objections had been centered not upon unrestricted immigration, but only upon the participation of the newcomers in politics. Nevertheless, as the Economic Revolution drew more and more people from all over the world, and the empty lands of the West began to fill up, Americans had second thoughts about the value of unlimited immigration. Workers, for instance, began to fear that excessive immigration might endanger their jobs or economic future. Others feared that traditional American values would be lost or diluted. The immigration of the 1880's, which reached peaks not duplicated at any other time in the century, made these apprehensions

One of the areas in the U.S. to which impoverished, illiterate immigrants were drawn was New York's Lower East Side, where they mingled with each other and with native Americans. Class distinctions, today largely invisible, were then obvious at once, even in such basic matters as dress.

seem more urgent than before. The number of immigrants who entered the United States in 1882, for example, was not equalled in any one of the succeeding 20 years.

The first manifestation of this new hostility toward immigrants was directed against the Chinese, who came to the United States in large numbers in the 1860's and thereafter to help build the transcontinental railroads. Most of them settled in the western states and territories, particularly California. In response to anti-Chinese violence in the West, as well as to agitation by labor organizations and by demagogues like Denis Kearney of the San Francisco "sandlots" (a group of workingmen, who, like their leader, were mostly Irish born), Congress passed the Chinese Exclusion Act in 1882. This was the first federal limitation on immigrants and the first (but not the last) measure to discriminate against an immigrant nationality. In that same year, Congress enacted another measure which prohibited the immigration of paupers, the insane, and the feebleminded, and placed a head tax on all immigrants. In the twentieth century, immigration reached even greater heights than it had in the nineteenth, and demands for its limitation grew correspondingly stronger, until, in 1924, Congress ended (up to 1965) the historic policy of unqualified welcome for all peoples.

The Great Strike of '77. The impact of the Economic Revolution was also felt outside the halls of Congress. In the summer of 1877, a great strike of rail-

IMMIGRATION, 1872-1896
(Selected Years)

NORTHERN, WESTERN EUROPE AND GERMANY

CENTRAL, EASTERN AND SOUTHERN EUROPE

TOTAL 788,992

TOTAL° 623,084

TOTAL 404,806

TOTAL° 334,203

TOTAL 343,267

GREAT BRITAIN (Excluding Ireland)
IRELAND
SCANDINAVIA (Norway, Sweden, Denmark)
GERMANY
* OTHER
ITALY
† OTHER
ASIA, AFRICA, AMERICA
ALL OTHER

TOTAL 141,857

HUNDRED THOUSAND

-8
-7
-6
-5
-4
-3
-2
-1

1872   1877   1882   1886   1892   1896

*Belgium, Switzerland, and France
†Austria, Hungary, Spain, Portugal, European Turkey, Russia, Poland, Finland
°Not including, British North America, Mexico

Until 1896 a majority of the immigrants who came to the United States each year were from Northern and Western Europe; in the peak year of 1882, for example, 250,630 Germans alone arrived. But in 1896 immigration from Southern, Eastern and Central Europe became predominant.

road workers protesting wage cuts erupted. The strike spread rapidly from West Virginia and Maryland to Pittsburgh, through the Middle West, on down into Texas, and out to the Far West. Strikers clashed with militia, burned trains, destroyed property, and set fire to roundhouses in a score of cities and a half dozen states. The great upheaval also ignited strikes by steel workers, coal miners, and canal boatmen in several states. Before the violence ended, lives were lost, and President Hayes had to send federal troops into a number of areas to restore order and to protect property. When measured by the number of men involved and amount of property destroyed, the strike of 1877 was the greatest in the nineteenth century. In its fitful light, thoughtful men suddenly caught a glimpse of a more troubled future for the United States. "The youth of the American Republic is over," wrote a Canadian observer. "Maturity with its burdens, its difficulties and its anxieties has come." When James Ford Rhodes, a former businessman who lived through the strike, wrote his multivolume history of the period, he remembered that the violence of the strike "seemed to threaten the chief strongholds of society and came like a thunderbolt out of a clear sky, startling us rudely. For we had hugged the delusion that such social uprisings belonged to Europe and had no reason of being in a free republic where there was plenty of room and an equal chance for all."

Haymarket Riot: Foreshadower of an Era. The strike of '77 was only the first of the labor upheavals that dramatized the human consequences of the Economic Revolution. While less impressive in size and less costly in damage than the strike of 1877, the riot in Chicago's Haymarket Square in 1886 was, nonetheless, more dramatic and even more significant. It caused Americans to recognize that they now lived in a new era. The riot began when a large force of police ordered the dispersal of a meeting of workingmen who were protesting the strikebreaking activities of the police on the previous day. Before the workingmen could heed the order, someone who was never identified hurled a bomb among the police, killing one officer outright and fatally wounding six others. During the ensuing riot, a number of workingmen were killed or wounded. In the confusion, several policemen shot one another. Since the meeting had been sponsored by anarchists, the episode was instantly interpreted as a conspiracy of radical workers against order and property.

Popular fear and anger spread far from Chicago. The *New York Times,* for instance, maintained, "No disturbance of the peace that has occurred in the United States since the war of the rebellion has excited public sentiment throughout the Union as it is excited by the Anarchist's [sic] murder of policemen in Chicago. . . . It is silly to speak of the crime as a riot. All the evidence goes to show that it was concerted, deliberately planned and coolly executed murder." One religious periodical even suggested that all such

The strike of 1877 began over wage cuts, but was also, to some extent, a protest of many Americans against the powerful railroads. In Pittsburgh, as shown in the picture below, the workmen expressed their grievances in particularly rampant destructiveness.

from Stefan Lorant's *Pittsburgh, The Story Of An American City* (Doubleday) future demonstrations be met with machine gun fire. The public outcry was so strong that organized labor cautiously repudiated any connection with the meeting, though the purpose had been to defend the rights of labor. The eight men who were tried for conspiring with the unknown bomb thrower were quickly convicted in a patently unfair trial, presided over by a judge determined to see them hang. Four were hanged, one committed suicide in jail, and three had their sentences commuted to life imprisonment. Once fears had subsided, many people admitted that the evidence against the convicted men was shockingly flimsy, and in 1893 a newly elected governor, John Peter Altgeld, pardoned the three men who were still alive.

The significance of the Haymarket riot lies not so much in the violence of the event nor even in the miscarriage of justice that followed. Neither was new. It was the sense of dismay and horror which gripped the minds of millions of Americans that was novel. Not even the great railroad strike of 1877 had produced such widespread alarm. With a shock, many Americans suddenly realized that a society they did not know or understand was developing in the United States. The Haymarket affair spelled it out all too clearly. The riot had erupted in one of the large and growing cities of the nation and its perpetrators were all anarchists who repudiated the accepted forms of government and the rights of property. Moreover, the criminals were mostly industrial workers who defended the strike as a legitimate weapon of labor, and their names seemed to indicate that most of them were foreign born. Historically, the riot symbolized the issues that would become the central concerns of an America transformed by the Economic Revolution—that is, the factory, the city, the foreigner, and the slum.

In Search of Solutions: Unions and Settlement Houses. The impact of the factory upon society in this crucial decade of the 1880's was also readily apparent in a less violent, but more permanent fashion in the spectacular growth of national labor unions and in a new militancy on the part of organized labor. Between 1877 and 1890, an organization known as the Knights of Labor rose to national prominence. Its membership reached 700,000 in 1886, a figure unmatched by labor organizations before the twentieth century. That same year, 1886, witnessed the founding of the American Federation of Labor, destined to be the successor to the Knights in importance and the dominant labor organization of our century. A further sign of industrial labor's militancy in the course of the 1880's was the tripling of the number of work stoppages and the doubling of the number of workers involved in strikes. Furthermore, during that same decade, labor organizations devised and widely used for the first time the weapon of the boycott, i.e., the refusal of workers to buy goods from firms believed to be unfair to labor. In short, the Economic Revolution even before the 1890's brought with it industrial conflict unprecedented in scale and intensity.

With their demands for higher wages, labor unions were indirectly attacking the evils of the urban slums. A more direct assault came from a different

In one of these Jacob Riis photos, the men, who might be poor job hunting immigrants saving to bring their families over, or drifters unable to cope with urban life, are paying "5¢ a spot" to get off the streets at night. Since little government welfare existed, such men were dependent on charity or unscrupulous landlords. The streets from which they fled into these hovels were often equally offensive — unpaved and full of refuse — since systematic street cleaning and garbage collection were still uncommon.

source. In 1886, Stanton Coit, a young graduate of Amherst College, opened the first settlement house in the United States in the slums of the lower east side of New York City. Coit, a middle-class American whose social conscience had been aroused by his investigation of the industrial slums of America and Europe, was inspired by Toynbee Hall, an English settlement house. Other middle-class Americans soon picked up his lead. In 1889, Jane Addams, Ellen G. Starr, and Julia Lathrop, who also wanted to put their college educations to social use, opened Hull-House amid Chicago's teeming immigrant slums. Like the many settlement houses that would follow its pattern, Hull-House sought to relieve the impoverishment of body and spirit that the poor, the foreigner, and the socially disinherited endured in the crowded, dirty slums of the nineteenth-century American city. It did so through elementary medical care, day nurseries, and other services. With Jane Addams and Hull-House began the effort to reduce the high human costs that the Economic Revolution entailed then and still exacts in our own time.

New Voices of Protest: George and Bellamy

The beginning of the intellectual response to the Economic Revolution also dates from those years between the end of Reconstruction and 1890. That response, as exemplified by Henry George's *Progress and Poverty* (1879) and Edward Bellamy's *Looking Backward* (1888), was both a denunciation of the inhumane consequences of the Economic Revolution and a vision of its potential benefits.

In some ways, these two influential books were quite different. Though couched in popular language, George's was a serious treatise on economics, while Bellamy's was an excellent piece of persuasion in the form of a mediocre novel. Moreover, Henry George's solution to the problems of an industrial society differed from Bellamy's. He concentrated his attack upon the undesirable effects of the monopolization of land, arguing that land should not be held out of production for speculative purposes. Force it into use, George counselled, and prosperity would follow. Because he saw the rise in land values as resulting primarily from the growth of population and society, he did not hesitate to call for the confiscation of rent (on land as distinguished from rent on buildings and improvements). All increases in the value of unused land, he argued, were "unearned increments" to the landholders and legitimately belonged to society. Because George thought that such a tax on economic rent would be sufficient to pay for all the costs of government, his scheme came to be called the Single Tax.

Bellamy's answer to the evils of the Economic Revolution was not only quite different but much less explicit. Describing an ideal society in A.D. 2000, he showed what cooperation and government ownership of the means of production could do to improve man's lot. In this society, competition among men was not practiced, and, since everyone received as much as he needed to

Jane Addams and Henry George exemplify two different approaches to the evils of 19th-century capitalism. Miss Addams dealt with the immediate problems that she found in the Chicago slums, while George attacked the root of the matter by suggesting a modification of the existing system.

live in comfort, work was easy and retirement early and honorable. Crime was nonexistent, and men worked not for gain but for honor to themselves and society. Bellamy's utopia was a variety of socialism, but it was devoid of foreign inspiration or connection and hence reached a much wider audience in the United States than the Marxian Socialist doctrine ever did.

Despite the differences between Bellamy's and George's approaches and the obvious inadequacies of both as solutions to the problems of an industrial society, the books of the two men had one important point in common. Throughout the history of mankind down to the age of machine production, the basic fact of economic life had been that the production of goods was never sufficient to permit more than a small proportion of men to live without persistent hunger, inadequate shelter, and intellectual poverty. Bellamy and George insisted that at last it was possible to change this ancient condition. The true meaning and promise of the Industrial Revolution, they asserted, was that poverty could be ended. Their great indictment of the society of their time was that the promise was not being fulfilled.

Why is it, George asked, that "in factories where laborsaving machinery has reached its most wonderful development, little children are at work?" Why is it that wherever machines are widely used "large classes are maintained by charity or live on the verge of recourse to it?" How paradoxical it is, he went on, that "the fruits of the tree of knowledge turn . . . to apples of Sodom that crumble at the touch. . . . This association of poverty with progress is the enigma of our times." Although George and Bellamy disagreed on the specific causes for this fatal association, they were in complete agreement on its general cause. The paradox of poverty and progress lay not in the immutable laws of nature or of God, but in men and the society they built. As George defiantly wrote in *Progress and Poverty,* "I assert that the injustice of society, not the niggardliness of nature, is the cause of want and misery." After George and Bellamy published these books, the poor could no longer be blamed exclusively for their poverty.

Such ideas, of course, constituted economic as well as social heresy; a whole generation of economists, businessmen, and clergymen had been preaching the immutable laws of economics. These laws, it was said, controlled prices and wages and made poverty inevitable no matter how regrettable it might be. Mere men and governments, which were only human, could not alter the principles that controlled the prices and distribution of goods or the cost of labor, and efforts to do so would result in violence and injustice. In fact, any governmental interference in economic affairs would make matters worse. Though there was a large degree of simple, selfish defense of the status quo in such arguments, there was reason behind them. Under the principles of laissez faire, the American economy, like that of the western world in general, had become more productive than at any earlier time in recorded history. Thus, to many men, government intervention in the economic process not only deprived businessmen of what they considered their personal liberty, it also threatened the continued operation of the most productive economic machine ever developed by man.

George's and Bellamy's trenchant criticism of the status quo and their disbelief in the immutability of the laws of economics aroused such widespread response that their books launched a whole generation of economic and social reform. *Progress and Poverty,* which was translated into several languages, sold more copies than any other treatise on economics up to that time. Almost overnight, George became a celebrated reformer both in America and England. In 1886, he ran on a workingmen's platform for mayor of New York City and, though he came in second, he ran ahead of the Republican candidate, Theodore Roosevelt, by thousands of votes. Bellamy's book was even more popular, if only because it was cast in the form of a novel. Within two years after its publication, 200,000 copies had been sold and weekly sales had reached 10,000. *Looking Backward* inspired a national magazine, *The Nationalist,* and brought into existence more than 150 clubs to propagate Bellamy's ideas.

Both books proved to be seminal in the thought of many later leaders of industrial reform in both the United States and Europe. Thorstein Veblen, a major critic of the American socio-economic system, for example, found Bellamy's book a "turning-point" in his life; Norman Thomas, for several decades the foremost spokesman for the American Socialist party, entered upon a lifelong commitment to socialism through the door of *Looking Backward.* Key figures in the Progressive movement of the twentieth century, like Tom Johnson and Clarence Darrow, later testified that *Progress and Poverty* helped to focus their attention on the inequities of industrial society.

Thus, by the time the American people entered the last decade of the nineteenth century, they had taken up the new issues raised by the Economic Revolution, while leaving behind a whole series of matters which once had engaged their attention, but now seemed irrelevant. These new problems constituted the challenge and controlled the shape of the future; for the next half a century the nation would struggle with their resolution. Though ensuing years would bring more social changes and fresh problems, few of them would come as a surprise after 1890. By then the nature of a society of factories and cities and the problems of life that confronted it were already apparent. Even some of the solutions had been suggested.

In the next two chapters we shall examine the character and impact of the Economic Revolution which brought the new age into being.

SUGGESTED READING

The subject of the Indians has been a popular one. A good and readable introduction to the topic is William T. Hagan, *American Indians** (1961), which, while brief, is knowledgeable and understanding. One of the grand old men of Indian studies was Oliver La Farge, whose *As Long As the Grass Shall Grow* (1940) provides a good introduction to his thought and work. Harold E. Fey and D'Arcy McNickle, *Indians and Other Americans* (1959), discusses the problem of the red man in white society yesterday and today. Also helpful in tracing the later development of Indian policy is *The Indian in Modern America,* ed. by David A. Baerreis (1956). Ralph K. Andrist, *The Long Death; the Last Days of the Plains Indians* (1964), is a very well written account of the shocking story. Paul I. Wellman's *Death in the Desert** (1935), and *Death on the Prairie** (1934), are earlier dramatic presentations of the destruction of the Indian. Stanley Vestal, *Sitting Bull* (1932), is an authoritative biography of the best known Indian leader. Loring Benson Priest, *Uncle Sam's Stepchildren: The Reformation of the United States Indian Policy, 1865–1887* (1942), is thorough and good. Henry E. Fritz, *The Movement for Indian Assimilation, 1860–1890* (1963), is important and informative. The standard work on the catalyst to Indian reform is Ruth Odell, *Helen Hunt Jackson* (1939).

On Chinese immigration see Mary Roberts Coolidge, *Chinese Immigration* (1909), and Elmer Clarence Sandmeyer, *The Anti-Chinese Movement in California* (1939). Gunther Barth, *Bitter Strength; a History of the Chinese in the United States, 1850–1870* (1964) provides the background to the hostility.

An excellent study on the eruption of labor problems is Robert V. Bruce, *1877: Year of Violence* (1959). A powerful companion volume is Henry David, *The History of the Haymarket Affair** (1936). The standard labor history is John R. Commons, et al., *History of Labor in the United States,* 4 vols. (1918–1936). Donald L. McMurry, *The Great Burlington Strike of 1888* (1956), further underscores the labor trouble of the 1880's.

*Available in a paperback edition.

The best biography of the founder of Hull-House is James W. Linn, *Jane Addams* (1935). Jane Addams, *Twenty Years at Hull-House** (1912) tells the first-hand story of the best-known and one of the earliest settlement houses. Broader in scope is Robert H. Bremner's excellent work, *From the Depths: the Discovery of Poverty in the United States** (1956). Arthur M. Schlesinger, *The Rise of the City, 1878 – 1898* (1933), also deals in some detail with the rise of the settlement house. Jacob A. Riis, *How the Other Half Lives,** which first appeared in 1890 but has been reprinted several times, is a striking description of tenement life.

A fine introduction to the reform sentiment of the 1880's and 1890's can be found in the opening chapters of Eric Goldman, *Rendezvous with Destiny** (1952). Daniel Aaron, *Men of Good Hope** (1951), has some penetrating remarks on Henry George and Edward Bellamy. A good study of Bellamy is Arthur E. Morgan, *The Philosophy of Edward Bellamy** (1945); it can be supplemented by Sylvia Bowman, *The Year 2000; A Critical Biography of Edward Bellamy* (1958). Undoubtedly the best biography of Henry George is Charles Albro Barker, *Henry George* (1955). George's ideas are examined in G. R. Geiger, *Philosophy of Henry George* (1933). Part I of Henry Steele Commager, *The American Mind** (1950) deals provocatively with the intellectual currents of the 1880's and 1890's.

The difficulties of terrain which had to be overcome in extending the railroad westward are apparent in this awesome photograph of the Diablo Canyon Bridge in Arizona. Only advances in technology and the use of steel made possible such engineering feats.   Photo: Santa Fe Railway

CHAPTER TWO

THE ECONOMIC REVOLUTION: RAILROADS, FACTORIES, AND CITIES

WHAT WAS THE Economic Revolution and how did it come about? It is perhaps most accurately described as three different, though closely interrelated, economic and technological developments which converged in the last half of the nineteenth century.

One of these developments was a revolution in power. The steam engine, though used for decades in both manufacture and transport, now came into its own. As recently as 1860, animals (chiefly horses and mules) supplied almost two thirds of all the nonhuman power consumed in the economy. By 1890, however, the horsepower generated by improved steam engines and steam turbines had increased six times and comprised over 60 per cent of all the nation's power; yet during the same period, the amount of animal power had doubled also. By 1900, two new sources of energy emerged: electricity and the internal-combustion engine. Industry in the twentieth century would rest upon them.

A second development was the enormous increase in both production (the quantity of goods produced) and in productivity (the efficiency with which they were turned out), principally through the greater use of machines. The growth in manufacturing will be discussed in the second half of this chapter. The upswing in farm productivity not only tripled the output of American farmers, but also freed large numbers of workers for labor in manufacturing. This revolution in agriculture is the subject of the first half of Chapter III.

A third development, which has been called the Communications Revolution, was a series of technological and economic innovations in transportation and communications, which, for the first time in history, linked together the four corners of the world into a gigantic market for bulk as well as luxury goods. In fact, the close interrelationships among these three developments can be seen most clearly in the Communications Revolution. One reason the United States made such rapid gains during these years was that its farmers found world markets for their mounting crop surpluses. Without a market of world dimensions, American agriculture would not have expanded as it did; without this marked increase in farm production, American industrial growth would undoubtedly have been retarded. In other words, without the development of a highly productive and efficient agricultural-machinery industry, farms could not have boosted their productivity. All three developments interacted to produce the Economic Revolution. Let us turn first to an examination of the Communications Revolution.

In the creation of the world market, improvements in transoceanic transportation and communication were central. The submarine cable, for example, accelerated business communication, while the completion of the Suez Canal in 1869 opened East Asian markets to shipments of bulk goods for the first time. Moreover, new improved types of ships now carried more goods farther, faster, and at less cost than the old sailing vessels or even the new wooden steamships. The compound steam engine, the screw propeller, and the steel hull halved the amount of fuel a ship needed to carry, a development which doubled freight capacity and reduced rates. While in 1860 it cost 12 cents or more to ship a bushel of wheat from New York to Liverpool, by 1888 the price had fallen to five cents. A similar reduction in passenger rates helped account for the great increase in immigration to the United States in the last half of the century. One measure of the increased productivity in marine shipping was the fact that the amount of trade carried by British merchant ships between 1870 and 1880 increased by 22 million tons, while the number of workers involved in shipping actually fell by almost 3000.

The Communications Revolution was also apparent domestically. Such devices as the typewriter and telephone, both invented in the 1870's, quickly ceased to be novelties as they found a ready use in the increasing volume and pace of business activity. With George Eastman's discovery of the process of dry-plate photography on paper-backed film, and Ottmar Mergenthaler's invention of the linotype machine, both in 1884, the cheap, mass newspaper and magazine trade expanded, offering new opportunities for widescale advertising and sales promotion among a growing number of urban-dwellers.

The keystone in the arch of the Communications Revolution, however, was the railroad. Its role in the economic growth of the United States is sufficiently strategic to warrant careful examination.

The Age of the Iron Horse

Railroad Construction: Boon to Communication and the Economy. As an invention, the railroad was old by 1860, but as a means of transportation, it was not widely used until after the Civil War. Because of the primitive character of the early trains, no railroad in the 1840's or even the 1850's could compete as a bulk carrier with river steamboats or canals. However, as more railroads were built, their potentialities as overland bulk carriers came to be recognized. Between 1870 and 1890, over 110,000 miles of railroad track were laid—more than existed in all of Europe (see map on page 24). As Sir John Clapham, the British economic historian, has written, "If a single national contribution towards the making of the new era [of industrialization] had to be selected for its world-wide economic importance," it would be the gargantuan railroad construction in the United States. By reducing costs of overland transportation, railroads widened the market for all goods. David A. Wells, an American economist, wrote in 1884 that a ton of goods "can now be carried on the best managed railroads for a distance of a mile, for a sum so small that outside of China it would be difficult to find a coin of equivalent value to give a boy as a reward for carrying an ounce package across the street."

The building of railroads also served as a catalyst to the economy through its voracious consumption of raw materials and finished products: wood for ties; coal for fuel; iron, steel, and copper for engines, cars, and rails. The railroads' extensive demand for these products boosted the expansion of the steel industry. This in turn lowered prices of steel, thus attracting new consumers and evoking new uses for the tough and resilient metal. In 1874, the first steel bridge was built across the Mississippi at St. Louis by James B. Eads; others soon followed. By the 1880's, American steelmakers were sufficiently versatile so that the federal government could use their plate and other products in building a new steel navy.

Despite the undeniable economic advantages of railroads, their construction presented problems to a new country short of capital and labor. Railroads require a long time to construct, during which there is no return on capital. Furthermore, the money for financing railroad construction cannot be invested piecemeal as it can be, for example, in installing spindles in a cotton textile mill where each spindle adds so much to productive capacity. Until at least two important points have been connected by track, no adequate traffic can move. Moreover, even when completed, railroads are not only expensive to operate, but their costs (such as maintenance of the tracks, the engines, and the roundhouses) also continue, regardless of the amount of business. It was these high fixed costs which forced railroads into the excessive competition that became the bane of the industry in the 1870's and 1880's.

These economic characteristics of railroads also explain governmental aid to railroad construction in the post-Civil War years. Where there was ample traffic, as on the eastern roads, private enterprise usually could manage the risks and costs of railroad construction. But in the West, where settlement was sparse, railroad building required government assistance. Actually, government aid to economic growth was not new. In the 1840's and 1850's, a number of states contributed funds to canal and railroad corporations, and in 1850 the federal government made its first venture in this field by providing land grants for the construction of the Illinois Central Railroad.

Through the Pacific Railway Acts of 1862 and 1864, the federal government encouraged western railroad construction on a large scale by offering millions of dollars in loans and millions of acres of land to the newly created Union Pacific Railroad Company and others for the joint construction of a road which would connect the east and west coasts. The act of 1864, typical of a number of such acts, granted the railroad the right to select, on each side of the track, ten alternate sections (that is, pieces of land one mile square) for every mile of track. Thus, the total of twenty square miles of land per mile of track would be arranged in checkerboard fashion. The plots were to be chosen within a strip twenty miles on each side of the right of way. While the road was being constructed, these tracts of land could be used by the builders as collateral for loans or supplies; once the railway was completed, they could be sold for cash to settlers. Between 1850 and 1872, the federal government together with nine states gave some 70 railroads about 183 million acres of land, roughly the area of the United Kingdom, Belgium, and Spain combined. A more appropriate way of describing it would be to say that the grants were equal to about one tenth of the Sahara Desert, for until the railroad came through, most of the West was a social desert, devoid of people or means for settlement. One economic historian has recently calculated that the building of the Union Pacific Railroad alone added roughly $16.5 million a year to the national income between 1870 and 1880.

The federal government also encouraged railroad construction by means of cash loans amounting to millions of dollars. Because the railroads obtained capital from the government instead of competing in the money market, federal loans saved them interest charges of as much as $48 million, while loans from 14 states probably netted the roads another $90 million. Furthermore, local communities often encouraged railroad construction by granting tax exemptions or by guaranteeing railroad bonds. Their reasoning can be found in the words of a public meeting in Iowa in 1865: "Resolved, that Johnson County donate half a million dollars rather than this Rail Road should be made twenty miles east or west of us." Whether a railroad came to a town or not often meant the difference between future prosperity and mere survival.

Since even honest men found railroad construction a risky business, the insecurity involved was magnified in an age of speculation and business recklessness. Hence, devices that now appear unscrupulous were often employed in an effort to compensate for the high risk. One such practice involved direct ownership of the construction company that built a railroad by some of the principal stockholders in the railroad company. The most famous of such construction companies was the Crédit Mobilier, founded in 1864 to complete the Union Pacific Railroad. Since many of the same men were executives in both companies, the "insiders" in the railroad were able to turn over the assets of the road to themselves, as constructors, through contracts to build at high prices. The result was that the construction company often obtained very high profits while the railroad was "milked" dry. In fact, the enormous profits of the Crédit Mobilier created a national scandal when the distribution of its stock to some congressmen was exposed in 1872. Despite the notoriety of that particular scandal, the widespread use of the construction company in the building of railroads was more indicative of the difficulties of accumulating capital than of general thievery in railroading. Indeed, like the government land grants and loans, the construction company was probably indispensable in accumulating capital for building railroads in the sparsely settled regions of the country. By the time the last of the four pioneer transcontinentals, James J. Hill's Great Northern, was constructed in the 1890's, private capital was able and ready to do the job unassisted by government.

Forging a Modern Railroad Network. For a quarter of a century after 1860, the railroads of the United States occupied themselves not only with laying track, but also with forming a network of rails, usable without interruption from one line to another. On a railroad map of the 1860's, the United States appeared to possess an impressive web of lines, but in fact, the absence of bridges over the major rivers, the diversity in gauges (the width between the rails), and the small size of engines and cars prevented railroads from

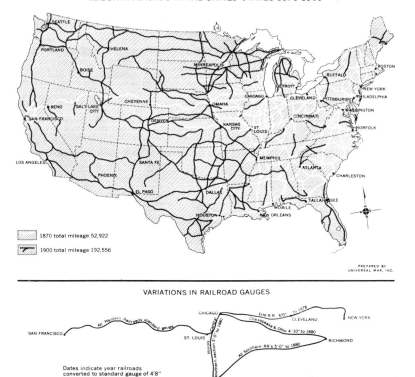

1870 total mileage 52,922

1900 total mileage 192,556

PREPARED BY
UNIVERSAL MAP, INC.

VARIATIONS IN RAILROAD GAUGES

Dates indicate year railroads
converted to standard gauge of 4'8"

While not all railroad lines are shown, especially in the Middle West and in the East, most of the period's nearly 300% growth in track mileage did occur west of Chicago and New Orleans, thereby stimulating growth in all areas.

effectively challenging canals and steamboats as long-distance freight haulers. Over four fifths of the traffic carried by the Pennsylvania and the Baltimore and Ohio railroads did not travel beyond their own tracks. Moreover, in the absence of double-tracking, two-way traffic on a single track sacrificed speed and efficiency to safety.

By the 1880's, the use of double-tracking, smoother roadbeds, steel instead of iron rails, and freight cars twice their previous size speeded up service and increased freight loads. Also, bridges now spanned the major rivers, and in 1886 the standard gauge of 4'8½" was finally adopted by every railroad line in the country. By the end of the 1870's, almost half of the nation's trains were equipped with the new Westinghouse airbrake, which provided a quick and efficient means of halting a whole line of cars, thus permitting greater speed while ensuring safety. The railroad by then had completely surpassed the canalboat and the steamboat as a long-distance hauler. Symbolic of the new long-distance function was the growing use of the Pullman sleeping and dining cars on passenger trains and the adoption in 1883 of uniform time zones across the country to avoid confusion in schedules. It was indicative of the importance of the railroads and of the influence of private institutions on public life that the time zones, still in use today, were first devised by the railroads and accepted by the country until 1918 without any legislation or governmental action.

By the end of the 1880's, the American railroad network was truly a communication system, for now a train could cross the continent virtually without interruption. The most obvious and important consequence was a steady decrease in transportation charges. On the run between New York and Chicago, for example, rates on the four highest classes of goods dropped more than 50 per cent between 1865 and 1888. On raw materials from the West, rates also fell sharply. The cost of shipping wheat from Chicago to New York declined from 65 cents to 20 cents per 100 pounds between 1866 and 1897. The expense of moving dressed beef fell from 90 cents per 100 pounds in 1872 to 40 cents in 1899. Since rates dropped 10 to 50 per cent even on local runs where there were no competitors, it is evident that lower costs and more efficient methods of handling freight were at least partially responsible for the general fall in charges.

The Railroad As Enterprise: Incentive to Fraud and Corruption. Railroads were more than economic institutions, binding producers and markets together; they were also the offspring of human labor, ingenuity, business acumen, and, sometimes, chicanery and greed. The prevalence of the last two factors has often been exaggerated. Daniel Drew and "Jim" Fisk, who are well known for their manipulation of the stocks of the Erie Railroad in the 1870's, were not typical of railroaders in this period, because they were not railroad men. They were swindlers who happened to be in railroading. Yet something in this business more than in others encouraged fraud and corruption. What one economic historian has described as the railroads' "insatiable and urgent demands for capital" led to many kinds of schemes to secure the necessary funds. For instance, in order to attract capital, railroads were often tempted to declare dividends larger than good management permitted or, as happened with the New York Central under Commodore Vanderbilt, dividends were maintained even if it could be done only by gouging the public with higher rates. The extraordinary appetite for capital also meant that railroads were usually corporations, which provided an opportunity for stocks and bonds to be issued as dividends or as a means of securing favors. Cornelius Vanderbilt, in building the New York Central system, often issued "watered stock," shares in excess of the value of assets, to buy out competing or connecting lines. In time, the more responsible roads like the New York Central squeezed out the "water" by reinvesting earnings in improvements.

In their stock manipulations, railroads also provided the first great example of separation of ownership from control in American corporations—a phenomenon now quite characteristic of American business. Ostensibly and legally the stockholders owned the railroad, but stockwatering and other financial manipulations revealed that the managers often ran the company and disposed of its assets as they saw fit. In short, regardless of chicanery, the public can own but not manage a large corporation.

Railroading was a risky business, but for those companies that did succeed high profits were not uncommon. The promoters of the Union Pacific, to cite one case, received profits of between $14 and $15 million for building the road alone, though actual construction costs totaled less than $60 million. Not all railroads bore the same high degree of risk as the Union Pacific, but most received high returns nonetheless. The great hazard of railroading was that the traffic might not justify the costly investment, and the history of the 1870's and 1880's is filled with stories of fierce competition and rivalry for traffic. John W. Garrett, who developed the Baltimore and Ohio into a major system, virtually ruined the road financially in the course of his titanic struggle with the Pennsylvania Railroad. In order to secure traffic, he cut rates so sharply that the road was kept financially afloat only by falsification of the records and by borrowing money at exorbitant rates of interest.

Not all railroad companies necessarily succumbed to dishonesty in order to survive and grow. J. Edgar Thomson's Pennsylvania Railroad managed to grow without scandal from a small line between Pittsburgh and Philadelphia in the 1850's to a thousand-mile giant in the 1870's, stretching between the Atlantic coast and Chicago. The Pennsylvania made a name for itself as being among the first to introduce new techniques into railroading such as the use of Bessemer steel rails, airbrakes, the block signal system, and the overhead crane.

The Great Race. To men of the time the great work of the age was the spanning of the continent by the Union Pacific and Central Pacific. For over a decade Americans had dreamed of building a line to the Pacific Ocean, but political rivalry between the North and the South had prevented it until the Civil War. After the war the North was free to do so without having to consider southern wishes for a terminus in New Orleans or Memphis. The acts of 1862 and 1864 authorized the Central Pacific to build eastward from Sacramento and the Union Pacific to work westward from Omaha. Aside from the heavy costs, which the transcontinentals encountered to an even greater degree than other roads, the dimensions of the construction alone were formidable. The Central Pacific ran into difficulties of terrain almost immediately. Since at that time there were no power drills to expedite railroad construction through the Sierra Nevada Mountains, the roadbed was carved out of the rock mainly by 9000 recently imported Chinese laborers using hand chisels and hammers. When gigantic snow slides covered the construction sites in the mountains, long sheds had to be thrown up to enable the work to proceed. After two years of heart-breaking labor in the mountain passes, the Central Pacific workers finally broke through to the Nevada plateau. Once in the open, the company drove the workers to prodigious efforts; they put down 362 miles of track in a single year — almost a mile a day.

The men behind the Central Pacific were the big four of nineteenth-century California history: Leland Stanford, later governor and founder of the university that bears his son's name; Collis P. Huntington; Mark Hopkins; and Charles Crocker. All four were recent immigrants to the West, attracted by the profits to be gained from selling supplies to the gold miners. Moderately successful as merchants, they seized upon the railroad venture as a chance to acquire substantial fortunes and fame.

The Union Pacific's task was only slightly easier. Although no mountains had to be scaled before reaching the Rockies, Indians were a constant menace. The armed guards who accompanied the construction crews could not always provide sufficient protection. In such cases the workers dropped shovels and picked up rifles to assist in repelling the attacks. Until 1867 construction was slow, but as the ribbon of steel and wood gradually grew longer and gave evidence that in fact the road would be completed, tracks went down with astonishing rapidity. At the end of 1867, with the Union Pacific crews on the eastern edge of the Rockies and the Central Pacific on the Nevada plateau, competition between the two groups became so keen that neither would take the usual winter break. The spring of 1869 found both crews working furiously in western Utah. Neither company, however, was willing to make the expected juncture, since governmental loans were paid on the basis of each mile of track laid. As a result, Congress had to intervene and designate Promontory Point, six miles west of Ogden, Utah, as the meeting place. There, on May 10, 1869, a golden spike (since removed) was driven into the last tie, while telegraph lines flashed the blows of the sledge hammer across the nation.

A second line to the west coast was not constructed until 1883, when the Northern Pacific was completed from St. Paul to Portland. Meanwhile, the Atchison, Topeka and Santa Fe joined with the Southern Pacific at Deming, New Mexico, in 1881, and a year later the latter road completed a juncture with New Orleans, thus giving the South its long-sought western connection. A fourth transcontinental line—James J. Hill's Great Northern, from St. Paul —was completed to Tacoma in 1893.

The Railroad As Menace: Monopoly and Rate Wars. A growing public interest in some kind of governmental regulation of railroads in the 1870's and early 1880's stemmed from two quite distinct characteristics of railroads. Where traffic was so limited that only one railroad was economically practical, it enjoyed a natural monopoly. In such situations railroads could, and often would, charge what seemed to be excessive rates, which were sometimes only an effort to make up for losses incurred at shipping points where they were forced to compete. Throughout the period there was public demand for governmental regulation of rates to cope with this situation. The most frequent and bitter complaints against the railroads centered on discrimination in rates among different classes of shippers. This practice of the railroads, which was usually stigmatized as an abuse by those who had to pay the higher rates, resulted not so much from monopoly as from the excessive competition in the industry. In its pursuit of traffic a railroad would allow lower rates to large, through-traffic shippers than to small, local-traffic ones, or would offer rebates (refunds of part of the charge), which amounted to the same thing. This kind of discrimination was so common that a railroad executive appearing before a Senate investigating committee in 1886 said that discrimination through "rebates is a part of the present railroad system. I do not believe the present railway system could be conducted without it."

Another form of discrimination in favor of the big shipper was to charge less for a long haul than for a short haul (included within the longer haul). This practice was justified by the railroads on the ground that long hauls cost less because they involved fewer stops, unloadings, and storage facilities en route and because they were usually for large quantities of goods. But in the eyes of the small, local shippers, who were usually individual farmers and local merchants and businessmen, it seemed like simple favoritism to large manufacturing and mining firms.

Excessive competition among roads also resulted in drastic rate wars that may have benefited shippers for a short time by cutting rates, but over the long term were disastrous to shippers as well as railroads. In fact, constantly changing rate schedules confused shippers, disrupted their marketing plans, and aroused suspicions of discrimination. Moreover, since rate wars could easily end in the bankruptcy of at least some of the railroads involved, the consequent disruption of service further weakened public confidence and deprived shippers of service. Some speculators in railroading in the late 1870's and 1880's deliberately sought to profit from excessive competition by increasing it. They constructed competing lines just to sell them at a profit to the established roads. William Vanderbilt dubbed a railway paralleling his own along the shore of Lake Erie the "Nickel Plate Line" because the purchase price was so high he could not believe that its rails were made of mere iron.

The rate wars and the drive for traffic during the 1870's and early 1880's made the public and railroads aware that competition was neither an effectual protection for the public nor was it conducive to the efficient functioning of a transportation system.

Sometimes the giant railroad companies, especially when they dominated a state or region, used their power not only against other companies but also in politics. Such activities often resulted in popular hatred of the railroads and political attacks against them. Both the Union Pacific in Wyoming and the Southern Pacific in California were highly influential and the objects of public animosity. Some railroads, like the New York Central under Commodore Vanderbilt, did not hesitate to bribe state legislators or to corrupt judges if it served their purpose.

Government Regulation. The movement for regulation of the railroads, though, did not stem primarily from such political activities, unsavory as they may have been. It resulted both from the much more widespread discriminatory practices and from the belief that rates were excessively high even when not discriminatory. (Actually, as has been noted, rates in general fell during the whole period, but never as much as shippers, especially farmers, would have liked.) As early as the 1870's, farmers and many businessmen, finding themselves dependent upon railroads, yet ineligible as small shippers for rebates or the benefits of the long and short haul discrimination, began to agitate for state regulation of the railroads. The beginning of the long decline in farm prices especially compounded the farmers' dissatisfaction with railroad rates. The railroads, of course, vigorously opposed such state intervention (although they were not always successful), and usually defended their position by invoking the doctrines of freedom of enterprise and laissez faire. Because of the pressure of farm organizations, a number of midwestern states did enact regulatory legislation, known as the Granger laws. Actually, many businessmen-shippers supported such laws, too.

At first, this legislation received support from the U.S. Supreme Court. In 1877, in the case of *Munn* v. *Illinois,* the Court upheld the right of an Illinois regulatory commission to set maximum rates for a grain elevator. The principle enunciated by Chief Justice Morrison Waite in that decision was equally applicable to railroads. Property "clothed with the public interest," the Chief Justice declared, "when used in a manner to make it of public consequence . . . must submit to be controlled by the public for the common good. . . ."

Nine years later, however, the Court, somewhat changed in composition and radically altered in economic philosophy, substantially modified the Munn interpretation of the interstate commerce clause of the Constitution. Waite in his 1877 decision had recognized that Congress possessed the paramount power over interstate commerce, but in the absence of Congressional action, he said, the state could regulate. Now, in 1886, the Court ruled that the power of the Congress was exclusive and that any traffic moving into, out of, or through a state was beyond state regulation. Inasmuch as over three quarters of the nation's rail traffic was interstate in character, the decision in *Wabash, St. Louis and Pacific Railroad* v. *Illinois* effectively ended state regulation.

By the same token, however, the *Wabash* decision challenged Congress to adopt some form of federal regulation of railroads, as advocates of regulation had been proposing for more than ten years. The proposed bills attacked both the problems of monopoly and of discriminatory rates. The most obvious form of monopoly was the pool—an agreement among supposedly competing railroads to divide the traffic on an agreed basis rather than compete for it. From the railroads' standpoint a pool was protection against ruinous rate cutting, but to the public it was an evasion of competition and therefore a source of high rates.

In Congress there was general agreement upon the need to prohibit pools and to prevent discrimination. It was the means of accomplishing these ends which was disputed. The House, led by John H. Reagan of Texas, favored simple prohibition of discriminatory rates and pools, while the Senate, less responsive to the shippers' demands, preferred an administrative commission that would oversee railroad practices and thus be less rigid in dealing with them.

The final Interstate Commerce Act, passed in 1887, accommodated both approaches. The act set up a five-man commission to regulate the railroads and determine rates in interstate traffic. No more than three members could be drawn from one political party. All railroad rates were to be reasonable and just, though the new Interstate Commerce Commission received no guidelines for judging them. The act categorically banned pools, but mentioned no other forms of monopoly or combination. With some exceptions it also outlawed discriminatory practices such as rebates and the long and short haul. To eliminate undercover arrangements, the act required the public posting of all rates, and changes were permitted only after giving the Commission ten days' notice.

The Interstate Commerce Commission, despite all the weaknesses that soon became apparent, was the first of a long line of similar administrative agencies which the federal government would find indispensable in dealing with the new problems of an industrial society. From that beginning came the Federal Trade Commission (1914), the Federal Communications Commission (1934), and the Securities and Exchange Commission (1934).

A Paper Tiger. If the act seemed to be a victory for those who opposed some of the practices of the railroads, for a time, at least, many railroads welcomed the stability which the Commission brought to transportation. Moreover, a modicum of regulation—and that is all the act contemplated—relieved some of the public pressure on the railroads. But the honeymoon was soon over. Many railroads were loath to abandon rebating, for example, since it constituted an important competitive advantage. The inexperienced Commission found it difficult to cut its way through the complications of rate determination and to overcome the refusal of an increasing number of roads to supply information. Furthermore, as a result of interminable appeals to the courts, the orders of the Commission often were not carried out.

Indeed, since the Commission's orders could be reviewed by the courts, the judiciary soon revealed itself as a quagmire that gradually reduced the Commission to impotence. This became clear in the Maximum Freight Rate case decided by the Supreme Court in 1896. For almost ten years the lower courts, despite a general friendliness toward the railroads' position, had recognized the Commission's claim to rate-setting powers. But in 1896 the highest court decided that the Interstate Commerce Act bestowed only the power to prohibit unreasonable rates, not the power to set new ones. Such a narrow definition of the Commission's power virtually ended any possibility of its maintaining effective controls over rates. The Maximum Freight Rate case was only the most outstanding instance of the courts' unsympathetic attitude toward the Commission's activities. In the first 15 years of the Commission's existence, over 90 per cent of the court cases involving rates went against it. The courts simply did not want to allow an administrative tribunal, which was so new in federal law, to assume control over important economic matters. Only time, experience, and further Congressional legislation would give the regulatory commission a chance to play its proper and full role in controlling the new forces released by the Economic Revolution.

The railroad, for all its importance in the Communications Revolution, was still only a part of the Economic Revolution. Of equal, if not greater, significance was a spectacular upsurge in manufacturing after 1870 which so dwarfed even the substantial industrial growth of the pre-Civil War years that it deserves to be called a Second Industrial Revolution.

The Causes of the Second Industrial Revolution

Some years ago, two identical-looking automobiles stood in a museum in Detroit. One car cost $700, the other $70,000. The first came off an assembly line; the second was its hand-built prototype. The exhibit demonstrated the advantage of mass production, but it also illustrated the social and economic gains obtained from producing goods by power-driven machinery. In essence, power-driven machines made the Industrial Revolution possible.

During the second half of the nineteenth century the United States became the greatest economic power in the world, toppling Britain from her long-held position of industrial preëminence and far outdistancing all other rivals. At the end of the century, for example, American steel production, the most convenient single measure of industrial power, was double that of Great Britain and almost twice that of Germany, England's most recent European rival. Other figures that measure the strides over the years are

IRON, COAL, AND STEEL PRODUCTION, 1870-1900

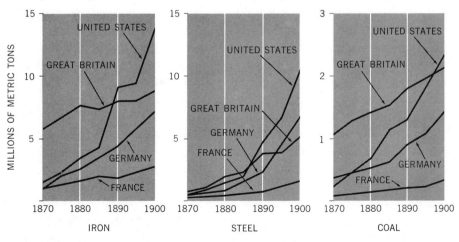

In the rapid rise of the United States to first place among the world's industrial powers, the achievements of the 1880's played a key role (see p. 131). By 1890, America had surpassed all contenders in iron and steel production.

equally impressive. The number of workers employed in manufacturing and construction quadrupled between 1860 and 1900; the value of manufactures increased over five fold; yet the population of the country during the same period advanced less than 2.5 times. The reasons for this burst of industrial activity are many; they merit examination because together they account for the most important single influence in American history since the Civil War.

Natural Riches. The story should begin with the land. Geographical circumstances do not in themselves cause industrialization, but they can facilitate or hinder that process. Fortunately, the United States possessed not only a vast expanse of territory, thereby avoiding population pressure upon the land, but also encompassed great stretches of rich farm land and ample, sometimes almost inexhaustible, deposits of most of the principal mineral resources needed by an industrial economy. Coal and iron ore were to be found in abundance. Americans did not have to import such raw materials, as did the Japanese or the French, for instance, in their rise to industrial power. Moreover, the Rockies and Sierras contained large deposits of the precious metals, gold and silver, and impressive stores of such industrial metals as lead, zinc, and copper. Petroleum, destined to be the great fuel and lubricant of the twentieth-century industrial age, existed in large quantities in western Pennsylvania, and in gargantuan amounts in Texas, as the spectacular gusher at Spindletop proclaimed in 1901. By the middle of the nineteenth century, this largesse of nature attracted and amply supported a rapidly growing population, which in turn constituted an enormous market undivided by tariffs, political boundaries, or language barriers.

Take-Off Years of Industrial Development. In accounting for the surge of industrial expansion after the Civil War, the preceding years of industrial development must certainly be included. Recent investigations by economic historians indicate that the 1850's constituted a true "take-off" period, as W. W. Rostow in his comparative study of economic growth has aptly named it. By 1860, American production of manufactures was over the billion-dollar mark and rising each year. States like New York and Pennsylvania had surpassed Massachusetts and the rest of New England as manufacturing centers. The rapidly lengthening internal waterways of canals and large rivers, supplemented by a developing railroad system, already marked the United States as a coming industrial power.

The Civil War in some respects, at least, interrupted that industrial development. Production continued to increase, but the rates of growth in production of important commodities like iron, cotton textiles, and railroads fell off between 1860 and 1870, presumably because of the war. However, the dislocation was not uniform. The rates of growth in the production of coal and woolen goods, to cite two examples, were unaffected by the conflict. In fact, the war inflation probably gave a fillip to business expansion, reflected in a great upsurge in business incorporations between 1860 and 1865. In Ohio, the number of incorporations rose from fewer than 40 in 1860 to over 300 in

1865. War orders by the government also stimulated standardization of production, since the Army, the greatest single consumer, favored uniformity. Rocketing federal expenditures gave a new push to the economy. Before 1860, the federal budget averaged about $60 million annually, while during the war it reached a high of $1.3 billion. Thereafter it seldom fell below $300 million. Thus the federal budget continued to support economic growth.

The war also made it politically possible for the Republican administration to enact legislation favorable to industrial growth, though the quantitative impact is difficult to assess. The banking acts of 1863 and 1864 secured a stable currency, while the issuance of greenbacks assured an adequate currency supply. The Contract Labor Law of 1864 encouraged the importation of cheap labor for industry, and the tariffs of the war years initiated the high protective policy of the late nineteenth century. The contribution of the tariff to the creation of the American industrial machine is open to controversy. The question is not whether the tariff encouraged industry—which no one disputes—but whether that encouragement was essential to economic growth. While the British economy industrialized without the aid of tariffs, it did not meet, at the outset, the international competition which the United States had to face as a late starter.

Equal Opportunity for All. Another important factor contributing to industrial growth was the general climate of opinion regarding economic activity. In the middle of the nineteenth century and for many years thereafter, most Americans (not just businessmen) believed that unfettered, individual self-interest was and ought to be the prime mover in the economy. Equal opportunity for all, special privileges for none, had been the Jacksonian motto, and so long as there was competition to protect society, most Americans believed in the practical consequences of the slogan. It seemed the best way to encourage rapid economic growth, even if it sometimes resulted in fortunes made in questionable ways or wasted natural resources. In the long run it would help the country grow. As one small-town newspaper stated the issue in 1871, "We can stand a pretty good 'steal' if we can get railroads in the state."

In practice, business enjoyed a great deal of freedom, spurred on by the carrot of high profits and the stick of bankruptcy. Government, as the agent of society, might well assist economic development when private enterprise could not do the job, as in the building of the transcontinental railways. Furthermore, government did little to restrict such individual enterprise or to increase costs of business operation. In fact, even when government helped to pay for railroads, as it did for some of the transcontinentals, it did not ask for a share in the ownership or control, but made grants to private corporations, vesting ownership in the companies. Regulatory measures like the Interstate Commerce Act were few on both the federal and state level, and they did not add to costs, as did workmen's compensation (for injuries sustained on the job) and sanitation laws in nineteenth-century England. The first workmen's compensation laws in the United States were not passed until the twentieth century—in Maryland in 1902 and in Montana in 1906.

Mechanization: The Key to Industrial Growth. The heart of the industrial process is mechanization. Thus, those general and particular factors that encourage a wider and more intensified use of machinery are crucial in explaining rapid industrial growth. Among such factors were the high wages in America relative to Europe, a result, probably, of the availability of land in the United States. In order to compete with cheap European labor, American manufacturers had to cut the costs of production without cutting wages; this they did by introducing machines. The availability of immigrant labor, which was mostly unskilled, also encouraged the use of machines in place of, or in the absence of, skilled labor. The more an employer depended upon unskilled labor the more he became committed to machines in his production.

To many Europeans who visited the United States around the turn of the century, the acceptance of the machine by both workers and management seemed to be the key to American industrial success. A group of British trade-union leaders who toured the United States in 1902 seeking the "secret" of American productivity thought they found it in the wide use of machinery in American factories. "The number of labour-saving appliances in use for almost everything is perfectly astounding," wrote one of them in his report.

Reaping the Benefits of Old World Technology and Capital. One reason American industrial production surpassed that of Great Britain was that America profited from English innovations and mistakes, just as Germany, Japan, and Russia—latecomers to the Industrial Revolution—in turn learned from American advances and errors. The Bessemer and the Siemens-Martin open-hearth processes in steel production—European inventions—were easily adopted by Americans. (William Kelly, an American, preceded Bessemer in using a blast of air through molten iron to produce steel, but Bessemer's process was used in American steel mills in the 1860's and after.) Europeans also invented the internal-combustion engine, which, in the automobile, was to play a central role in the American economy during the twentieth century. The wide acceptance of machinery resulted in a great advance in American productivity and wages over those of Europe. By 1900 the productivity of the *average* American worker in the steel industry was twice that of the *best* European.

Americans benefited from their late start in the industrial race in still another way. In addition to its own accumulation of wealth, the United States had access to European capital (mainly English). By 1900, Europeans had invested over $3.4 billion in this country, mostly in railroads, mines, and municipal bonds, thereby releasing American capital for manufacturing. European capital was readily available to American enterprise largely because the years 1815 to 1914 afforded the western world an unprecedented era of peace. Rapid communications, profitable industrialization, and an international gold standard permitted capital to flow across international boundaries more easily and safely than at any other time in history. The resulting availability of capital is one reason why Americans have faced fewer difficulties in building an industrial society than the Russians, the Indians, or the Communist Chinese. It has been estimated, for example, that Americans had to invest only 11 to 14 per cent of their national income during their years of industrialization as compared with the 20 per cent the British and the Russians had to save during their period of industrial growth. Western scholars estimate that Communist China in 1956 invested as much as 23 per cent of its total national income in industrial growth.

The Power of Machines. Along with the acceleration of communications, the invention of new machines was one of the principal causes for industrial growth after 1870. Sometimes, inventions spawned completely new industries, as in the case of the telephone, invented by Alexander Graham Bell in 1875. By the end of the century telephone communication was a major industry, and the Bell Telephone Company had become one of the burgeoning giants of big business. Thomas A. Edison's invention of the phonograph (1877) and the electric light bulb (1879) also created new industries. Indeed, Edison's successful, if laborious, discovery of a proper filament for an incandescent lamp prompted several industries, for in order to utilize his invention, Edison and his associates also had to invent machinery for generating electricity and new devices and techniques for transmitting and applying the new source of power. By 1890 the three electrical companies in the United States operated more than 1000 central power stations which lighted 1.25 million lamps.

It was George Westinghouse, though, who expanded the use of electricity through the introduction of alternating current. Using the inventions of a recent immigrant, Nicholas Tesla, Westinghouse showed that, because alternating current (unlike direct, which Edison favored) could be transmitted over long distances, it permitted the tapping of sources of hydroelectric power such as Niagara Falls. Before the century was out, the great falls at Niagara were harnessed for electric power.

The introduction and use of electric motors in manufacturing made electricity the most convenient and the cleanest form of industrial power the world had known. By the 1890's, electric power was widely used in transportation. In Richmond in 1888, Frank J. Sprague successfully demonstrated the first electrically driven street car, which, since it filled a definite urban need, was soon used in many other cities. It was rapid, cheap, and easy to operate, and did not pollute the air or present a fire hazard as steam trains did. Sometimes, inventions permitted a new and much wider use of a resource, as in the case of the electrolytic process invented by Charles Hall and others for refining aluminum — a metal which, despite its unique and desirable properties, until then had been too expensive to be widely usable. Out of Hall's patents came the Aluminum Company of America.

Not all inventions that advanced industrialization were as dramatic as these; yet many were as instrumental in expanding production and lowering prices. One example was the use of Michael Pupin's mathematical formula to prove that properly spaced inductance coils could greatly expand telephonic transmission, thereby reducing costs and facilitating modern long-distance telephoning. Yet another was the invention of the sterile tin can and Gail Borden's development of sanitary canned milk, which not only sparked a new food-processing industry, but stimulated a canning industry as well.

The machine tool industry provides a good example of the importance of small, unspectacular inventions for, despite the lack of major innovations, the advance of this business was central to rapid mechanization. Machine tools, which are power-driven contrivances that cut, shape, and mold metal, are machines that literally make other machines; lathes and milling machines are the most common examples. They also involve a "transfer of skills," since with them unskilled workers can make parts for machines that otherwise only highly skilled metal-craftsmen could cut or shape. Their use on a wide scale waited upon two developments, both of which came only after the middle of the nineteenth century. The first was the production of high-quality steel at low cost, made possible by the Bessemer process. The second was the invention of devices to cut and shape metal with speed and precision. One of the many innovators in this field was Frederick W. Taylor who, in the 1880's and 1890's, invented a whole series of important machine tools, but whose major contribution was the development of techniques for making high-speed machine tools. The higher the operating speed of a machine tool, the greater the amount of work it could perform, but high speeds also heated the tool to the point where it softened and lost its cutting ability. Working with J. Maunsel White at the Bethlehem Steel Company, Taylor, in 1898, developed a process whereby the steel tool retained its hardness even when running very fast and hot. Taylor's processes and tools are still standard in the machine shops of the world.

Innovators and Organizers. American industrial growth was not accomplished by machines and inventions alone; indispensable in that process were men—the entrepreneurs who organized the businesses, gathered the capital, recruited the labor, systematized the production, and sold the finished products. The names of the most famous, like Andrew Carnegie, Philip Armour, Gustavus Swift, John D. Rockefeller, George Westinghouse, John S. Pillsbury, and others, are well known today, if only because their industrial creations still carry their names. These were the true innovators, the men who broke with the old patterns of industrial production and distribution to strike out in new directions. Sometimes the contribution of these giants was in accumulating capital and in organizing vast new enterprises as did J. P. Morgan with United States Steel and Edward Harriman with railroads. Partly because these entrepreneurs were innovators, Charles and Mary Beard, the well-known American historians, once argued that they were a new social class come to power. The Beards saw the typical industrial leader as a farm boy of poor social origins who rose to power without the advantages of much education.

 (*Continued on page 41*)

Artifacts of an Industrial Society / Pictorial Essay

The Economic Revolution was the work of machines that augmented the work of men's hands, not of their brains, as computers do today. Because of their limitations, early machines often required a great deal of human assistance. Even the chain store of the late nineteenth century was a personal affair. Modern pre-packaged goods, guaranteed untouched by human hands, are quite different in form from the products of the past, which were not only handled by customer and clerk, but were sometimes prepared in the store itself.

In the big cities complicated logistics were involved in getting men from their homes to their machines and back again. Partial solutions were provided by elevated railways and electric trolleys; in New York these used the great steel suspension bridge, built by J. A. and W. A. Roebling, which stretched from Manhattan to Brooklyn. This type of construction had just been made possible by the invention of stronger steel cables. Even though people could be moved fairly expeditiously by the trolley after its invention in 1888, the

Interior of a steel plant, Braddock, Pennsylvania. *Photo: Brown Brothers*

Harvest time near Devil's Lake, North Dakota, ca. 1890. *Photo: Culver Pictures*
Below: Advertisement for barbed wire. *Photo: Carl S. Dentzel Collection*

movement of goods within the city was still dependent upon the slow and cumbersome horse-drawn wagon. On the farm as well, horses brought grain to the new steam-powered threshers from the fields where it had been cut by the horse-drawn harvesters. The mechanical age was not yet full-grown; the machine was still too often dependent on horse or human power.

Most machines which could be improved upon have been, and many have disappeared in the process, so there are no longer trolley cars or handpulled carts for molten steel. The telephone and the typewriter, however, have become more popular and necessary than ever. Both devices, so essential to the growing bureaucracy of the expanding business enterprises of the late nineteenth century, were inventions of the 1870's. By the end of the century, the manufacture and operation

Curve at Brooklyn terminal, showing New York City and the Brooklyn Bridge, 1898.
Photo: Library of Congress

A. & P. Store, 1898. *Photo: The Great Atlantic & Pacific Tea Company*

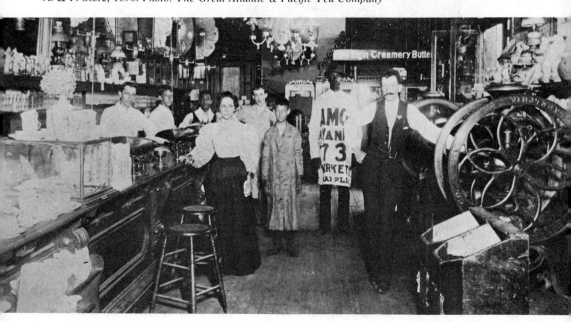

of telephones was a big business. When the American Telephone and Telegraph Company was established in 1900, there were already over 1.3 million telephones in use.

With industrialization came advertising, and by the 1890's advertising had become an important and necessary means of disposing of the ever-increasing quantities of consumer goods that poured from American factories. Industrial empires like those in tobacco, bananas, baked goods, and meat were built on advertising and in 1898, it has been estimated, the proportion of the gross national product spent on advertising by American industry was greater than in 1956. Advertising is a measure of the consumer economy, for it is at the consumers' dollars that the catchy phrases and colorful designs are directed. At a minimum, the increase in advertising indicates that the Economic Revolution brought an improvement in the ordinary citizen's standard of living, as he earned more dollars by working the machines that turned out more and cheaper consumer goods.   *End*

Office of the Galt, Missouri *Sun*, showing the editor using a Remington typewriter, ca. 1900.
Photo: Charles Phelps Cushing

Reassessment of the Entrepreneur. A larger sample of industrial leaders, however, reveals a quite different composite picture of the social character of the new men of power. An investigation of the background of 51 railroad leaders, for instance, indicated that 21 of the men attended college and that all but six had attended high school. This is especially striking since few American boys at the time could boast more than a grammar-school education. None of these railroad leaders came from the working class. An even broader investigation of 300 industrial leaders of the 1870's concluded that the typical magnate was native-born; Congregational, Presbyterian, or Episcopalian; and had a New England father who was a businessman of English descent. The majority of these leaders came from well-to-do homes. Instead of going to work at an early age, as the myth would have it, most of these executives took their first regular jobs at 18 and then only after educations far above average for the time.

If the concept of the self-made man as the typical entrepreneur of the period needs some modification, so does its corollary that these men were "robber barons," who ruthlessly crushed their competitors, exploited their workmen, and defrauded the nation. Certainly it is true, as one historian has shown, that many of these industrial captains, such as John D. Rockefeller, Cornelius Vanderbilt, and Andrew Carnegie, went to almost any lengths to expand their enterprises. Thirteen of the 46 leaders examined by this historian gained favors through political corruption, and 16 profited at the expense of their own companies. Nor can one deny the power and ruthlessness of an individual organization like the Standard Oil Trust, which Rockefeller formed in 1882 and which, thereafter, virtually monopolized the oil-refining industry. Certainly, Standard Oil, with its undisguised threats of economic extermination, compelled small oil-refiners to sell out at a low price. Rockefeller also took advantage of the railroads at every opportunity. In the notorious (if short-lived) South Improvement Company episode, he actually secured rebates not only on the oil his own company shipped, but on the shipments of his competitors as well. With unmistakable ruthlessness, John D. Rockefeller admitted that in the Standard Oil Trust he wanted "only the big ones, those who have already proved they can do a big business. As for the others, unfortunately, they will have to die."

Instilling Order into Competitive Business Practices. Yet even after recounting such examples, there remains another side to the activities of the robber barons, as Matthew Josephson called them in a book by that name. Rockefeller's management of the Standard Oil Company marked the beginning of order and stability in an industry notorious for chaos. Prices, the supply of raw materials, and the employment of labor fluctuated so widely and wildly that companies rose and fell abruptly, leaving production neither systematized nor dependable. Consumers, especially, suffered from such instability. In 1873 illuminating oil sold for 17.9 cents a gallon, wholesale, in New York; a year later the price was 13 cents. In 1876 it was back up to 19 cents. After Standard Oil took over the industry, however, the price never rose above 8.5 cents for the remainder of the century, and sometimes it fell below that point. (At the same time, it should be noted that Standard's rate of profit during the last 20 years of the century was very high, between 15 and 20 per cent of the net assets annually.)

The social implications of an example like Standard Oil are broader than mere reduction in consumer prices, though that is certainly important. At a time when the public was acutely suspicious of any governmental regulation of industry, certain powerful corporations imposed private regulation to instill order in an excessively competitive economy. Defenders of private enterprise have traditionally denounced collectivism; yet private enterprise itself imposed a kind of collective control over some American industries during the late nineteenth century.

As the example of Standard Oil suggests, a variety of motives drove these entrepreneurs to create their industrial empires. Certainly they wanted money; certainly they sought power—just as the man who runs for President or governor. But they also wanted something more socially useful. John D. Rockefeller sought to organize a chaotic industry; Henry Ford wanted to produce a serviceable car which the average American could afford. Edward Harriman strove to encircle the globe with his steamship and railroad lines, but also worked to make his Union Pacific a well-run, up-to-date railroad with double-tracks and smooth curves to improve service and increase safety.

The Growth of Big Business

The giant corporate enterprise has been the hallmark of American economic development. In the nineteenth century no other industrialized people used the corporation so widely as Americans, and no nation, except perhaps Germany, was so well known for the large size of its industrial firms.

The business corporation is an old legal institution that stems from the English joint-stock company of the sixteenth century. In the 1800's, the corporation replaced the partnership or the individually owned company for several sound business reasons. Being a permanent legal entity, the corporation, unlike the partnership, is not disrupted by the death of one of its members. It enjoys limited liability; that is, those who invest (buy stock) in it are not legally liable, as partners are, for the debts of the corporation beyond the amount of their investment. Furthermore, the corporation provided the means to attract the very substantial investment capital required by the large enterprises of the time.

The corporation did not become a prominent form of organization in manufacturing until after the Civil War, though it had been used widely in canal and railway construction. By 1900 the corporate form dominated American business; 86 per cent of the output of mines and quarries and two thirds of manufactures were produced by corporations. Considering the

English origins of the joint-stock company, British manufacturers, unlike those in America, made surprisingly little use of the corporation; in fact, before 1862 not all kinds of economic enterprises were legally entitled to enjoy limited liability. Until the end of the nineteenth century most British industrial firms were owned by individuals or by partnerships.

But it is the size of the enterprise, rather than its form, which distinguishes American business, for the British did not develop the giant company even when the corporate form became more popular. (The British, as a result, never engaged in the battles over monopoly and concentration of industrial power so prevalent in American economic and political controversy during the late nineteenth century and after.) Large-scale enterprise in Britain became prominent only after 1914.

Before 1870, American industry was made up chiefly of small firms, whether incorporated or not. By the opening of the new century, however, the picture had altered substantially; the great company, grown large either by expansion or by buying out competitors, had become prominent, foreshadowing an even larger role in the future. In the iron and steel industry, to cite one example, the capital and production per firm increased 500 per cent in these three decades, while the number of firms actually decreased five per cent. In some industries, giant enterprises, like Standard Oil, the American Sugar Refining Company, United States Steel, International Harvester, and Armour and Company, controlled 50 per cent or more of the total production. Moreover, many of these giant companies were vertically integrated. That is, they owned everything that they needed, from their sources of raw material (oil wells, sugar plantations, and coal and ore mines), to the transportation facilities (railroads, pipelines, steamship companies, Great Lakes ore boats), and marketing facilities (warehouses, retail stores, and wholesale distributing agencies). This kind of ownership is contrasted to horizontal integration in which a company controls only one phase of production.

Basically, the reasons for the growth of the giant industrial enterprise in the United States lie in the enormous market created by the railway network and the burgeoning cities. Cities contained not only millions of consumers for "soft" goods, but, in their construction, created a large demand for concrete, brick, iron and steel, transportation equipment, and other capital goods. Aside from this general basis for growth, individual firms had their own motives for expansion. Sometimes, as in the case of Standard Oil, growth resulted from the desire to cut competition; hence, small firms were bought out and joined to the big ones. At other times, vertical integration promised greater efficiency and cheaper access to raw materials, which also resulted in growth. This, apparently, was the motive behind the purchase of the ore-rich Mesabi range in Minnesota in 1896 by the Carnegie Steel Company and in the purchases of ore fields by the Anaconda Copper Company. In such other industries as explosives, paper, and coal mining, mergers were prompted by a desire to lower production costs through the wider use of existing machines and techniques.

Development of a Nationwide Market. The careers of Gustavus Swift and Philip D. Armour in meat-packing reveal the difficulties that confront entrepreneurs seeking to build a nationwide industry, as well as some of the reasons why these businesses soon mushroomed into large-scale ventures. Prior to the invention of the refrigerator car in the 1870's, a nationwide fresh meat-packing industry was not possible; only pickled or salted meat could be shipped long distances. Fresh meat arrived in the cities on the hoof, was slaughtered in evil-smelling abattoirs on the outskirts, and then distributed through local butcher shops. But even the ice-cooled refrigerator car did not solve all the problems of a fresh-meat industry seeking a national market. Finding local outlets for such meat was not easy; butchers and abattoir owners vigorously fought the introduction of "imported" meat, and the public could not be persuaded that meat from animals killed a thousand miles away and days earlier could be either as fresh or as sanitary as meat from newly slaughtered animals. A cook book compiled in 1889 by a chef at Delmonico's, a fashionable New York restaurant, for example, advised that refrigerated beef was unsatisfactory for good cuisine, and in the nineties many a New York butcher proudly displayed a sign reading "No Chicago beef sold here."

To surmount this and other opposition, Swift and Armour set up their own distribution and transportation agencies. They sent out salesmen, bought out butcher shops, and opened retail outlets. Because the railroads refused to introduce refrigerator cars, the packing houses bought and maintained their own. In order to be able to undersell local butchers and abattoirs, the meat packers cut costs by making use of waste products, thereby projecting themselves into new fields. Buttons were made from bones, glue from hoofs, combs and ornaments from horns. By the 1890's both Armour and Swift owned glue, soap, glycerine, and fertilizer factories. And because waste products constituted 35 per cent of an animal's weight, the packers saved on transportation costs. This, in combination with vigorous selling, permitted them to undersell locally dressed meat virtually anywhere in the United States. By the 1890's most of the abattoirs had been eliminated by the competition; it was clear that only large firms, necessarily few in number, would dominate the industry thereafter.

Other consumers' goods firms like the American Tobacco Company, United Fruit, and the National Biscuit Company, displayed the same pattern. If size was often the result of trying to buy out competition and to stabilize production, continued growth just as often stemmed from the need to find markets for the enormous potential output of the machines.

One of the major characteristics of American industry by the end of the century was the large size of its firms. At the same time that American business was developing its capital goods industry, it was also building a giant consumers' goods industry, to satisfy the market created by the growing urban population. Thus, one result of industrialization was that Americans became a people of plenty as well as a people of power.

Corporate Organizational Experiments. Historically, it took a number of decades for the giant industrial combinations to discover the most practical organizational structure. One of the earliest devices, the pool, proved to be among the least satisfactory, as we have seen in the case of the railroads. A pool in the distilling industry in 1881, for example, lasted scarcely a year before one of the companies broke away—a common danger since no pool agreement was legally enforceable. A device almost as transitory was the trust, which John D. Rockefeller introduced in 1882 with Standard Oil. Although the name "trust" later came to stand for any large firm of whatever legal form, it originally had a quite restricted meaning. It was simply a group of men who held in trust, on behalf of the stockholders, the stocks of a number of companies. This arrangement allowed the trustees to coordinate the operations of what otherwise would have been competing firms. The trust was obviously superior to the pool as a device for checking excessive competition and production. As its popularity grew, this organizational structure found favor in other industries besides oil, notably distilling, which had experienced disastrous results with the pool. As a form of industrial organization, however, the trust soon was severely limited by the state courts, particularly in Ohio and New York, which declared it contrary to the prohibitions of the common law against restraint of trade.

The legal device that superseded the trust and has remained the typical form of organization of the giant firm is the holding company, which is simply a corporation empowered to hold the stock of other corporations. However, this type of organization was not legal until New Jersey made it so in 1888. Soon thereafter, New Jersey earned the reputation as the home of trusts, since so many big companies used its generous incorporation provisions. In time other states followed New Jersey's lead, if only to secure the incorporation fees.

Corporate Financing: The Investment Bank. Like the development of American enterprises, the growth of investment banking was at once a measure and a characteristic of industrial evolution in the United States. Investment banks are companies that devote themselves to marketing the securities of railroad and industrial properties, some of which by the late nineteenth century had become too large to be financed from earnings or by direct appeals to the public. Large accumulations of capital were especially important in financing the mergers and the purchases of other firms that were essential to business expansion of the late nineteenth century. Foremost among investment houses was J. P. Morgan and Company of New York, which played a central role in the reorganization of a number of railroads and other companies in the 1890's. Obviously the growth of such investment houses was both a consequence and a cause of the large size of American businesses.

Investment bankers were heavily involved in financing American industry and exerted a strong influence upon its development; usually they decreased the amount of competition. Once a house like J. P. Morgan had secured an interest in a firm, it also acquired some control over that firm's operations, perhaps by naming a member of the banking establishment to the firm's board of directors. Often the representatives of the House of Morgan would sit on the boards of two or more competing firms. In cases where the House of Morgan had an interest in both firms, the degree of competition would obviously be muted. Such interlocking directorates, as they were called, became common in the twentieth century as investment houses played an increasing role in the financing of American industry.

Not all American industrial firms, of course, were compelled to look to the bankers for funds; the Ford Motor Company was the classic instance of one which did not. But there were enough such financial arrangements to arouse concern over their threat to competition. Many public figures in the early twentieth century began to denounce the "Money Trust" for reducing competition in industry and having a near monopoly on capital. In 1911, Congress finally undertook a major investigation of investment banking for just those reasons.

The Antitrust Movement

Despite the ability of the large industrial enterprises to produce great quantities of goods, often at reduced prices, their rapid growth and great power aroused hostility and fear among broad segments of the public. Small businessmen suffered from their competition, workers felt overwhelmed by their domination of the labor market, and farmers protested their control of transportation facilities and monopolization of the manufacture of agricultural machinery. Moreover, political leaders and others saw them as potential monopolies capable of destroying small businesses and victimizing the consumer through excessive prices. And it was a fact that the size of the giant corporation often permitted it to operate beyond the controls of competition, since three or four big enterprises might produce almost the entire output of a whole industry. In such cases, it was asked, what would prevent them from agreeing on prices far above the cost of production and realizing large profits at the expense of the public? In the sphere of government and politics, Americans had long been accustomed to thinking that power needed to be constantly checked, and that diffusion of power was one of the best ways to do it. It was natural, therefore, for them to demand that similar checks be placed upon the unprecedented economic power of the new and rapidly growing industrial combines.

During the 1880's public concern over the burgeoning trusts reached a high point. The Cullom Committee of the Senate, investigating railroad abuses, concluded in 1885 that "no general question of governmental policy" was more prominent among the people than "that of controlling the steady growth and extending influence of corporate power and of regulating its relations to the public. . . ." Already a dozen or more states had written prohibitions against monopolies and trusts into their constitutions, and several others had passed statutory prohibitions. Most of these states were in the West or the South, where declining farm prices had made the dominant agricultural population particularly sensitive to the power of the railroads and the industrial combinations. Legislative investigations by state and federal authorities publicized new and sometimes shocking examples of monopolistic activities by some of the giants. An investigation of trusts in New York in 1888, for instance, turned up evidence of such ruthless suppression of competition that it inspired a suit against the Sugar Trust in that state and one against Standard Oil in Ohio; the result was the legal dissolution of trusts. President Harrison, in his first annual message in December 1889, urged Congress to take action against combinations that crush competition, for "they are dangerous conspiracies against the public good, and should be made the subject of prohibitory and even penal legislation."

The Sherman Antitrust Act. At the first meeting of the Fifty-first Congress in December 1889, Republican John Sherman of Ohio proposed an antitrust measure, Senate Bill No. 1. The people, Sherman said in defending his bill, were anxious about "the concentration of capital into vast combinations to control production and trade and to break down competition." In view of the size of these organizations, he went on, "Congress alone can deal with them." After five days of debate the bill passed overwhelmingly, and a short time later it passed the House without dissent, though some 85 members did not vote. It became law on July 2, 1890.

The Sherman Act, as the first antitrust statute came to be called, declared illegal "every contract, combination in the form of trust or otherwise, or conspiracy, in restraint of trade or commerce among the several states. . . ." Conviction under the law could bring a fine of $5000 and one year's imprisonment. Section 7 authorized private persons to institute civil suits for injuries arising from unlawful combinations and provided that triple damages, including court costs, might be awarded a successful plaintiff.

The vagueness of the definition of monopoly in the law has occasioned much subsequent criticism, including the accusation that the ambiguity reflected an insincere motivation on the part of the sponsors. But the vagueness was apparently deliberate. The language was actually that of the common law, which had traditionally forbidden monopolies and restraints on trade. By bringing the common law definition into the federal courts, Sherman and his supporters hoped to utilize its flexibilities and thus avoid spelling out in the act all the varieties of illegal industrial combinations. Unfortunately, this approach depended upon the courts, and they did not cooperate. Instead they chose to interpret the statute narrowly, thus necessitating further antitrust legislation in the twentieth century.

The Sherman Act, which, after the Interstate Commerce Act, was the second attempt to deal nationally with some of the new problems of an industrial society, offered a quite different solution. In place of a regulatory commission, Congress simply used the power of government to enforce competition, the traditional protector of the consumer. The different approach of the new act can be explained by the contemporary belief that railroads were public utilities and therefore subject to regulation by public authority, while manufacturing enterprises were not, and thus should continue to be controlled by competition. Moreover, the provision for triple damages to injured parties suggests that the sponsors of the act thought prohibitions of monopolies would be self-executing and not actually dependent directly upon government action. In this regard the Sherman Act reflected the prevalent belief in the social virtues of individual self-interest as well as the popular distaste for government intervention in the economy.

Until American influence in Germany after World War II inspired the enactment of a similar antitrust statute, no other industrial country followed the United States example of legislating to ensure competition. Pre-war Germany, for instance, was so unconcerned with the question of the concentration of economic power that it officially encouraged large enterprises, called cartels, and other forms of combination.

For ten years or more after its passage, the government rarely invoked the Sherman Act, and was seldom successful when it did. Of the 26 suits instituted between 1890 and 1903, only ten were won by the government, and four of those were against labor unions and not business corporations. Basically, the administration of President Grover Cleveland saw little reason for the act, and at first the Supreme Court was not much more enthusiastic. This attitude is well illustrated by the case against the Sugar Trust, *United States v. E. C. Knight Company,* decided in 1895. The government lawyers presented an unnecessarily weak argument, and the Court took an incredibly narrow view of the meaning of the act. Although both sides in the case admitted that the company controlled 98 per cent of the production of sugar in the country, the Court announced that manufacture was not trade and therefore the virtual monopoly of production was not a restraint of trade prohibited by the act. Upon learning of the decision in the Knight case, Attorney General Richard Olney, who was responsible for the government's case, wrote privately, "You will have observed that the government has been defeated in the Supreme Court on the trust question. I always supposed it would be and have taken the responsibility of not prosecuting under a law I believe to be no good. . . ." Thereafter, Olney employed the act solely against labor unions. The Attorneys General under the succeeding McKinley administration were scarcely more active; they entered three suits in four years.

In two cases at the end of the decade, however, the Supreme Court put back into the Sherman law some of the teeth it had drawn in the Knight case. In *United States v. Trans-Missouri Freight Association* (1897), the Court applied the Sherman Act for the first time to railroad combinations by upholding the government's argument that combinations to fix rates were illegal. Then in 1899, in *Addystone Pipe and Steel Company* v. *United States,* the Court unanimously held that a pool among manufacturers of steel and iron pipes was illegal even though, in this instance, the pool controlled only 30 per cent of the nation's production of pipe. This decision, when taken together with the Knight decision, which the Court did not overrule, placed the judicial definition of monopoly in an ambiguous position. In effect, the Court said that combinations among independent companies to fix prices were illegal *(Addystone),* but that if a single company monopolized production in a given industry, such an action did not restrain trade and therefore was not a violation of the Sherman Act *(Knight).*

Such an approach possessed a certain narrow logic, but it evaded the intention of the Act to deal realistically with economic monopoly. Not until well into the twentieth century, and then only after much public and Congressional agitation, would the Court take a more realistic view of the meaning of the Sherman Act and of the problem of industrial monopoly. In short, when the United States achieved the position of the chief industrial power in the world, it had only begun to wrestle with the question of controlling and channelling the new forces and institutions emerging from the Economic Revolution.

The Rise of the Industrial City

The site of the Economic Revolution was the industrial city. Even though cities have been the center of man's culture throughout his history, never before the nineteenth century have they been the focus of his economic life. Theretofore, in all civilizations and at all times, the great majority of men had tilled the soil. Then, about a century and a half ago, a momentous change began. Under the impact of industrialization, first thousands, then millions of people in western Europe and in the United States uprooted themselves from the land to move to the cities.

During the 1880's both European and American cities grew rapidly. In Prussia, for example, the population of cities increased by two million, while the rural areas gained a mere 500,000; in England and Wales during the same period the cities added 3.75 million people while the countryside actually declined by 200,000. In the United States, as we have already seen, the rate of urban growth in that decade was among the highest in history.

At the time of the Civil War, barely one fifth of the population of the nation lived in towns of 2500 people or more, but by the turn into the twentieth century 40 per cent of the American people were classified as urban-dwellers. In fact, even in 1890 the eight largest cities of the country accounted for one tenth of the total population. Perhaps more significant than the number of people in cities was the concentration in urban areas of the nation's wealth. Whereas in 1880 the value of urban and of rural real estate was

POPULATION DISTRIBUTION 1870-1900

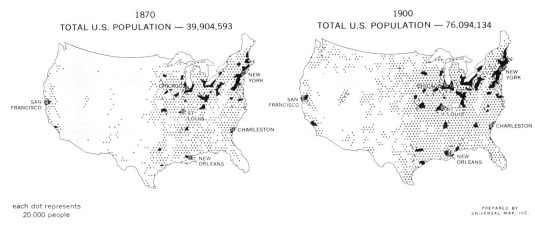

1870
TOTAL U.S. POPULATION — 39,904,593

1900
TOTAL U.S. POPULATION — 76,094,134

each dot represents
20,000 people

PREPARED BY
UNIVERSAL MAP, INC.

During this short period the most striking changes in population distribution include the general westward movement of settlers and the expansion of urban industrial areas, especially in the Middle West and Northeast.

estimated to be approximately equal — about $10 billion each — in 1890 the value of farms was placed at $13 billion; all other real estate was calculated at $26 billion. This change was as good a measure of the shift of social power from country to city as might be found.

Figures that encompass the whole nation, however, obscure the important fact that urban civilization was not evenly spread across the country. In the plains and mountain states and in the South, cities were scarce and widely scattered, for they developed principally where industry was expanding. On the other hand, in areas where industry flourished — such as the Northeast, the states bordering the Great Lakes, and the Pacific coastal states — cities often blended into one another, forming sprawling metropolitan centers that extended the influence of the large metropolis far beyond its corporate limits. "Dormitory cities" — suburbs which served as homes for employees of the industry and trade in large neighboring cities — were already emerging in the 1880's. Lake Forest was a "bedroom" for Chicago, as Greenwich, Connecticut, was for New York City and Brookline for Boston.

A large part of the urban growth of these years must be related to the great immigration. After the Civil War the stream of immigrants, especially from eastern and southern Europe, widened, until in the 1880's it became a flood equalled only in the early twentieth century. Most of these millions of immigrants (over five million entered in the 1880's alone) settled in the expanding industrial cities, for the economic opportunities that the newcomers sought in America were located there. The rapid growth of many cities during the 1880's was the result of immigration. The populations of industrial centers such as Fall River, Massachusetts; Paterson, New Jersey; and Rochester,

New York; as well as those of big cities—Chicago, San Francisco, Milwaukee, Providence, New York City, and Minneapolis—were from a third to a half foreign born.

Urban Health Hazards. Any city presents problems of organization and social control because of its concentration of people in one place; the spectacular growth of American metropolises in the 1880's compounded the problems. To take one example, as the number of people increased, the disposal of human and industrial wastes changed from an insistent problem to a positive danger. Despite the threat to health, nearby rivers and bays were tempting places in which to dump garbage and sewage, and there the wastes were commonly deposited. In Indianapolis, where only ten per cent of the homes in 1880 possessed water closets, the excrement from the privies was collected periodically to be dumped into the local river. The soil of New Orleans was reported by the Census of 1880 to be saturated "very largely with the oozings of foul privy vaults," while the porous soil in Baltimore (population 332,000) made the 80,000 cesspools a menace to the wells from which the drinking water was drawn.

Such conditions inevitably fostered disease. In fact, death rates in cities were notoriously higher than they were in rural areas. Of course the concentration of people made the spread of infectious diseases painfully easy. During 1869 and 1870, for instance, Philadelphia experienced a scourge of scarlet

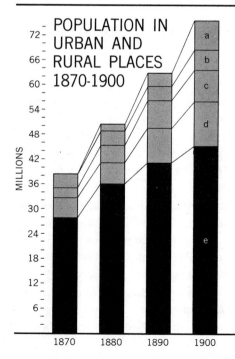

POPULATION IN URBAN AND RURAL PLACES 1870-1900

(MILLIONS, years 1870 1880 1890 1900)

NUMBER OF URBAN AND RURAL PLACES

none	1	3	3	a
7	7	8	12	b
45	69	113	145	c
611	862	1224	1577	d
— not available —		6490	8931	e
1870	1880	1890	1900	

		1870	1900
Striking changes occurred in the percentages of the total urban population which each of the various categories of cities comprised in 1900 as opposed to 1870.	a	00.0	21.3
	b	31.7	14.9
	c	27.1	29.1
	d	41.1	34.6

Two categories increased their percentages: cities of over one million, and cities from 25,000 to 250,000, with the most significant increase occurring in the largest cities. The percentages of the other two categories, cities from 250,000 to one million, and cities from 2,500 to 25,000 dropped significantly, with a particularly noticeable decrease in the former category.

a) Places over 1,000,000
b) Places 250,000-1,000,000
c) Places 25,000-250,000
d) Places 2,500-25,000
e) Rural (Places 2,500 and less)

fever that killed over 1700 people and left many more deaf, crippled, and debilitated. Half the children of Chicago, it was reported in 1882, died before reaching five years of age because of unhealthy living conditions.

Standing Room Only. Concentrations of people presented new housing problems to which the tenement house was the most obvious response. This multi-family dwelling was four or five stories high, usually made of wood, and contained small, often windowless rooms, serving as bedrooms. In 1883 the Health Department of Chicago reported that deaths in the tenement districts outnumbered those in the residential wards almost three to one. The interior of a one-room Boston tenement in the 1870's was described in an official report as "unspeakably filthy; the furniture: two or three old chairs and an old table. No fire, and the room, damp, dark and cold. . . . The two oldest children were dirty and ragged and leaning against the window on the side of the room. . . . The youngest was . . . about worn out and apparently half-starved. . . ."

New York introduced the so-called dumbbell tenement in 1879 as an improvement in mass housing, only to see it become the name for the worst in tenements. The structure took its title from the shape of the floor plan, which showed a shallow indentation along the sides to form an air shaft when the buildings were placed side by side. In practice, however, the air shaft proved to be much too narrow to offer any air or light to the apartments below the top floor. Moreover, the few toilets provided were wholly inadequate for the large number of families crowded into the building. Yet the dumbbell plan continued to be used throughout the remainder of the century. The menace to health and to morals that the tenement represented was already biting at the consciences of some people when Jacob Riis, a Danish immigrant, published his book, *How the Other Half Lives,* in 1890. By using the recently developed techniques in photography as well as vivid descriptions of life in the slums, Riis graphically portrayed the depressing and demoralizing conditions of tenement life. Yet in 1900 some 2.4 million people were packed into tenements in New York City alone. Other kinds of housing for the industrial working class were not much better in other large cities. In Chicago the immigrant poor were often reduced to living in back-lot shanties or in lofts, which one Chicago inspector described as "unfit for habitation by civilized people."

Although buildings occupied more and more of the available land in the cities, urban authorities were slow to compensate for the loss of recreational space or to provide new facilities. It is true that New York City in the late 1850's opened its magnificent Central Park, but some large cities, like Brooklyn (not yet a part of New York), Newark, Pittsburgh, and Cleveland, actually devoted more land to cemeteries in 1890 than they did to public parks. Not until the twentieth century would it be widely recognized that recreational facilities, once readily available and taken for granted in the countryside and the small city, had to be planned and provided for in the new environment of the industrial city.

Breeder of Crime and Corruption. The wealth and poverty that existed side by side in the city seemed to stimulate crime, or at least there was more crime in urban than in country districts. Moreover, in the 1880's and 1890's urban crime rates rose sharply. In a three-square-mile section of Chicago in 1893, one quarter of the population was arrested at least once in the course of the year for some infraction of the law. Another measure of the social disorganization of the cities was the legislation passed against homeless unemployed. Between 1876 and 1893, some 21 states passed laws specifically against tramps, which imposed such punishments as jail sentences, public whippings, and temporary forced labor. Gangs and gang warfare also became more common, though big cities like New York had long been plagued with lawlessness and violence.

Unfortunately, police operations which were intended to check such developments were too often lax, when not actually corrupt. An investigation in 1894 revealed that jobs in the New York Police Department had been up for sale to the highest bidder and that the police had been exacting blackmail from bawdy houses and gamblers instead of enforcing the laws against them. Two potent sources of crime and corruption, the prostitute and the liquor dealer, were at home in the city as nowhere else. In the late 1860's it was estimated that there were 12,000 prostitutes operating in New York City alone, and the Census of 1880 showed that the 500 cities with populations of 5000 or more supported 80,000 liquor establishments.

Since most buildings in the growing industrial cities were of wooden construction, fire was a constant and horrifying menace. The most famous fire of the period occurred in Chicago in 1871. It virtually gutted the central part of the city, leaving thousands homeless and inflicting damage estimated at almost $200 million. Only the next year, 65 acres of buildings were burned out in Boston, to be followed by another fire in 1873, the damage from which exceeded one million dollars. Each year the nation set new records for fire losses. As in dealing with deficiencies in recreation, police protection, and sanitation, the cities turned only slowly to meeting the mounting danger of fire. The proper answer was full-time, paid firemen instead of volunteer companies, but as late as 1871 the large metropolis of Philadelphia was still depending on volunteers; St. Paul, Minnesota, did not shift to paid firemen until 1881. As in so many areas of urban development, other aspects of the Economic Revolution supplied some help. New technology—the telegraphic fire alarm system, the fireboat, the water tower, the sprinkler system in buildings, and fire-proof construction materials such as steel, brick, and terra cotta—all of which were introduced in the 1870's and 1880's—helped to diminish the loss of life and property from fire.

Everyone recognized that the big cities with their overcrowded tenements, dirty streets, and high crime rates were unattractive, but the smaller, more slowly growing cities were not much prettier. Lord Bryce, the English scholar and political commentator, although in general favorably impressed with

American institutions, waxed sarcastic over the monotonous appearance of urban America. The cities, he wrote, "differ from one another only herein, that some of them are built more with brick than with wood, and others more with wood than brick. In all else they are alike, both great and small. . . ." Most American cities, he might have added, lacked even paving, except on a minority of their streets. Less than one fifth of the streets of an old and large city like New Orleans were paved in 1880; in the rainy season they were a sea of mud, and in the dry months the dust rose in clouds. Of Chicago's almost 2000 miles of streets in 1890, only 628 were paved and less than half of those with asphalt. It was not until the middle eighties that asphalt paving — smooth and long-lived — began to replace the cobblestone or brick paving that was used in the few places where pavement had been introduced.

The Urban Spirit. Although cities responded slowly to the physical problems inherent in rapid urban growth, their real importance lay in their reshaping of men's values and attitudes. As one minister said of cities in the 1880's, "The evil of them is not in their size, but in the avarice, luxury, oppression, and vice that haunts them." Although he was mistaken in implying that cities hold a monopoly on vice, he was right in seeing city people as different. In contrast to rural folk, the vast majority of whom were farmers, city-dwellers were remarkably diverse in national background, occupation, standard of living, and education. The source of urban diversity, of course, was the enormous range of economic opportunities provided by the city. That opportunity was the magnet that drew millions of farmers from the American countryside and from the peasant farms of Europe in the last quarter of the nineteenth century.

Life in the city was highly competitive and fast-paced; people were constantly on the move; some businesses prospered while others failed. The very face of the city was constantly changing as men tore it down, expanded, or rebuilt it. Living in a city involved frequent contact with many people; yet, paradoxically, that contact was less intimate than in rural life. One met so many people in stores, at work, and in school that one could know them only in passing, if at all. Hence the urban dweller's relation with others was less personal, and human relationships tended to be based more on utility than on sentiment; thought and action tended to be increasingly rational rather than traditional. Urban people, therefore, were more willing to accept change, to tolerate differences, and to welcome new ideas; after all, they saw change and differences all around them every day. One general result was that reform movements often got their start and a better hearing in cities than in rural regions. The price the city man paid for this greater receptivity to change, however, was often increased anxiety and insecurity. The loosening of traditional values and morals weakened that sense of social cohesion from which security derives.

The Metropolis: Center of Socio-Economic and Cultural Progress. The late nineteenth-century cities, it should be emphasized, were not simply a source of problems. They were a necessary part of the Economic Revolution. They provided not only markets for agricultural commodities and a labor supply for industry, as we have seen, but also an important fillip to economic growth. As the railroad boom of the eighties subsided, the expanding cities, with their need for new housing, public buildings, street construction, municipal lighting, and intra-urban transportation lines, provided one of the principal new sources of activities that kept the economic machine going.

The education of millions of newcomers — foreign-born and native — should also be recognized as one of the achievements of the late nineteenth-century city. Despite the problems that the rapid growth of cities produced, the educational opportunities in cities even during those very difficult years were always considerably better than those offered in rural areas. In 1891, for example, the typical elementary school year in the cities of the United States was 180 – 200 days as compared with 70 – 150 days in rural areas. Moreover, it was the cities of the 1870's and later that provided secondary education for the masses for the first time; some even provided college education. In short, the cities of the nineteenth century were centers of cultural as well as social advancement.

Having examined the industrial aspects of the Economic Revolution, let us now turn to the transformation of agriculture and its effects upon the people who manned the Economic Revolution.

SUGGESTED READING

For a general account of the Economic Revolution there is no better place to begin than the contemporary David A. Wells, *Recent Economic Changes* (1895). The fullest modern account is Edward C. Kirkland, *Industry Comes of Age; Business, Labor, and Public Policy, 1860–1897* (1961). Ida Tarbell, *The Nationalizing of Business, 1878–1898* (1936), emphasizes social history. Highly provocative in analyzing the meaning and impact of laissez-faire thought is the short but incisive study by James Willard Hurst, *Law and the Conditions of Freedom in the Nineteenth-Century United States* (1956). Equally provocative and widely influential is W. W. Rostow, *Five Stages of Economic Growth** (1960); it compares American development with that of other countries.

The literature on railroads is voluminous. John Moody, *The Railroad Builders* (1919) is old, but still the only synthesis. Also published many years ago, but readable, is Robert Riegel, *The Story of the Western Railroads** (1926). A brief, yet important study is George R. Taylor and Irene Neu, *The American Railroad Network, 1861 – 1890* (1956). The pioneer article on the evaluation of the land grants to railroads is Robert S. Henry, "The Railroad Land Grant Legend in American History Texts," *Mississippi Valley Historical Review,* **XXXII** (September, 1945), 171 – 94. For

* Available in a paperback edition.

railroad men's conception of themselves see Thomas C. Cochran, *Railroad Leaders, 1845–1890* (1953). Oscar Lewis, *The Big Four* (1941) is an interesting account of the men who built the Central and Southern Pacific railroads. A knowing summary statement on aid to railroads can be found in Carter Goodrich, *Government Promotion of American Canals and Railroads, 1880–1890* (1960). Robert Fogel, *The Union Pacific Railroad: A Case in Premature Enterprise* (1960) measures the gain to the economy from the Union Pacific. His more recent *Railroads and American Economic Growth* (1964) questions the importance usually assigned to railroads in American economic development. A valuable study in the reevaluation of the origins of the demands for regulation of railroads is Lee Benson, *Merchants, Farmers, and Railroads* (1955). Virtually the only general study of the relationship between technology and society is the popular Roger Burlingame, *Engines of Democracy* (1940). More informative, but narrower in conception is W. Paul Strassmann, *Risk and Technological Innovation: American Manufacturing Methods During the Nineteenth Century* (1959); he concludes that not much risk was assumed. A very important, though somewhat technical study is H. J. Habakkuk, *American and British Technology in the Nineteenth Century; the Search for Labour-Saving Inventions* (England, 1962). A monumental study of an important practitioner of technological innovation is Matthew Josephson, *Edison** (1959).

The many works on the entrepreneurs and individual businesses are too numerous to cite here. Among the most important is Matthew Josephson's readable although biased *The Robber Barons** (1934). Equally readable but more sympathetic are the portraits of Ford, Edison, Carnegie, Harriman, and J. P. Morgan by economist Jonathan Hughes, *The Vital Few* (1966). Of the several studies on the social origins of business leaders perhaps the most convincing is F. W. Gregory and I. D. Neu, "Industrial Elite in the 1870's" in *Men in Business,** ed. by William Miller (1952). Chester Destler, "Entrepreneurial Leadership Among the 'Robber Barons': a Trial Balance," *Journal of Economic History,* VI (Supplement, 1946) 28–49, points up their failings. Edward Chase Kirkland, *Dream and Thought in the Business Community, 1860–1900** (1956), does justice to the various aspirations and limitations of the so-called robber barons.

A seminal article is Alfred D. Chandler, Jr., "The Beginnings of 'Big Business' in American Industry," *Business History Review,* XXXIII (Spring, 1959), 1–31. The best study of the movement to limit business is Hans B. Thorelli, *The Federal Antitrust Policy* (1955). John Moody, *The Truth About the Trusts* (1904) provides important information on the consolidation movement.

Adna Weber, *The Growth of Cities in the Nineteenth Century* (1899), though very old, is still useful for its factual data; the most recent compendium of urban history is Blake McKelvey, *The Urbanization of America, 1860–1915* (1963). Still helpful is Arthur M. Schlesinger, *The Rise of the City 1878–1898* (1933). Constance M. Green, *American Cities in the Growth of the Nation** (1957) deals with several cities. A fine collection of sources on urban history is *The American City: A Documentary History,** ed. by Charles N. Glaab (1963).

CHAPTER THREE

THE ECONOMIC REVOLUTION: THE WEST, FARMERS, AND INDUSTRIAL WORKERS

THE DEVELOPMENT of machines, their application to manufacturing, and the growth of large-scale industrial enterprises constituted only one aspect of the Economic Revolution. Another was the opening up and exploitation of the hitherto untouched far western regions of the country, which contributed new resources to the nation's economic growth. Still a third element was an agricultural revolution that raised the production of food and fiber to unbelievable heights in a few years, releasing a flood of American foodstuffs upon the markets of the world.

Meanwhile, the expanding manufacturing sector converted millions of native American farmers and European peasants into an industrial labor force, attracted by the new opportunities in the cities and factories of America. But the Economic Revolution, for all its promise, had such a profound impact that both those who stayed on the land and those who went into the factories felt impelled to form organizations to help them adjust to the new economic order. The growth of these organizations of protest and adjustment is also a part of the story of the Economic Revolution.

The Challenge of the Far West

When the Civil War began, the continental boundaries of the United States were approximately the same as they are today, but less than half of the area of the country was occupied by white men. White settlements extended just slightly beyond the tier of states west of the Mississippi River. Once a westward traveler left those states behind, he came upon virtually no settlements for over 1000 miles with the exception of a few settlers in the Sante Fe region of New Mexico and a cluster of Mormons in Utah. Most of the enormous expanse of land that lay between the great bend of the Missouri River and the Sierra Nevada Mountains was given over to the Indian, the buffalo, the prairie dog, and the coyote. The opening and settlement of this vast area about the size of Europe west of the Soviet Union was the work of the next 30 years.

A Forbidding Territory. Why was this region the last frontier when California and Oregon, located much farther west, had been settled long before? The primary reason was the difficulty faced by settlers accustomed to the moist, forest frontier of the older regions of the country. What could men from the East do with the vast, grassy plains where the sod was so tough that it could snap off the blade of a plow, and where the scarcity of trees deprived them of the wood they had depended upon for fuel, homes, and fencing? Furthermore, although the soil was undoubtedly rich in many places, other portions of the Great Plains and the Great Basin were little more than sandy wastes, on which dust storms had raged long before the first furrow was cut.

Photo: Deadwood, South Dakota in 1876—a gold mining town which had mushroomed in the wilderness —consisted of a few makeshift shacks filled with would-be millionaires, and not a woman in sight. All these factors added up to the almost legendary loneliness and violence which existed in such areas.

Early travelers and explorers were so struck by the aridity and treelessness of the plains that maps of the 1840's and 1850's designated large sections of this terrain as the Great American Desert. Though this title was a misnomer, rainfall on the Great Plains, even in the grassy regions, is much scantier than in the East, and west of the 100th meridian, on the so-called High Plains, the average annual precipitation is not enough for farming as customarily practiced in the humid East.

West of the formidable Rockies, the pioneer encountered a landscape that to one nurtured in forested, humid lands was at once breathtakingly beautiful and vaguely forbidding. The Great Basin and Plateau provinces, especially including what are now the states of Nevada, Utah, western Colorado, northern Arizona, and portions of southern Wyoming and Idaho, are the driest regions in the United States. In fact, large sections are literally deserts. Instead of oceans of rippling grasses, as on the plains, these regions have only sparse vegetation, unattractive and useless, consisting largely of cactus, sage brush, and a few short grasses. The most striking characteristic of the southern two thirds of the region is the craggy face of the land. Stark, eroded mesas, wind-carved rock pinnacles of curious and wonderful shapes, deep parched gullies, and broad alkali flats made the area a wonderland to the first explorers and a nightmare to the first farmers. Confronted by such poor economic opportunities, most American pioneers passed over the Great Plains, the Rockies, and the Great Basin, not settling down until they reached the wet and fertile valleys of Oregon and California.

Up to the Civil War, of all the men of European culture and tradition, only the Mormons, after being hounded out of the East, had displayed the industry and imagination necessary to bring to fruit the empty and discouraging lands of the Great Basin. They showed that irrigation, carefully planned on a large scale, could resuscitate the seemingly dead soil. Although no others attempted such a task, it is probably accurate to say that the Mormons' efforts, though successful in a small area, could not have been applied with equal results to the whole region. Even today, thousands of acres of the Great Basin lie uncultivated because of a dearth of water, despite the fact that the region now boasts a large number of dams and irrigation projects. But the dams have made clear that only a new technology could meet the challenge of the Far West. Hence its settlement and exploitation waited upon industrial developments elsewhere in the nation.

By the 1860's, the forces that would open these regions were in motion. The discovery of gold and silver was the first incentive for men to venture into the hitherto neglected reaches between the Missouri River and the Pacific coastal states.

The Mining Impetus: Gold! More than any other commodity, gold has fascinated men and excited their cupidity; the prospect of acquiring it has drawn them from the ends of the earth and the most comfortable lives. Recognizing this power, Johann Sutter, a Swiss immigrant living quietly in

California, tried to suppress knowledge of the discovery of gold on his land in 1848. But his effort to preserve his tranquil and almost idyllic life in the Far West failed. Within a year, the news of the discovery triggered a world-wide movement of fortune seekers, which soon propelled California into statehood and enormous wealth. By the summer of 1850, when California became a state, the taxable property of San Francisco alone was said to be worth $40 million; in 1852, eager miners extracted from the ground over $81 million worth of precious metals.

In the early days, gold mining was an individual enterprise. A man staked a claim near some water, which he used to flush buckets of dirt through a sluice or over a pan. The gold, being heavier than the dirt, sank to the bottom, while the water washed away the stone and gravel. The work was arduous, monotonous, and time-consuming, for actual nuggets of gold were hard to find. Most miners, if they discovered any gold at all, had to labor countless hours to accumulate a few fine particles. Despite these drawbacks, placer mining, as this process was called, attracted many because it demanded little capital and virtually no skill; moreover, the miner, if he was lucky enough, did not have to share his good fortune with anyone. Placer mining, however, was only a passing phase of the industry, for gold occurs naturally in rock formations, not in a free state. The loose gold found in streambeds and in the soil was the result of earlier erosion and might be recovered by a single prospector working alone. But no individual miner could extract the large sources of gold which were imbedded in rock formations; working such deposits required many men, elaborate rock crushing equipment, and substantial capital.

As early as 1855, gold seekers were fanning out into the Great Basin and Rocky Mountains. These prospectors and the people who followed when word of new strikes spread were the first settlers in the vast expanse of land between the Great Plains and California. Many of the present-day towns and cities of the Far West are as truly their creation as are the ghost towns for which the miners are more often remembered.

The push of the miners into the region began before the Civil War and continued right through it. The two earliest thrusts extended into what is now Nevada and Colorado. In the Washoe district of western Nevada, Henry Comstock in 1858 stumbled upon the great gold and silver lode that still bears his name; within 20 years, the mine yielded $300 million worth of precious metals. Almost at the same time, gold was discovered in eastern Colorado, near Pike's Peak. Thousands of fortune seekers flocked to the region in 1859; many came from great distances, as attested by the signs on the sides of their wagons, "Pike's Peak or Bust." Since gold-seeking was a speculative business, many of them did go broke and had to return as best they could. Gold and silver continued to be discovered at various Colorado sites through the early 1890's, thus gradually opening the whole region to settlement.

The ceaseless search for quick wealth drove miners and settlers into both the Northwest and the Southwest. Gold discoveries in 1862 along the Colorado River in what is now Arizona laid the foundations for the town of Tucson. In the North, on the banks of the Columbia and Snake rivers, other prospectors discovered "pay dirt" in the present-day states of Montana, Idaho, and Washington. Idaho's first permanent settlements grew out of the mining activities along the Snake River between 1861 and 1865. Gold also opened up Montana, for one of the biggest strikes of the 1860's was at Alder Gulch, later Virginia City. In 1864, another strike, this time on the upper Missouri River in Montana, started the city of Helena; when mining died out, it remained a commercial center and later became the state capital. The last new area of the West to be settled as a result of the miners' roving and unceasing quest for wealth was the Black Hills, in the southwestern corner of South Dakota; in 1876, perhaps as many as 15,000 gold-hungry men flooded into the region. Almost overnight they founded notorious Deadwood City, where Calamity Jane and Wild Bill Hickok were real people, and the robbing of the stage and even murder in the streets at high noon were common events.

What the rough and transient miners began, others finished. Soon after the miners arrived, merchants, craftsmen, cattlemen, and farmers moved in as permanent residents. Indeed, as the first placer sites became exhausted, mining itself rapidly changed. In place of the miner's pan and shovel, gold mining required crushing machinery, drills, hoists, and large crews of men. Such large equipment and labor demanded capital, knowledgeable entrepreneurs, and engineering skills. As a consequence, the mining corporation, financed by interests in the East or abroad, rapidly supplanted the individual miner in the same way (and for the same reasons) that the individual craftsman or small businessman was superseded in manufacturing. Under the new order of things, the miners became wage workers, paid by the hour and subject to the control of clock and foreman. Many of them were now family men, living a settled, if dangerous, life similar to that of any factory worker in a large manufacturing center.

Although the development of large-scale mining enterprises indicated that a stable society was growing in the Far West, the population increased slowly. Most of the mining districts achieved territorial status soon after the first strikes, but none of the mountain and Great Basin territories, with the exception of Nevada (1864) and Colorado (1876), acquired statehood until 1889 or after.

The exploitation of the precious metals was only the first way in which mining stimulated the population growth of these areas. Industrial ores, which were often found in association with gold and silver deposits, provided another reason for capital and people to flow into these barren and once-scorned regions. In northern Idaho, at Coeur d'Alene, the search for gold uncovered enormous lead deposits, which in the 1880's yielded millions of dollars. Copper mining in Utah and Montana also attracted capital and people. At Marcus Daly's Anaconda Silver Mine, purchased in 1881, miners uncovered a gigantic seam of copper instead of silver, which provided the

PHYSICAL REGIONS OF THE UNITED STATES
WITH CATTLE TRAILS AND MINING AREAS 1870-1900

PREPARED BY
UNIVERSAL MAP, INC.

Mining Area

Cattle Trail

MESABI RANGE, MINN.
IRON, 1884

BLACK HILLS, S.D.
GOLD, 1874

ANACONDA, BUTTE, MONT.
SILVER, COPPER 1875-76

BALD MTN. WYO.
GOLD 1890

COEUR D'ALENE, IDAHO
SILVER, LEAD, 1882

HAILEY, IDAHO
SILVER 1879

BONANZA, IDAHO
GOLD 1875

CARIBOU MTS. IDAHO
GOLD 1870

ROSLYN, WASH.
COAL 1883

BINGHAM, UTAH
COPPER 1887

EUREKA, NEV.
GOLD, LEAD 1872

VIRGINIA CITY
GOLD, SILVER 1859

LEADVILLE, COLO.
SILVER 1878

CRIPPLE CREEK
COLO. GOLD 1878

OURAY, COLO.
SILVER 1875

SILVERTON, COLO.
GOLD 1874

PRESCOTT, ARIZ.
GOLD 1870

GLOBE, ARIZ.
COPPER, SILVER 1873

TOMBSTONE, ARIZ.
SILVER 1879

LORDSBURG, ARIZ.
COPPER 1870

SEDALIA

ABILENE

BAXTER SPRINGS

DODGE CITY

OGALLALA

PUEBLO

CHISHOLM TRAIL

WESTERN TRAIL

SEDALIA AND BAXTER SPRINGS TRAIL

GOODNIGHT-LOVING TRAIL

Hudson R.

Lake Ontario

Lake Erie

Lake Huron

Lake Michigan

Lake Superior

ALLEGHENY PLATEAU

CUMBERLAND PLATEAU

APPALACHIAN HIGHLANDS

PIEDMONT

UPLAND

COASTAL PLAIN

ATLANTIC

Ohio River

Cumberland R.

Tennessee R.

INTERIOR PLATEAUS

OZARK HIGHLAND

Mississippi River

GULF

COASTAL PLAIN

Red River of the North

CENTRAL LOWLANDS

Red River

SUPERIOR UPLAND

Missouri River

CENTRAL LOWLANDS

Arkansas R.

Red R.

Rio Grande

Pecos R.

G R E A T   P L A I N S

R O C K Y   M T S.

BLACK HILLS

WYOMING BASIN

COLORADO PLATEAU

GRAND CANYON

Platte R.

Colorado R.

Green R.

Gila R.

WASATCH RANGE

G R E A T   B A S I N

DEATH VALLEY

MOJAVE DESERT

COLUMBIA PLATEAUS

Snake R.

Columbia R.

CASCADE RANGE

COAST RANGES

SIERRA NEVADA

Sacramento R.

San Joaquin R.

COAST RANGES

foundation for the later, very successful Anaconda Copper Company. The production of lead, copper, and zinc from these and other western sites, along with gold and silver, gave an additional thrust to the Economic Revolution that was transforming the United States.

Conquest of the Great Plains. Just as mining was the prime impetus for the settling of the mountain and Great Basin regions, so the cattle industry provided the incentive for the exploitation of the Great Plains. The true Great Plains begin along the line of the 98th meridian and continue to the Rockies. With only the interruption of the Black Hills, they stretch from Canada to the Rio Grande. For a generation, the topographical and climatic conditions of these plains had discouraged settlers; but what was forbidding to farmers was paradise for cattle and sheep. More important, by the 1860's, the growing industrial society of the East was ready to sustain a cattle industry. The railroad, which was then just entering the plains, provided the necessary transportation, and a growing urban population's demand for meat supplied the necessary markets.

The Long Drive. The cattle industry began in southern Texas. As a result of the Spanish introduction of cattle to the New World, a tough breed of wild cattle, the so-called Texas longhorns, roamed the southern plains in great herds, waiting for equally tough men to round them up. As early as the 1840's, some Texas cattle had been driven to markets in Ohio and elsewhere, but their numbers remained small. The Civil War temporarily disrupted the moving of cattle. In 1865 and 1866, however, the northbound herds became so large that farmers in Missouri and Arkansas, who did not want great numbers of transient cattle trampling their crops or transmitting cattle diseases, interfered with the drives. But the measure of success that attended the "long drive" clearly indicated that if a route farther west could be found, such drives could provide a practical means for bringing together Texan cattle and the growing appetite for beef in the eastern cities.

The enterprising cattleman who worked out the scheme was Joseph McCoy. In 1867, he arranged with the Kansas and Pacific Railroad to make the little town of Abilene, Kansas, into a loading depot for cattle driven up from Texas. A cattle trail (Chisholm's), located far to the west of any settlements, led straight from southern Texas to Abilene; from there the railroads transported the cattle to the slaughterhouses in Chicago and elsewhere. Between 1867 and 1880 alone, some four million Texas steers, it has been estimated, made the long drive to Abilene or other railheads.

Herding cattle on the drive was a specialized job, which was done by a worker who was neither a boy nor a driver of cows. Like so much else in the new environment of the plains, the cowboy displayed the marks of adaptation. His wide-brimmed hat protected his eyes and head from the merciless heat and glare of the sun; in rain it served as an umbrella; at a waterhole, it substituted for a bucket. The bandanna around his neck was really a mask to shield his mouth and nose from the clouds of dust kicked up by cattle on the move; the "chaps" *(chaparejos)* or leather leggings protected him in case of falls and against the stings and thorns of the sagebrush and cactus; the high-heeled boots enabled him to cling to the stirrups or to dig his heels into the ground when a vigorous thousand-pound steer romped on the other end of his lasso. Despite the romance that has since surrounded the cowboy's life, it was in fact a hard one. He was a migratory worker without a home or family, who worked long hours, frequently encountered danger from stampeding cattle or wild animals, and suffered the monotony and loneliness of the long drive. Hence, upon arrival at Abilene, Dodge City, or Wichita, at the end of the drive, he indulged in a little aimless shooting to let off steam, and carousing and gambling to break the monotony and relieve his loneliness.

When the necessity for the long drive ended in the late 1880's, the cowboy's specialized function also ceased; he became a mere cowhand, who lived on a ranch, patrolled the fences, mended the breaks, and sorted the cattle for shipment to market by railroad. Yet despite the limited time span during which the true cowboy flourished—no more than a generation—he has remained, in television shows, movies, magazine serials, children's games, and books (in the United States, Europe, and even parts of Asia), the most distinctive of American figures.

The long drive provided not only a way to get the cattle to the railroad, but also a means to stock the ranches of the northern plains. Just before the Civil War, men discovered that the grass, ostensibly frozen and killed by the severe winters, was actually excellent year-round fodder for cattle, and could enable them to subsist through even the winter without care. Inasmuch as the whole region was virtually unsettled and the amount of grass seemed unlimited, enterprising cattlemen recognized an unparalleled opportunity for gain. Like gold mining, early cattle raising required only a small amount of capital; it encouraged individual enterprise and attracted large numbers of people in a short time. The usual procedure was to obtain 160 acres through the Homestead Act (1862) or to buy a similar amount from the government for $200. On this piece of land, the enterpriser built a crude ranch house and a corral. Usually the ranch included a water hole, or some good source of water. The cattle were then brought up from Texas, put out to feed and fatten on the unfenced government lands, and a new cattleman was in business.

Cattle and Sheep Raising: Profits and Risks. Making a profit in cattle raising was deceptively easy. Cattle bought for five or ten dollars a head in Texas and raised on the northern plains could later be sold for at least $25 and sometimes for as much as $50. The sole expense was that of driving them from Texas to the northern plains, but that cost less than a cent per mile. In the words of one old cowhand: "It figured good on paper. Borrow money at ten per cent, buy a few cows, and the herd will double every three years." How could a man fail to make money?

And for a while many people did in fact get rich. The Texas longhorns spread into all the plains and mountain territories and states. As early as

1869, Colorado counted a million head, and by 1880, Kansas and Nebraska between them supported over 2.5 million. Cattle raising was so profitable that eastern and even English and Scottish capitalists invested in the flourishing industry. Theodore Roosevelt, with his ranch in the Black Hills in the 1880's, was only one of a number of Easterners who showed a lively financial interest in the booming cattle business. To the optimistic eye, there seemed to be no discernible end to the bonanza; to the shrewd and thoughtful, however, it was evident that even the seemingly endless plains of America could support only a limited number of cattle.

Actually, raising cattle was not as devoid of expense and risk as it appeared. Storms, drought, animal diseases, and misadventures often seriously reduced a costly herd or even wiped it out. Moreover, by the 1880's prudent ranchers were stiffening the competition. In order to meet the eastern demand for better beef and to obtain higher prices for their meat, some cattlemen were already improving upon the lean and often rangy longhorns by introducing Herefords and other less "wild" strains. New breeds and the fencing necessary to keep them true also added to expenses. While the investment costs of the industry were rising, the winters of 1885 – 1887 delivered their blows to the cattle industry. Both of those years brought blizzards which left the snow so deep on the plains that thousands of cattle starved to death because they could not get through to the grass. The disastrous effects of the winters were compounded by the intervening summer, which was uncommonly dry, thereby reducing the usable grazing lands. These calamities almost wiped out the investments of many ranchers. Hundreds of marginal producers sold out to large ranchers, many of whom were fencing in their lands rather than depending upon the open range.

Thus, even faster than it shot into prominence, the open-range cattle industry contracted to the dimensions of a stable, conservative business, shorn of its romance and potentiality for sudden wealth. To succeed at it now required the same ingredients as other businesses: determination, capital, and entrepreneurial ability. As a result, the corporation came to cattle raising for the same reasons it had come to mining—the need for capital and entrepreneurial skill.

Paradoxically, the growing industrial society, which had fostered the development of the cattle industry, also caused the elimination of its two early characteristics, the open range and the long drive. The mass production of barbed wire in the 1870's and 1880's permitted fencing in the treeless plains at a reasonable cost and terminated grazing on the open range. Railroads during this period gradually penetrated all sectors of the plains. As they did so they rang the deathknell for the long drive by offering an economical means of transporting cattle that didn't wear off pounds of saleable meat.

Sheep raising on the Great Plains and in the mountain regions also helped to open the Far West. Like the cattlemen, the sheepherders freely used the government lands as pastures. Because sheep are more tractable than cattle, a single herder with a dog or two could watch over hundreds as they munched their way over the plains and through the valleys of the Rockies. The shepherds followed their animals in a kind of covered wagon, which provided crude living quarters. By 1900, there were more sheep than cattle grazing on the Great Plains, though the comparison is misleading since the cattle were systematically slaughtered while the sheep were kept alive to bear wool. In general, by the close of the century, the cattle industry dominated the plains, and sheep raising dominated the mountain states. In Montana, for instance, sheep outnumbered cattle six or seven to one.

Farming the Plains. As sheep- and cattlemen began to settle on ranches in the 1880's, the sedentary farmer, last in the procession of frontiersmen, made his entrance onto the western plains. Some farmers, it is true, had already moved into western Kansas and Nebraska in the late seventies, but not until the early 1880's did they reach sizable numbers, and it was even later before there were many in the Dakotas. (Both of the Dakotas became states in 1889.) Like the ranchers before them, the farmers fenced in their lands, thus making their contribution to the closing of the range.

Unlike the ranchers, however, the farmers found the scanty rainfall of the Great Plains a constant threat to their existence. For a few years in the late 1870's and early 1880's, rainfall in the western plains was more plentiful than normal, luring farmers into the region. Then in the middle 1880's, the more usual dry conditions returned, forcing thousands of farmers in western Kansas and Nebraska to abandon their farms and flee eastward again. Indeed, part of the farm discontent of the early nineties that became known as Populism was rooted in the economic difficulties encountered in trying to adjust to the unfavorable environment of the Great Plains.

In time, new techniques and devices from the industrial East would help the farmers to make the Great Plains the breadbasket of the United States. The barbed wire, which permitted the cattlemen to fence in their breeding herds, also could be used to keep wandering cattle out of the farmers' crops. Improved seeds that could survive the climate of the plains also aided agriculture, as did "dry farming," a new technique of conserving water through quick and shallow cultivation of the soil after a rain. Inexpensive windmills, capitalizing on the steady winds of the plains, provided power for deep wells to fill the cattle and horse troughs. Nevertheless, even to the present, drought and dust storms have recurrently plagued the farmers of the western plains.

Far Western Frontiers: Molders of a New Breed

In a sense, the history of the United States is the story of the frontier, but for most of American history prior to the Civil War, the frontier was the farmers' domain. The trappers and herdsmen who preceded the farmers into the wilderness were transitory figures, leaving few marks of their passage upon the civilization that followed. Not so with the frontiers of the Far West.

There the farmers came late; to some of the regions of the Great Basin they never came at all, and even where they did settle, as we have seen, their tenure was precarious. Largely because the mining and cattle frontiers were so different, they contributed unique and colorful elements to American culture, leaving in folklore and literature monuments to their short history.

The mining and cattle frontiers provided many sharp contrasts to the traditional frontier of the East. For one thing, unlike the Atlantic frontier, the mining frontier moved from west to east, since the pioneers in the opening of the Rocky Mountain and Great Basin country were miners and other migrants from the Pacific coastal settlements. Furthermore, compared with even the most primitive farmstead communities of the forest regions, the mining frontier fostered an unstable society, of which the ghost town is an extreme example. Basically, of course, this instability stemmed from the nature of mining—that is, the town usually lasted only so long as the ore did. But there were other factors that made life in the mining town unstable, rough, often violent, and frequently lawless. Because of the remote places in which gold was often found, and because most miners hoped to make a quick strike and return to civilization with their new wealth, few brought their families with them. Indeed, the world of the miner, like the world of the cowboy and cattleman in the days of the open range, was without women, except for the dance hall singer, the barmaid, and the prostitute. It lacked, therefore, the stabilizing influences of home and family. Furthermore, the prospect of quick wealth attracted all kinds of men to the diggings and to the towns of the mining regions. Farmers, college boys, and physicians came; but so did gamblers, speculators, thieves, army deserters, and other undesirable persons who, drawn by the easy money of the mines, brought instability and violence.

Because of the great diversity of social types and the essentially transitory character of mining, local government consisted of only a few, primitive institutions. Justice in the first few years of the mining frontier was meted out by a "folk court" composed of all the miners of a given region; of necessity it tended to be rough (there were no judges), quick (the men wanted to get back to the diggings), and simple (there were few lawyers). Punishments, in the absence of jails, were limited to death, flogging, fines, or banishment, depending on the seriousness of the crime. The informal institutions of government and justice attracted thieves and thugs who further aggravated the problems of law and order. Indeed, the lawlessness of the new western frontier became legendary.

Violence as a Way of Life. In almost all periods of their history, Americans have displayed a taste for violence that belies their belief in law and the fact of their political stability. Many examples of such violence can be found in the 30 years before the Civil War in the riots of nativists and in the mobbings of antislavery agitators by Northerners as well as Southerners. But considering the sparseness of settlements in the trans-Missouri West, the law was probably broken more frequently in that region than in any other. For example, in the West between 1882 and 1903, the number of white people lynched in proportion to the population far exceeded that of either the South or the East. During that period, some 80 people were lynched in Montana, though the population of the whole state was only 143,000 in 1890; in the three states of Indiana, Ohio, and Illinois, 62 white people out of a population of 9.7 million were killed by mobs during those 23 years.

Lawlessness more significant than lynching, which the West inherited from the eastern frontier, occurred in the form of the vigilante, who, if he did not originate in the West, was certainly characteristic of it. Some vigilante groups, such as the San Francisco committee of 1851, actually improved the administration of justice, since the established authorities were corrupt. But many other vigilantes hanged alleged murderers after only a pretense of a fair trial, and some, in their haste and ignorance, clearly killed innocent men. On occasion, vigilantes interfered with the process of established justice, not because it was weak, but because they believed it was too lenient. In such cases, vigilante justice sank to the level of a lynch mob.

Like the cowboy, the vigilante is a uniquely American figure in history; Canadians and Australians moved into unsettled land at about the same time as Americans, but the vigilance committee did not appear among them. Violence was common on both the Canadian and Australian frontiers, but there justice was meted out by the constituted authorities without the interference of people's courts or extra-legal tribunals. The contrast can be explained by the different processes of settlement. In both Australia and Canada, a strong executive authority moved into the unsettled areas ahead of the pioneers, thus establishing the rule of law and the maintenance of order from the beginning of settlement. The circumstances were exactly the reverse in the United States, where the local communities made their own laws and provided their own officials without much assistance from the central government. Simply because authority on the American western frontier was local, it was susceptible to popular pressures and whims. In Canada, on the other hand, the Royal Mounted Police (founded in 1874), as agents of the central government, were independent of local pressures and armed with more than adequate powers to discipline and control unruly frontiersmen.

"Century of Dishonor." The story of the relations between the western Indians and the invading white men also differed strikingly in the United States and Canada. As we have seen, the subjugation of the Indian and the securing of the West took a great toll in money, lives, and self-esteem. The Canadian West was settled at less cost, though the Indian tribes and even the topography were very much the same. Canada experienced no Indian wars; no more than 300 Northwest Mounted Police maintained order in the West even after the settlers came. Even when Sitting Bull and hundreds of his followers fled from the United States into Canada after the massacre of Custer's force in 1876, there was no war; the Sioux kept the peace during their five years in Canada.

A good part of the difference stems from the meticulous fairness of the Canadian officials in working out and honoring agreements with the Indians for their lands. The record of the United States stood in unhappy contrast. But of equal importance in accounting for the difference in Indian and white relations was the dissimilarity in processes of settlement, already described. Government arrived in the western United States only with the settlers and on a local basis. Thus the same men who threatened the Indians' lands constituted the government that was responsible for bringing to justice those white men who violated the Indians' rights. Only considerably later did the more disinterested authority of the central government arrive with a measure of justice. By then, the relations between the races were suffused with memories of conflict, treachery, and distrust. In Canada, on the other hand, the Mounties, as the representatives of the central government, preceded the settlers. Furthermore, the Mounties' license to both apprehend and judge lawbreakers in the West, powers which certainly assisted them in keeping order, constituted a degree of governmental authority that no United States official possessed and which Americans with their firm belief in local home rule would never grant. For that reason the "century of dishonor" is a failure of American frontier institutions as well as a failure of morality.

The Agricultural Revolution

During the long history of man's cultivation of the soil, there have been only a few great improvements. The first was the beginning of agriculture itself, sometime around 6000 B.C., when men found that they could grow their own crops instead of gathering them from wild plants. Another was the great revolution in techniques in the late eighteenth century, which, by greatly increasing production, freed the majority of the population, for the first time in history, from the necessity of tilling the soil. It was this agricultural revolution that permitted the development of an urban, industrial society. In the years between 1870 and 1900, agriculture in the United States passed through another great revolution that is still going on, one which has enabled a very small proportion of the population to feed the rest. In the late nineteenth century, this agricultural achievement made possible the industrializaton of the economy.

Land of Plenty. There were two important elements in the agricultural revolution of 1870–1900. The first was the enormous increase in total farm output. During those 30 years the production of major crops—corn, wheat, cotton, and livestock—increased between 130 and 150 per cent. The second part of the revolution was that this increase in production was achieved without a comparable increase in the number of farmers. During this period, the agricultural working force rose only 69 per cent.

The long-term cause for this increase in both production and productivity was, of course, the enormous demand from the world market newly created

(Continued on page 75)

The Real West / Pictorial Essay

The fabled West—of song and story, movie and television—is in many ways a far cry from what actually existed there. The legendary lusty, brawling miners, for example, spent most of their time at the arduous work of panning or shoveling soil into sluices, always hoping to find the elusive riches they sought, but seldom succeeding in doing more than earning a bare living. As mining became a more conventional business, requiring costly equipment and large investments of capital, the earlier romantic aspect vanished. All that remained of the past was the hard work, to be done not for oneself but as a wage earner for some employer.

The miners spent relatively little of their time in the saloons and dance halls of such towns as Goldfield, Nevada. Nevertheless, whether they served miners, cattlemen, or farmers, towns were a vital part of life in the West. They were the nexus to which even the most independent had to return in order to purchase supplies, sell gold or silver, register a claim, send or receive mail, get medical attention, or simply talk with other human beings. For western towns to become established, more was required than just the dis-

Main Street of Goldfield, Nevada, ca. 1900. *Photo: Library of Congress*

California miners using a "long tom" (sluice) and pan in their search for gold. *Photo: Library of Congress*

covery of gold or the construction of a railroad spur. There had to be men who were willing to travel long distances, often still clad in Eastern clothes, and live in tents for weeks on end to hold town lots on which they could build stores and offices to supply the services the community needed.

Like the miner, the cowboy and rancher of the era also led hard, unglamorous lives. Whether he rounded up cattle in Kansas or served as a member of a vigilante group such as the Montana Manhunters, the cowboy seldom resembled the stereotype of the glamorous hero. Instead, he was usually very ordinary in manner and appearance and, like the miner, worked long and lonely hours.

The settler, too, played an important role in the development of the West. In a few cases he was able to build a house that contained such luxuries as sizeable glass windows or to build a windmill to draw water from deep beneath the dry earth. However, his life was generally an arduous and limited one, isolated as he was from most of humanity and from the comforts of his former home.

The person who suffered most in the settlement of the West was the red man. His usual payment for the land the white man took from him was poverty

Round up in southwest Kansas, 1890. *Photo: Kansas State Historical Society, Topeka*

Montana Manhunters,
ca. 1876. *Photo: L. A.
Huffman Collection*

HOLDING A TOWN LOT

Homesteader holding a
town lot. *Photo: Cun-
ningham Collection,
Stillwater, Oklahoma*

A family of settlers on
their farm. *Photo: Li-
brary of Congress*

and banishment to successively smaller reservations. The proud and fierce Apache, Geronimo, one of the last Indians to resist the white man's encroachments is shown below, in bewildering and humiliating captivity at Fort Bowie, Arizona.

Despite the hardships almost all endured and the injustices some perpetrated, the West continued to be a magnet. It drew miners, ranchers, cowboys, farmers, shopkeepers, in fact all who had a dream of better things and believed that where the sun set, there lay greater opportunity. By and large opportunity did exist, and many were able to fulfill their hopes by dint of faith and hard work. The settlement of the West remains, therefore, one of the best remembered and most cherished sagas of our past.   *End*

Indians at Fort Bowie, Arizona. *Below:* Geronimo and Natchez at Fort Bowie, 1886, with the 4th Cavalry Band on the right. *U.S. Signal Corps photos, National Archives*

by the Communications Revolution. The immediate increase in production was made possible by the conquest of the Great Plains and by the growth of an industrial society with improved technology.

One way in which farmers were able to meet the new demand for foodstuffs and fiber was by cultivating virgin lands. Between the establishment of Jamestown in 1607 and the year 1870 American farmers brought 408 million acres under cultivation; in the 30 years after 1870, an additional 431 million acres were put to the plow, approximately 23 million more than in the preceding 263 years! One result was that during these 30 years American agricultural exports increased enormously. For instance, in the 1860's, the annual export of wheat was about 35 million bushels; by the 1880's, it was up to 120 million, and at the turn of the century, 200 million bushels were exported. Pork exports shot up from 128 million pounds in the 1860's to 500 million in 1900. Immediately after the Civil War, cotton exports amounted to a billion pounds a year; in 1901, they reached almost 3.5 billion. The United States was feeding not only its own burgeoning industrial population, but the industrial workers of Europe as well. Much of the new farm land opened up in those years was in the Great Plains, for that was an untouched frontier, but old sections as well as new saw great increases in land under cultivation.

Once the incentive of a world market and a new technology existed, opening untilled land to cultivation and exploitation was fairly easy to accomplish under the liberal land laws of the United States. Contrary to popular impression, the Homestead Act of 1862 did little to help the landless settlers, for whom it was intended, but it did bring new acreage under cultivation. The principal reason the Homestead Act failed to do much for the small farmer was that the best land in the West already had been excluded from the operation of the act by previous legislation. Moreover, the provisions of the act were easy to evade; thousands of acres of homestead land fell, through fraud and deception, into the hands of large holders, cattlemen, and speculators. Hence, the Homestead Act assisted in the transfer of government lands to private hands, even if not in a manner intended by its sponsors. The spirit of the times in agriculture, as in industry, was to expand production under private auspices as quickly as possible, and the Homestead Act, like other land acts of the period, helped achieve that goal. In all, the government gave away 500 million acres, most of it during the last 40 years of the nineteenth century. The extensive land grants to railroads also encouraged agricultural settlements, since the companies, especially the Burlington Lines and the Northern Pacific, carried on advertising campaigns in the United States and Europe to entice farmers and immigrants to buy railroad lands in the West.

The Homestead Act was but one of several acts that facilitated the rapid opening of the Far West. The Timber Culture Act of 1873, for example, awarded 160 acres to anyone who would plant a quarter of his land with trees in ten years. A later amendment, which further modified the requirements, was of little significance, since few grantees bothered to plant trees in any case, though they obtained the land. The Desert Land Act of 1877 granted 640 acres of land at 25 cents an acre to anyone who would try to irrigate a portion of it within three years. When the plot was deemed watered, the payment of a dollar an acre completed the transaction. In this case, as well, few took the trouble to irrigate their new lands, but complied with the provisions of the act only enough to obtain cheap acreage for the expansion of their cattle ranches or timber sites.

Both of these acts of the 1870's were attempts by men familiar with the humid and forested East to deal with the alien environment of the Great Plains. The purpose of the Timber Culture Act was to grow trees where none grew naturally, and the aim of the Desert Land Act was to make up for the small amount of water on the Great Plains and in the Great Basin. As efforts to transplant the agriculture of the East to the Far West, they were notably unsuccessful.

A third piece of legislation, the Timber and Stone Act of 1878, provided that if a buyer would swear there were no valuable minerals in the land, he could purchase as much as a quarter section (160 acres) at $2.50 an acre for the timber and stone to be obtained from it. Through this invitation, several million acres of timberland passed into private hands.

Increasing Productivity. As the opening of new lands was the principal way in which farm production was increased, so the increasing use of farm machinery and the development of new techniques explains the improvement in agricultural productivity. This increase in production per farmer is of prime importance, for it permitted a transfer of labor to industry without reducing the nation's supply of raw materials and food. The best known example of the new laborsaving machinery is the McCormick reaper, which came into prominence during the Civil War. Later the combine, as the name suggests, made it possible for one machine to perform uninterruptedly several operations of harvesting grain. A government witness told the United States Industrial Commission in 1901 that to reap, bind, and thresh a bushel of wheat by hand consumed 160 minutes; with a combine the three operations could be completed with four minutes of human labor. By 1880, as much as 80 per cent of American wheat was being harvested by machine. Before the turn of the century, mechanical harrows, fertilizer spreaders, and corn harvesters contributed further to the mechanization of agriculture. This mounting use of agricultural implements was reflected in the census figures. In 1850, the value of farm implements and machinery was $6.8 million; by 1870, the figure was up to $42.7 million; and by the close of the century, it was over $100 million. Improved seeds, better fertilizers, and new knowledge gained through agricultural experiments by the Department of Agriculture, which was established in 1862, also helped to increase productivity.

Farm machinery was usually powered by animals, principally horses, but now steam was introduced for exceptionally large pieces of equipment like threshers, combines, and corn shellers. A steam-operated corn sheller, for instance, could handle a bushel in one and a half minutes as compared with 100 minutes required by hand work. Steam tractors the size and weight of railroad locomotives were used for a while on some of the large farms of the Dakotas and the flat valley lands of California; however, their excessive weight and the sparks that flew from their chimneys, threatening fire to the dry grain, doomed them to only limited use and early abandonment.

Another source of agricultural efficiency was crop specialization. As the railroad and distribution network of the nation improved, those regions best suited to growing a particular crop could supply the nation with increased quantities of a better quality, thus lowering prices. The concentration of cattle and sheep raising in the plains and mountain states respectively, discussed earlier, was one example. Others were the development of corn and hog production (in the Middle West) and the cheese industry (in Wisconsin.)

Changing the World Market. As already stated, the enormous increase in American production was a response to a new world-demand that was brought within reach by the new technology of the Communications Revolution. It is not surprising, therefore, that American production profoundly affected Europe. The fall in world farm prices in the 1870's and 1880's was followed by a fall in land values in the agricultural countries of Europe, causing a migration to European cities or to the United States. The decline in food prices facilitated the industrialization of England and Germany as well as that of the United States, for cheaper food meant workers could survive on lower wages.

EXPORTS AND IMPORTS, 1870-1900

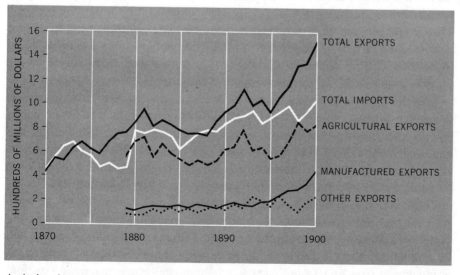

Agricultural exports played the major role in maintaining America's almost continuously favorable balance of trade between 1870 and 1900. Despite industrialization, not until 1900 did manufactured exports rise appreciably.

The United States benefited from the agricultural revolution in another way. In an economy seeking to industrialize, foreign imports are indispensable, but they must be paid for by exports of equal value. In all but two years between 1873 and 1900, the United States was able to maintain a favorable balance of trade, thanks in large measure to the farmers, whose products each year constituted three quarters of total United States exports. Without those exports the United States would have had to curtail its imports and reduce its rate of industrialization.

Cash Crops: Development of Commercial Farming

New Commercial Farmer. The agricultural revolution was gradually transforming many farmers into businessmen, who devoted all their time, resources, and energy to the raising of a commodity for profit. Admittedly, farmers had long been selling some of their produce, but to a much greater extent they had farmed "for a living" — that is, for subsistence. Never before had so many of them participated in the market, especially to the almost total extent that they did in the last three decades of the nineteenth century. Although subsistence farm families had sold some of their crops for money, they had relied primarily on growing their own food, canning or preserving their own vegetables, baking their own bread, and making their own clothes, as well as, perhaps their own shoes and agricultural implements. But when agriculture became commercial, many of these items, usually of much better quality, could be purchased from stores and traveling merchants with the cash earned from the sale of one or two staple crops, to which farmers devoted their full time and skill. Moreover, with cash, the commercial farmers could partake of the amenities of life, usually unavailable to the subsistence farmers. They could buy books, medicines, better tools, finer clothes, trips to distant places, and a host of other benefits. The considerably higher standard of living to be gained from commercialization easily outweighed whatever objection farmers might have had to involvement in the market.

But there was another side to the lot of commercial farmers. By committing themselves almost entirely to production for the market, they became vulnerable to all the downward swings in the price curve. Unfortunately, after the middle 1870's, falling farm prices were characteristic of the American and world economy. Wheat which sold for $1.19 a bushel in 1881 brought only 49 cents in 1894; corn, priced at 63 cents a bushel in 1881, fell to 28 cents in 1890. At such prices, farmers grimly pointed out, it was cheaper to burn corn for fuel than to buy coal. It is true that prices in general fell during the same period. However, the prices of agricultural commodities always fell faster than the others, leaving the farmer in the position of Alice in Wonderland, producing "faster and faster" just to maintain the same economic position. The more successful he was in increasing production, the more supply outran demand and the lower the prices fell.

The productiveness of the American farmer was but one of several causes of the increasing supply of farm products, for the Communications Revolution was bringing into the world market producers in other lands, old and new. Canadian and Russian wheat, Argentine beef, Indian and Egyptian cotton, and Australian beef and wool now competed with American products.

Growth of Tenant Farming. Falling prices constituted one measure of the farmers' worsening condition; another was the report by the 1880 Census of widespread farm tenancy. Throughout most of their previous history, Americans had been proud of the broad distribution of landownership and the merely temporary role tenancy played in the life of the vast majority of farmers. The Census of 1880, however, reported that a quarter of America's farmers did not own the land on which they labored. A large proportion of the tenancy in the South, it is true, stemmed from the presence of former slaves who had never owned land, but the high level of tenancy in the northern states, where there were few Negroes in agriculture, showed that the heritage of slavery was not the whole explanation. Because of falling prices, many farmers obviously lost their land or were unable to purchase it. In Indiana, Illinois, Iowa, and Nebraska, for example, between 17 and 24 per cent of the farmers were tenants. As the century wore on, the situation only worsened; in 1900, a third of America's farmers were tenants.

Organization and Protest. Ordinarily in a free-enterprise economy, when an excess of production causes prices to fall disastrously, producers withdraw until the relationship between supply and demand is more favorable to them. That is what usually happens when there is a surplus of a manufactured commodity. But farmers were reluctant to leave their occupation. Unless a farmer actually abandoned his work, no action of his own could affect prices, whereas a large manufacturer might raise the price of his commodity by cutting production. Many farmers during this period of stress migrated to the cities, but not nearly as many as the low economic state of agriculture would have seemed to warrant.

Most farmers refused to act upon the danger signals of falling prices and instead sought ways that would enable them to stay on the land. As a result, during the last 30 years of the nineteenth century, farmers held meetings, issued protests, and formed organizations, even though previously they had always been distrustful of organization or collective action. But the falling prices brought about by the Economic Revolution threatened the farmer as nothing had before: organization seemed capable of meeting the danger.

There were two broad explanations for the decline of the farmers' income. One was overproduction. The other was a group of reasons that included high costs of credit, transportation, and farm equipment, and a shortage of currency leading to lower prices. The farmers based their protests almost entirely upon the second explanation and largely ignored the effects of overproduction. Yet subsequent history suggests that overproduction was in fact the principal cause for farm distress. The only times that farm income in the

United States has risen significantly have been either when demand expanded, as in the first decade of the twentieth century, or when supply was cut by governmental action, as under the New Deal. Although there was some validity in the accusations of high interest rates and excessive transportation costs, these factors were not enough to account for the fall in the farmers' income at the end of the nineteenth century. Furthermore, recent research into the level of farm mortgage rates in the plains states suggests that interest rates were not excessive, considering the high risks to the lenders.

Since few farmers would admit that their own prodigious production lay at the root of their troubles, they emphasized the disadvantages that an independent producer faced in an age of large enterprise. They quickly grasped that in the marketplace the individual farmer was no match for the railroad companies, grain elevator operators, and agricultural machinery manufacturers, who were backed by vast resources and sometimes enjoyed a virtual monopoly. Consequently, in the last 30 years of the nineteenth century, the farmers concentrated not on limiting or controlling their production, which was probably beyond their power anyway, but on controlling and regulating the great business enterprises.

Short of curtailing production, there were only two ways in which the farmer could meet the problem of falling income. One was to try to raise the prices he received for his goods; the other was to cut his own costs of production in an effort to offset the fall in prices. Between 1870 and 1900, a variety of organizations were formed among farmers for achieving one or both of these goals.

The Grange Movement. The earliest of the principal farmers' organizations was the Patrons of Husbandry, founded in 1867 by Oliver H. Kelley. In the beginning, the Grange, as this organization was popularly known, concentrated on educating farmers in better methods of cultivation. But inasmuch as such efforts to cut costs proved inadequate to meet the steady fall in farm income, the Grange in the early 1870's (with membership at a peak of 500,000) turned to other solutions. In order to reduce the costs of farm machinery, insurance premiums, interest on loans, and other items required by farmers, the Grangers formed cooperatives to supply these needs. None of the cooperative and other efforts proved very successful, but the talk and agitation aroused by the Grange meetings led to other activities by farmers, some of which, like political activity, the Grange would never officially sanction.

It was through political agitation that farmers in several midwestern and western states, including Illinois, Iowa, and Wisconsin, succeeded, in the 1870's, in getting their legislatures to set up commissions to supervise and regulate railroads and grain elevators, which many farmers thought charged excessively high rates and thereby reduced farm income. In 1877, these Granger laws, as they were called, were upheld by the Supreme Court in *Munn* v. *Illinois.* Sometimes the aroused farmers in this early period turned briefly to third-party political activity, such as supporting the Anti-Monopoly party of the 1870's and the Greenback party of the late seventies and early eighties. The latter party, as its name implies, also bespoke the farmers' new interest in cheap money as a means of raising farm prices. But third parties and inflationary schemes, both of which farmers would turn to with enthusiasm in the next decade, were still premature in the 1880's. The bulk of the nation's farmers preferred to stick with strictly economic measures to lower costs of production, as had been advocated by the Grange.

Other Self-Help Schemes. Though its philosophy still dominated farmers' organizations in the 1880's, the Grange was being superseded by new and more vigorous groups. The important farm organizations in the South were the Agricultural Wheel and the National Farmers' Alliance; in 1888 they coalesced to form what was popularly known as the Southern Alliance, with over a million members. Negro farmers were united in the Colored Farmers' Alliance, which in 1891 claimed to speak for a million members spread over 30 states. The western farmers, mainly of the plains states, organized themselves into the National or Northern Alliance, founded in 1880 in Chicago.

The several efforts to unite the Southern and Northern Alliances failed, even though their answers to the farmers' plight were very similar. Both demanded close governmental regulation of the railroads, economy in government (to cut the farmers' taxes), and limitation on public land grants so that government land would be given only to settlers and citizens. Like the Grange before them, the Alliances advocated farmers' cooperatives to eliminate the cost of the middleman and thus permit cheaper purchasing of agricultural supplies and marketing of farm goods. By the close of the 1880's, the two Alliances were also advocating cheap money in an effort to raise farm prices and to make it easier for the farmer to obtain loans. Indeed, the farmers' unending need for credit to buy such items as machinery, land, fertilizer, and seed made the supply of credit a central concern of all farmers' organizations by the end of the 1880's. Both the Northern and Southern Alliances, for example, opposed the National Banking System because only banks in larger cities could qualify as members, and it severely curtailed the supply of paper money.

The Southern Alliance also sought to satisfy the farmers' perpetual need for credit through a so-called subtreasury plan, the brainchild of a leading Texas Alliance man, Charles W. Macune. The plan provided for government loans to farmers at one per cent interest against the collateral of crops, which would be stored in government-provided warehouses. The farmer could borrow up to 80 per cent of the value of his stored crop, which he was permitted to leave in the government storage facility up to one year. From this scheme the farmer would gain not only an easy and cheap source of credit but also the opportunity to hold his crop off the market if prices were depressed at harvest time. To many people, the grave drawback in the subtreasury plan was that it brought government into economic affairs to a degree hitherto unknown in the United States. However, similar devices to aid the farmer have since been enacted and accepted, suggesting the plan was practical.

Into Politics: Populism. Inasmuch as the subtreasury plan and other such efforts to improve the farmers' income could be realized only through government action, the farmers, by the end of the 1880's, moved increasingly into direct political action. In 1890, for example, in Kansas and Nebraska, candidates sponsored by farmers' groups ran under the label of a newly formed People's party. Southern farmers, who were worried about the effects of a third party upon white supremacy, remained inside their traditional Democratic party, but succeeded in getting a hearing for their demands for legislation and reform favorable to agriculture. In the elections of 1890, southern farmers scored notable successes; they controlled eight state legislatures, elected several governors, and sent 44 representatives to Congress. Western farmers, that same year, using the vehicle of their new Populist party, were conspicuously successful in Kansas, Nebraska, and South Dakota, sending ten congressmen and two senators to Washington.

The farmers' victories at the polls in the South and the West encouraged the Northern and Southern Alliances to look sympathetically upon the agitation for creating a new national reform party. On July 4, 1892, just in time for the presidential election of that year, the two farmers' organizations joined with other reform groups in a convention at Omaha to complete the organization of the People's (Populist) party. A platform was approved and candidates were nominated for the forthcoming election. This party was the farmers' last great effort to meet the challenge of the Economic Revolution, the forces and direction of which they feared and only partly understood. Not many years after the Omaha convention, the farmers would learn that a third party was no more the answer to falling prices than cooperatives had been. But that story is more properly a part of the political and economic history of the 1890's than of the farmers' movement and will be discussed in chapter five. In voicing their protests, the farmers had done more than any other social group to focus national attention on the need to control the forces released by the Economic Revolution, if a just and humane society was to prevail. Thus, they had achieved something even if their understanding of the problems and their solutions were inadequate. The farmers' agitation and protests were an important beginning in teaching Americans to cope with a new society of cities and factories.

The Recruitment of an Industrial Labor Force

Surplus Farm Labor. Through most of American history, the great majority of people in the labor force has been engaged in agriculture; indeed, as late as 1870, farmers made up 53 per cent of the workers in all occupations. Yet that census year was the last in which they constituted a majority, and by 1910, only 37 per cent of the nation's workers were farmers. Since 1910, the absolute number as well as the relative proportion of farmers has grown smaller until, in 1960, workers on farms constituted less than six per

LABOR FORCE DISTRIBUTION, 1870-1900

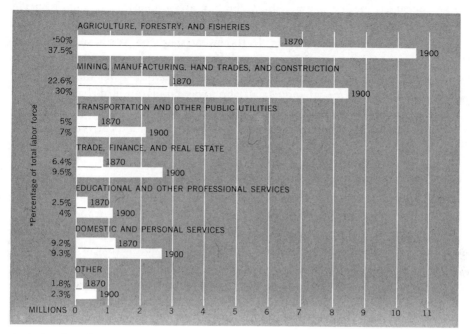

Agricultural employment increased and remained dominant during this period, but its percentage of the total labor force, unlike those of the other categories, decreased. The most significant employment growth occurred in manufacturing and trade, areas likely to expand sharply in an industrial economy, though even then not enough to challenge agriculture's preeminence.

cent of the nation's labor force. This steady decline was the consequence of the continuing revolution in agriculture. The principal source of labor in the new industrial cities of the 1880's was the surplus native farm population. The exodus from the rural regions was so great that between 1880 and 1890 almost 40 per cent of the nation's townships reported an absolute drop in population. In Indiana the figure was 50 per cent, in Illinois 54 per cent, and in Ohio 58 per cent. Two thirds of the rural townships of New York and New England reported declining populations during the 1880's.

Industrial growth also drew women and children into the labor force, if only because they worked for lower wages than men. The number of women gainfully employed jumped from 1.9 million in 1870 to 5.3 million, 30 years later. Most women worked in factories, but the increasing number of working women in business offices was reflected in the 825 per cent increase in clerical workers between 1870 and 1900. The number of working children below the age of 15 also rose significantly—from 750,000 in 1870 to 1.75 million in 1900. Thereafter the number gradually fell off as laws prescribing higher minimum working ages and stricter compulsory school attendance were enacted by the states. Textile mills, coal mines, and meat-packing houses were among the conspicuous employers of children in the 1880's and 1890's.

"In the Southern cotton mills," the Industrial Commission of 1901 reported, "12 appears to be the age at which children are ordinarily expected to begin work; but some of the mills employ children under that age, sometimes as young as 9, 8, and even 7 years. In the sweat shops of Northern cities, also, very young children are often employed."

Immigrant Labor. Second to the native population from the farms, the most important source of industrial labor was immigration, principally from Europe. Although immigration had been mounting ever since the 1830's, the last 30 years of the nineteenth century saw more immigrants arrive than in the whole preceding 70 years. Almost 12 million immigrants entered the United States in those three decades (see page 10).

Although at various times in history, some Americans have been fearful of the effects of large numbers of aliens flocking into the country, most Americans in the nineteenth century placed great value upon the European—but, as we have seen, not the Asian—immigrant. For example, in 1871 an official report of the federal government estimated that "the average worth of each permanent addition to our population . . . was $1000."

Well might native Americans celebrate the immigrant, for, as a class, he performed more of the work of an industrializing economy than did the natives. As one writer pointed out in 1893, although a little over 13 per cent of the population in 1880 was foreign born, the immigrants constituted almost 32 per cent of those engaged in manufacturing and mining. In 1890, immigrants constituted 14.6 per cent of the total population but made up 26 per cent of the total working force. This disproportionately large role the immigrant played in the labor force can be explained by the special and, from the standpoint of American industrialization, favorable character of the immigrant population. Most immigrant workers who came to the United States were adults, yet with many years of productive labor ahead of them. Thus, as John R. Commons, an economist, wrote in 1906, "Over four-fifths of the immigrants are in the prime of life—the ages between fourteen and forty-five." Two fifths of the native population, he pointed out, were below the age of industrial employment. Therefore, Commons concluded, "Immigration brings to us a population of working ages unhampered by unproductive mouths to be fed. Their home countries have borne the expense of rearing them up to the industrial period of their lives, and then America without heavy expense, reaps whatever profits there are on the investment."

American industry also benefited from the industrial skills which some of the immigrants brought with them, such as the glassmaking of the Belgians and the mechanical crafts of the English. But with the notable exception of Russian Jews, most of whom had been in trade or manufacturing before they emigrated, the great majority of immigrants were peasants who brought few industrial skills to their new country.

Simply because of their peasant background, many of the immigrants, if they had the necessary resources, sought out the new lands of the Far West, and helped in settling the Great Plains. The Dakotas, for example, were peopled largely by immigrants from Norway and Russia. As late as 1910, foreign-born adults constituted 27 per cent of the population of North Dakota, while their children made up another 43 per cent.

But by the last decades of the nineteenth century, good farm land was not as readily available as it had been in the first half of the century; besides, the rising industry in the cities now offered ready jobs for the eager, if impoverished newcomers. As a result, after 1880 the typical immigrant was a worker in a factory or mine. In 1910 only 14 per cent of the foreign born were employed in agriculture as compared with 43.5 per cent in manufacturing. By the opening years of the twentieth century, immigrants supplied most of the labor in a number of industries basic to American industrialization. People born in foreign lands constituted more than 60 per cent of the labor force in iron and steel, coal mining, construction, copper mining, and oil refining. The cotton textile industry, once staffed largely by native New England farm girls, now depended upon a labor force that was 70 per cent foreign born.

Some industries counted very few immigrants among their employees, often because of the high degree of skill required, but sometimes simply because of ethnic discrimination. The boot and shoe industry is an example of low immigrant participation for, though it was highly mechanized, the foreign born made up only 28 per cent of the employees. As might be expected, because of language differences, immigrants did not share significantly in the great increase in clerical jobs. On the other hand, immigrants dominated the fields of domestic service and day labor, calling attention to the important role immigrants have always played in filling the unskilled, but necessary jobs at the bottom of the economic pyramid. In fact, by moving in at the bottom, the immigrants permitted native workers to move up to more skilled and better-paying jobs.

The Condition of the Industrial Working Class. Even if wages had been high and hours short, the adjustment of erstwhile European peasants and American farmers to industrial labor would have been hard. Work on the farm, to be sure, had been physically demanding, but work in the factory was no less so, and its pace was often faster and more rigorous under the relentless pressure of the clock, the foreman, and the tireless machine. Paid holidays and summer vacations, now commonplace among all workers, were virtually unknown in the nineteenth century. The work week was six full days, so that Sunday was truly a day of rest.

For the newcomers from farms, the world of the factory was not only strange, it was often poorly paying. It is not easy to generalize about the wages and hours of industrial labor, since they varied according to location and occupation. Nevertheless, for many workers the hours were certainly long, the pay low, and the work exhausting. Steelworkers often labored 12 hours, six days a week, in front of blazing furnaces even in the heat of summer for wages that sometimes barely covered living costs. Silver miners in

Nevada worked in such heat in the deep shafts that they had to be splashed with water periodically to enable them to endure the temperatures. In 1902, the annual wage for the highest-paid mine worker in the anthracite coal fields was $560, which was about the yearly cost of maintaining a family. This pay was the highest wage in an industry that was among the most dangerous. Because most wages in coal mining were low, young sons of miners, usually less than 12 years of age, attempted to bolster the inadequate family income by working as slate pickers at 39 cents for a ten-hour day. A study of industrial workers in Massachusetts in 1883 revealed that one third of the families investigated required the earnings of their working women and children, meager as they were, in order to make ends meet. In 1884, factory investigators in Illinois, where the cost of living was reputed to be considerably lower than in Massachusetts, reported that a quarter of the breadwinners did not earn sufficient income to cover household expenses.

Despite the many examples of low wages and long hours that might be cited, the general picture, taking in the whole country, was less grim and suggests that the workers were sharing in the spectacular industrial growth. Real wages for industrial workers—that is, the actual buying power of the money the workers earned—rose significantly between 1870 and 1900. Moreover, hours declined for the average worker from 66 per week in 1860 to 59 in 1900. And for such occupations as the building trades, the work week, on the average, fell to 48 hours—the eight-hour day—by 1900. Even leaders of organized labor, appearing before the United States Industrial Commission in 1901, admitted this decided improvement, though usually they argued it was not sufficient—which it was not—or that it was the result of union activity—which was dubious. To cite one example, the president of the Cigar Makers Union noted that few workingmen in his youth had more than a rag rug in their homes. "Today," he explained, "you can go into the average workingman's house and find several carpets on the floors and a piano. I never saw many pianos in workingmen's homes when I was a boy and I am 42 years old. I want to say, and I am frank enough to really admit, that we can live better today. . . ."

Even immigrant workers—admittedly less well off on the average than the native workers—must have shared in the benefits of the tremendous production of the Industrial Revolution, for they were able to send back to Europe sizeable amounts of money, which helped to finance further immigration into the United States. A small group like the Greeks remitted over $4.3 million in the single year of 1910; Italians sent back $85 million in 1907. In the 50 years before 1900, one authority has estimated that the Irish in America sent over $250 million to relatives and friends in the old country.

The Rise of Organized Labor. If, in the long run, conditions for most workers were improving, in the short run, as the tripling of the number of strikes and other measures of labor dissatisfaction in the 1880's attest, workers had a number of reasons to be discontented with their lot. Wages might be adequate in a given industry, but long periods of layoff reduced a good hourly wage to an inadequate annual income. A survey made in Massachusetts in 1885 reported that 30 per cent of the state's wage earners lost one third of their potential income because they were unemployed four months of the year. Even if the annual income was adequate, working conditions might be intolerable, and there were few government regulations of labor conditions designed to improve them. Workingmen's compensation for injuries on the job was only a twentieth-century innovation, and even sanitary inspection and sanitary codes came slowly during the 1880's and 1890's.

The power of the boss over most workers was almost unlimited, and the prevailing view among employers was that labor was a commodity to be purchased when needed and to be laid off when business declined. Most employers pressed their employees to produce as much as possible for their wages. A witness before the Industrial Commission of 1901 reported that in the textile industry the machines were run at a much faster rate than they had been 40 years before. Some employers even charged the workers for the machinery on which they worked. Anyone caught organizing a protest committee or a union was usually fired and then "blacklisted" from other jobs in the vicinity. As a consequence, early unions, like the Knights of Labor, often operated secretly in order to protect their members against reprisals. Unions were a direct response of the workers to the impact of the factory system. Only by collective action could workers expect to contest the power of the growing business enterprises of the time.

Despite the many sound reasons that can be adduced for the growth of unions in the late nineteenth century, the trade union movement in the United States developed slowly. (Even today, unionization in the United States lags behind that of many European countries. In 1956, for instance, less than 34 per cent of those people employed in nonagricultural jobs in the United States were members of unions as compared with 90 per cent in Sweden, 66 per cent in Austria, and 50 per cent in the United Kingdom.) Part of this slowness undoubtedly stemmed from the hostility of employers to trade unions, but a comparable hostility in European countries suggests that such an explanation is far from the whole story. In fact, two other factors were more influential. One was the great diversity of nationalities in the American working class, which spawned antagonisms and suspicion within the house of labor that European unions did not have to contend with. The second influence was the strong sense of individualism in the American worker, which probably resulted from his recent rural background. Most American workers simply lacked that sense of identification with their fellow workers which acceptance of a labor union requires. They believed that social mobility and financial advancement would come more rapidly to them as individuals.

The small size of the unions also meant that they were too weak to withstand downswings in the business cycle. In periods of prosperity, workers joined unions, only to leave during hard times when jobs became scarce. Such had been the case in the panics of 1837 and 1857 and again after the Civil War. In America, unionism has been so vulnerable to economic crisis that not until the 1890's could organized labor be sure that a majority of its unions would be able to weather a severe depression. When the long depression of 1873 struck, the promising union movement across the country collapsed under the impact. In 1878, labor union membership in the United States was estimated by Samuel Gompers to be 50,000 as against 300,000 in 1872. Throughout the nation during the depression, wages plummeted and hours lengthened as unemployment mounted. In the building trades in New York City, for example, wages fell from a high of three dollars a day in 1872 to a low of $1.50 in 1875, while the working day jumped from eight to ten hours. Not until the middle eighties was organized labor able to regain the position it had held prior to the depression.

Because employers often refused to deal with a union, workers sometimes resorted to violence to gain recognition or to protest poor working conditions and low pay. The most extreme example of violence in labor relations took place in the anthracite coal fields of Pennsylvania in the late 1860's and early 1870's, where Irish miners organized themselves into a secret labor organization popularly known as the Molly Maguires. Very little has ever been learned about the organization, except that it probably grew out of the Irish fraternal society of the Ancient Order of Hibernians and that it carried on a fierce struggle against the mine owners; this violence included the extensive burning of mine property and even the murder of company officials. Although the terrorism of the Mollies attracted wide attention at the time and eventually resulted in the hanging of 19 of the organization's leaders, it brought no substantial gains for the workers. It did, however, leave in the public mind an association between violence and labor organization that was reinforced by the great railroad strike of 1877 and the Haymarket riot of 1886.

The Evolution of an American Philosophy of Labor Organization. The association of unions with violence was essentially unjust because the philosophy of the major labor organizations of the time clearly repudiated violence or lawlessness. Broadly speaking, two philosophies of trade unionism dominated the thought of organized labor. The first type, idealistic, sometimes Utopian, sought through the union to improve not only the worker's position, but the condition of society in general. This kind of union advocated a comprehensive membership including all types of workers. It also supported broad social reforms, such as education, temperance, women's rights, and cheap money, and not merely those which would be beneficial to labor. The second type took the view that unions existed not to improve the lot of all, but to gain advantages for their members. Such unions accepted the economic and social system of their time, but wanted to increase their own returns from that system. They would have nothing to do with broad programs for social amelioration and confined their membership to skilled workers who could negotiate from strength with employers. The National Labor Union (NLU) and the Knights of Labor represented the first kind, and the American Federation of Labor (A.F. of L.), the Railroad Brotherhoods, and the craft unions represented the second.

Utopian Approach to Unionism. The National Labor Union, founded in 1866, was the first truly nation-wide organization of labor unions in the United States. Its leading figures, William Sylvis of the Iron Molders Union and Richard A. Trevellick of the Ship Carpenters, were skilled workers who had long been active in labor organization. Just before the depression of 1873, the NLU boasted a membership of 300,000 and some success in gaining better conditions for its members. Moreover, in 1868 it influenced Congress to repeal the Contract Labor Law of 1864, which, in the opinion of the NLU, had encouraged the importation of cheap, competitive immigrant labor. But like many of the unions before the Civil War, the NLU also believed in the use of government action to aid the cause of labor. For example, it advocated cheap paper money (though it is questionable whether a wage earner actually gained anything from inflation). The NLU also agitated, with some success, for a working day limited by law to eight hours. Six states passed laws limiting working hours, and the federal government ordered an eight-hour day for workers at its workshops and arsenals. However, only the federal government's response to the NLU's agitation proved effective, since the state laws were riddled with loopholes. By the 1870's and even before the depression of '73, the reformist interests of the NLU split it asunder. To many workers and to craft union leaders within the organization, general reform was of relatively little interest. The onset of the depression finished off even the remnants of the NLU.

One labor organization that did survive the panic of 1873 was the Noble Order of the Knights of Labor, founded in 1869 by a Philadelphia tailor, Uriah Stephens. Destined to be a much more important union than the NLU, the Knights, nevertheless, reflected a similar reformist ideology. Stephens' reformist bent was evident in the Knights' practice of opening membership to any gainfully employed workers, including farmers, and excluding only lawyers, stockholders, liquor dealers, and physicians. To emphasize the fraternal, almost mystical unity of all working men, the Knights insisted upon an elaborate ritual, and for a time operated as a secret society.

In some respects, the Knights anticipated the modern industrial union in which all workers in a given factory are members of the same union, regardless of their craft or occupation. The basic unit of the Knights was the district, a kind of territorial "local," to which all workers of a given locale belonged, even including members of the traditional craft unions, if they wished to join. Unquestionably, Stephens wanted to obtain better working conditions for his Knights, but his central purpose was more far-reaching, looking to a renovation of society and the economy. On principle, the Knights opposed "the wage system," which they believed was transforming the independent craftsman into a dependent and degraded proletarian. To Stephens and his followers, the proper course for labor was the formation of workers' cooperatives in which each member could be at once a worker and an employer, sharing in the profits as well as receiving wages. Between 1884 and 1886, when the Knights were at their peak of membership and success, some 135 producers' cooperatives were in operation; a third of them in mining, coopering (making or repairing wooden casks and tubs), and shoemaking.

Certainly in retrospect and even in the light of conditions evident at the time, a cooperative approach to the problems of industrial labor was exceedingly Utopian. Business enterprise, as we have seen, was fast moving in the direction of larger units of production; to have expected the small, weak cooperatives of the Knights to compete successfully with the giant corporations already in the field was illusory if not foolhardy. American labor unions took a long time to evolve the "bread and butter" unionism that today is axiomatically considered the purpose of labor organization.

Exclusive attention to economic issues may well have been the key to any labor organization's success in America, as shown by the history of the Knights in the 1880's. After 15 years of activity as a Utopian union, the Knights could count no more than 52,000 members throughout the country. But in 1884 and 1885, the Order's energetic organizer, Joseph Buchanan, carried off successful strikes against the Union Pacific and the Wabash railroads, thereby bringing thousands of new members into the ranks. Never before had an industrial giant like Jay Gould, the financier who controlled the Wabash Railroad, been forced to engage in collective bargaining. By 1886, membership in the Knights reached 700,000, making it the largest and strongest national labor organization the United States was to see during the entire nineteenth century. (It was ironic that the Knights' greatest success should result from strikes, for the Order's Constitution of 1884 condemned strikes as affording "at best . . . only temporary relief" for the difficulties of labor; cooperatives were judged to be the only permanent help.)

The spectacular success of the Knights, however, was only temporary. Most American workers were still not prepared to bear the risks and costs of unionization. A new strike on Gould's southwestern system of railroads in 1886 failed. With the winning streak of the Knights over, many workers left the union as abruptly as they had joined only a few months earlier. Moreover, many workers were scared away from the Knights because several of the anarchists hanged for the Haymarket bombing had been members of the Order. But perhaps most important in accounting for the decline in membership was the refusal of the Knights to abandon their strong interest in reform and to confine themselves to issues of direct concern to the ordinary workingman. Skilled workers, for example, discovered that the rising craft or trade unions were much more suited to their needs; even the unskilled workers, who really had nowhere else to go, found the Knights unsatisfactory because the Order was reluctant to support the movement for an eight-hour day. Furthermore, continued support for the producers' cooperatives, which the public did not patronize, drained the resources of the Knights. By 1890, membership in the Order had fallen to 100,000 and was still decreasing.

In 1893, Terence V. Powderly, who had been Grand Master Workman since 1879, resigned his office. In his letter he summed up the Knights' difficulties in the preceding ten years and voiced the Order's continuing Utopian concerns. "Teacher of important and much-needed reforms, she has been obliged to practice differently from her teachings. Advocating arbitration and conciliation as first steps in labor disputes, she has been forced to take upon her shoulders the responsibilities of the aggressor first and, when hope of arbitrating and conciliation failed, to beg of the opposing side to do what we should have applied for in the first instance. Advising against strikes we have been in the midst of them."

The Triumph of Bread-and-Butter Unionism. As the Knights declined, the membership of the trade unions continued to rise steadily. With the trade union, labor organization had reached its final stage of evolution in meeting the needs and outlook of the ethnically heterogeneous and individualistically minded working class in the United States. The essential character of the trade or craft union was typified by the Cigar Makers Union, reorganized on its modern lines by Samuel Gompers and Adolph Strasser, both of whom would later be active in the formation and leadership of the American Federation of Labor. Gompers and Strasser were immigrants, who, though once interested in socialism as an ideology for labor, soon abandoned the idea as impractical for American conditions. Instead, they turned to strong union organization. In accordance with their conception of the trade union, the locals were put under tight control of the national officers; and dues, deliberately set high to permit the accumulation of substantial funds for strikes and organizing activities, were also given over to the national office. Backed by such a structure, labor would have a fighting chance in controversies with employers. As a further inducement to membership, the new craft unions of the 1880's, which followed the Cigar Makers' model, usually offered accident, sickness, and death benefits.

In 1886, a group of trade unions formed the American Federation of Labor, which, as the word "federation" in its title implies, was really a loose association of strong unions, free from centralized control. Unlike the NLU or the Knights, the A.F. of L. was made up of national unions in which each trade in North America (there were a few locals of some unions in Canada) was represented by a single union only, thereby avoiding rival groups whose conflicts in the past had often shattered attempts at national organization. For the most part, the constituent unions of the A.F. of L. were craft unions composed of skilled workers, though in the 1890's, the United Mine Workers, an industrially organized union, also affiliated with it.

At its founding, the A.F. of L., with a mere 140,000 members in its dozen or so national unions and lesser organizations, was distinctly weaker than the Knights, who were then at a peak of membership five times greater than the

A.F. of L. But the newer labor organization was destined to survive and grow in the United States, while the Knights would pass from the scene entirely within a decade. Thus an examination of the differences between the two great rival national organizations reveals something of the institutional requirements for success in labor organization in America.

Aside from the differences in organization that have already been mentioned, there were important differences in membership. The A.F. of L. concentrated on organizing the skilled trades, and, though professing to recognize no barriers against women and Negroes, it in fact mobilized few of these marginal workers. The Knights, on the other hand, included unskilled workers and thousands of women and Negro workers. Such an approach, while it was democratic, endangered survival, both because such marginal workers were easily replaced during a strike, and, as objects of the prejudice of other workers, they created internal dissension. By limiting its membership to the skilled and the "acceptable," the A.F. of L. built a strong union for a few rather than a weak union for the many. As practical men, Gompers and his A.F. of L. members saw survival as the first test of validity.

It was in their philosophies that the two labor organizations differed most radically. The Federation, for example, would have nothing to do with the kind of long-range social goals that the Knights had long and proudly stood for. Gompers and the A.F. of L. even opposed any government interference in the conflicts between capital and labor, simply asking that government treat each side equally. Primarily concerned with preserving the worker's job, the trade unions of the A.F. of L. were eminently, if narrowly, practical. That practicality stood in clear contrast with the fraternalism of the Knights, who, by taking in all workers, sacrificed survival to principle. Gompers instinctively recognized what labor historian Selig Perlman later described as the deadliest disease of American labor unions: their fragility, their inability to endure. Only by the elimination of as many divisive elements as possible, Gompers reasoned, could a national labor movement of consequence be created. And it worked.

Gomper's practical approach, in pragmatic and materialistic America, worked better than the idealism of the Knights, but it exacted a price. The resulting labor movement was narrowly based. By failing to organize the unskilled, immigrant workers in the growing mass industries, the A.F. of L. ignored the great majority of American industrial workers.

Indeed, not even all of organized labor was affiliated with the Federation. As late as 1900, a third of the organized workers of the country had not joined the A.F. of L., and some of these unaffiliated unions were strong and influential, like the Railroad Brotherhoods, the bricklayers, and the plasterers. By the First World War, however, the principal unions and the overwhelming majority of unionized workers were a part of the Federation. Yet only 15 per cent of nonagricultural workers in the United States, even in 1914, were members of any union.

Thus by the opening of the new century, the American working class had at last determined the permanent form of its response to the impact of the industrial system. It was a fragile creation, closely fitted to its practical, conservative, and individualistic temper. Neither the radical Industrial Workers of the World nor the Socialist party, both of which appealed to American workers for support in the early twentieth century, could dislodge the Federation from its favored place. Not until the Great Depression of the 1930's would American workers be prepared to accept a broader and less individualistic conception of labor organization than that which the A.F. of L. represented in the late nineteenth century.

SUGGESTED READING

Walter Prescott Webb, *Great Plains** (1931), is still the outstanding historical study of man's relationship to his physical environment in the American West. A less readable, but no less informative work on the same region is James C. Malin, *The Grasslands of North America* (1948). Social history of plains settlements is told in Everett Dick, *The Sod-House Frontier, 1854–1890* (1937). The most recent study of the Far West is Rodman Wilson Paul, *Mining Frontiers of the Far West, 1848–1880* (1963). Equally authoritative but dealing only with the years before 1860, is Ray Billington, *The Far Western Frontier: 1830–1860** (1956). Old, yet still valuable, is Charles Howard Shinn, *Mining Camps, a Study in American Frontier Government** (1885). Paul F. Sharp, *Whoop-Up Country: The Canadian-American West, 1865–1885* (1955), shows that the border was only an imaginary line insofar as migration was concerned. Wayne Gard, *Frontier Justice* (1949), brings together much material on vigilantism in the Far West. The standard study on the original vigilante committee is Mary Floyd Willams, *History of the San Francisco Committee of Vigilance of 1851* (1921). A systematic study of vigilantism in the United States is greatly needed. The emphasis is on the human side of the cattle ranchers in the very good study by Lewis Atherton, *The Cattle Kings* (1961); the fullest scholarly investigation of the cowboy is Joe B. Frantz and J. E. Choate, Jr., *The American Cowboy: The Myth and the Reality* (1955).

A fine overall account of agriculture and farmers in the last half of the century is Fred Shannon, *The Farmer's Last Frontier* (1945). For the extent of mechanization in agriculture see also Leo Rogin, *The Introduction of Farm Machinery . . . During the Nineteenth Century* (1931). Undoubtedly the fullest, though not the most readable survey of discontent on the farms is Carl C. Taylor, *The Farmers' Movement, 1620–1920* (1953). John D. Hicks, *The Populist Revolt** (1931), is the best general study, though it is weak on the South. Theodore Saloutos, "The Agricultural Problem and Nineteenth-Century Industrialism," *Agricultural History*, XXII (July 1948), 156–157, neatly sums up the great agricultural revolution at the end of the century. Allan G. Bogue, *Money at Interest: The Farm Mortgage on the Middle Border* (1955)

*Available in a paperback edition.

calls into serious question the oft-heard complaint that the farmer was exploited by money lenders.

There are many single-volume surveys of American labor history; one of the best and most recent is Joseph G. Rayback, *A History of American Labor** (1959). More critical is Philip S. Foner, *History of the Labor Movement in the United States*, 4 vols. (1947–1965). The story of the Knights of Labor is told well, if unsympathetically, in Norman J. Ware, *The Labor Movement in the United States, 1860–1895** (1929). Philip Taft, *The A. F. of L. in the Time of Gompers* (1957) is the best work on that national union. A more critical approach to Gompers is taken in Bernard Mandel, *Samuel Gompers, a Biography* (1963). Lloyd Ulman, *The Rise of the National Trade Union* (1955), treats the unions as institutions. The ideological conflict within the nineteenth-century house of labor is discussed in Gerald N. Grob, *Workers and Utopia* (1961). The older, seminal work on the distinctive outlook of American labor unions, Selig Perlman, *A Theory of the Labor Movement* (1928) is still valuable. Charlotte Erickson, *American Industry and the European Immigrant, 1860–1885* (1957) is an important study of industry's interest in immigrant labor. Herbert G. Gutman, "The Worker's Search for Power" in *The Gilded Age: A Reappraisal,** ed. by Howard Wayne Morgan (1963), qualifies the usual view that small business opposed labor organization. A valuable study that shows the reality of social mobility among the working class of an industrial city of the late nineteenth century is Stephan Thernstrom, *Poverty and Progress* (1964).

On violence in American labor relations see Vernon H. Jensen, *Heritage of Conflict* (1950), which treats the Far Western miners, and Wayne G. Broehl, Jr., *The Molly Maguires* (1965), which reexamines the labor upheavals in the Pennsylvania coal fields in the 1870's. The two great leaders of nineteenth-century labor organizations have also left their edited testimonies: Terence V. Powderly, *The Path I Trod* (1940), Samuel Gompers, *Seventy Years of Life and Labor*, 2 vols. (1925).

One of the weaknesses of the campaign for free silver by William Jennings Bryan and others was that, as the cartoon indicates, achieving their goal would inevitably profit the silver mine owners, who had only a pecuniary rather than an ideological or sociological interest in the spread of free silver.   Photo: Culver Pictures

CHAPTER FOUR

THE LAG IN NATIONAL POLITICS, 1877–1892

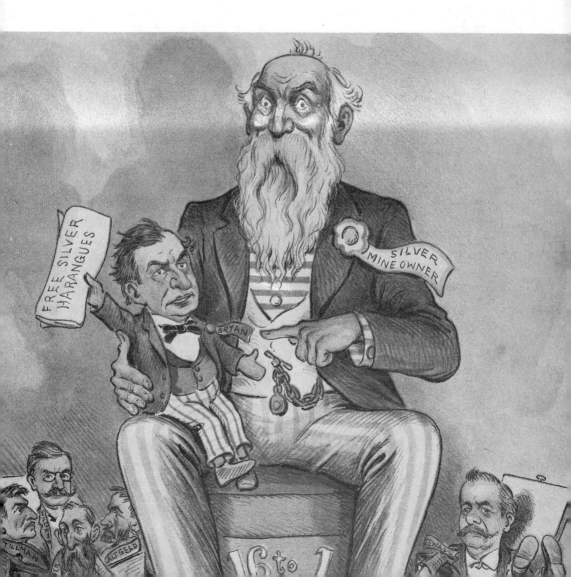

N EARLY EVERY historian who examines American politics from the time of the election of Rutherford B. Hayes (1876) to the close of Benjamin Harrison's term (1893) arrives at the same judgment. It was a low point, both in the quality of the candidates and Presidents and in the level of campaigns and issues. In the midst of the Economic Revolution, politics remained untouched. It is the purpose of this chapter to explain why this was so. Let us look first at the national elections and parties between 1877 and 1892.

Candidates and Campaigns

Presidents Without Political Personality. One measure of politics' unresponsiveness to the Economic Revolution was the dependence of the Republicans upon Union generals for success; they still looked to the past for their appeal. Rutherford B. Hayes, James A. Garfield, and Benjamin Harrison all had served as general officers in the Civil War. Even Chester A. Arthur, who merely succeeded to the presidency following the assassination of Garfield, was quartermaster general of the New York State Militia during the war. In the campaign of 1880, the Democrats also turned to a Union general, Winfield Scott Hancock, for their presidential candidate in an attempt to repeat the Republicans' success. As a hero at the Battle of Gettysburg, Hancock possessed the standard military requirement for President, but lacked any experience in political office. Yet his contest with Garfield that year was the closest election in the history of the country. Hancock came within 9000 votes of Garfield's winning plurality.

On the other hand, when the Republican party in 1884 finally abandoned its practice of nominating a Union general it lost. James G. Blaine was no Union officer, but he was the most popular Republican of his generation and an ardent seeker of the presidential nomination. Prior to 1884, however, his dubious political morality denied him the nomination, since he had been involved in accepting favors from railroads when he was a congressman in the 1870's. Nevertheless, his magnetic, almost flamboyant personality inspired devotion from a legion of followers. As a newspaperman, congressman, Speaker of the House of Representatives, senator, and Secretary of State in Garfield's Cabinet, Blaine had a rich experience in government, but like many of the candidates and Presidents of this era, he had no cause to which he was dedicated. His name is not associated with any important piece of legislation. Later, though, he would serve with distinction as Harrison's Secretary of State, actively promoting business with Latin American countries through reciprocal trade agreements.

The man who defeated Blaine, Grover Cleveland, was the only successful Democratic presidential candidate during the last 40 years of the nineteenth century. Like Blaine, Cleveland had not served in the Army, but by 1884 he had made a good, if unexciting record as an honest, hard-working, and conscientious public servant; he served terms as sheriff of Erie county, as mayor of Buffalo, and as governor of New York State. His principal attributes were humble ones: forthrightness, a willingness to learn, and stolidity. Imagination and flexibility were conspicuously absent from his activities while governor, as they would be later when he was President. At the time of his nomination he was welcomed as a fresh new face on a political stage that was sorely in need of something other than the leaders and issues left over from the war and Reconstruction. Moreover, he was untainted by any of the scandal of corruption that still clung to Blaine.

Actually, despite the odor of corruption that pervaded politics in these years, none of the Presidents was personally corrupt. In fact, the personal rectitude of some set a high standard for the nation. Hayes, for example, who entered office under the cloud of the disputed election of 1876, was referred to by hostile newspapers as "His Fraudulency" and "Rutherfraud B. Hayes." Yet, he soon made the White House a symbol of simple living and quiet republican dignity. Mrs. Hayes even refused to serve alcoholic beverages at official functions; her temperance may have amused some sophisticated foreign diplomats, but it warmed the hearts of many rural and earnest Americans. Even Chester A. Arthur, who succeeded to the presidency in 1881 upon the death of Garfield, did not disgrace the office, despite his past. Prior to being nominated for the vice-presidency in 1880, Arthur had been a notorious spoilsman in New York, where he was a loyal lieutenant of Senator Roscoe Conkling, the Republican boss of the state. George W. Curtis, a well-known civil service reformer, told a reporter in 1881 while President Garfield lay dying: "I presume that if Mr. Arthur should become President, in his ignorance and inexperience he would be compelled to rely on some one more capable than himself. Obviously that person would be Mr. Conkling, and he would be the controlling influence of that administration."

Yet once in office, Arthur proved to be independent of both Conkling and his own past. In 1882, he vetoed a rivers and harbors bill that was clearly a pork barrel for spoilsmen, and the following year he supported the first civil-service legislation ever enacted. It also fell to his administration to prosecute the perpetrators of the so-called Star Route frauds in the Post Office, which had been uncovered during Garfield's brief term. The prosecution of the accused Republican leaders by Arthur's Republican administration was commendably vigorous, though no convictions were secured.

The Presidents of this era may have been personally beyond reproach, but not one was a true political personality in the manner of Andrew Jackson or Abraham Lincoln. None, however, was less of a personality than Benjamin Harrison. His quiet, almost cold manner could not ignite any warmth of feeling even in his friends as the hearty, if bluff, ways of a Cleveland clearly did. Even the imposing Chester A. Arthur, with his love of company and his impeccable attire, appeared a warmer and more gracious person than Harrison. One who knew him wrote later, "President Harrison was the only man I ever saw who could do another man a favor in such a way that all the sweetness and appreciation and sense of gratitude was gone from it. . . ." Admittedly, Harrison, a successful lawyer and politician, spoke in public with fire and enthusiasm; but the glow quickly dissipated once he finished speaking. His handshake, it was said, chilled the blood of those whose hearts had only recently been warmed by his fiery words.

Campaigns Without Important Issues. The election campaigns of these years lacked substance and meaning; personalities, rather than large issues, were the staple appeals. Certainly this was true in 1884, when a Buffalo newspaper revealed that Cleveland, the Democratic candidate, had fathered an illegitimate child many years before. Cleveland's courageous admission of the accusation probably won as many votes as the revelation originally lost for him, but the hustings rang with the issue for weeks. Meanwhile the Democrats exploited the fact that James G. Blaine had received favors from railroads when he was a congressman in the 1870's. The personal slip that was assumed, then and since, to have determined the outcome of the election was Blaine's failure to repudiate a fellow Republican's intemperate denunciation of the Democrats as the party of "rum, Romanism, and rebellion." The remark was considered a slur on the Irish who were supposedly about to vote Republican because Blaine was of Irish descent and his mother was a Roman Catholic. Actually, there is good reason to believe that the decisive factor was quite different but no less personal. Roscoe Conkling of New York, who had long opposed Blaine within the party, simply refused to support him for President. The record shows that Blaine lost sufficient votes in Conkling's county to throw the state to Cleveland; the decision in New York determined the close election.

Even when personal indiscretions or slips were absent from a campaign, the level of political discourse rose no higher, for important issues still were not discussed. Garfield, in the campaign of 1880, his biographer has written, "never once referred in public to any political question that might be supposed to be before the American people for solution." Often, after making a campaign speech, Garfield would write in his diary, "I think no harm has been done." Indeed, issues were sometimes deliberately manufactured. In 1880, for example, the Democrats produced a forged letter purporting to show that Garfield did not support the Republican plank favoring restriction of Chinese immigration. Similarly in 1888, a Republican party worker, posing as a British national, asked British minister Sackville-West his preference in the election. When Sackville-West fell into the trap by naming Cleveland as his choice, the Republicans gleefully twisted the British lion's tail, hoping to wring out a few Irish votes.

When all else failed, there was always fraud. Probably no election in the whole nineteenth century was so infamous for the buying of votes and stuffing of ballot boxes as that of 1888. Harrison won the crucial state of Indiana that year only because thousands of campaign dollars were poured into the state and because the Standard Oil Company threw its employees' campaign efforts and votes behind him. In fact, the extensive fraud in the election of 1888 sparked a long-overdue move to introduce the Australian ballot into American elections. This reform replaced the "ticket" (supplied by the party) with the ballot (provided by the state). The change greatly enhanced the secrecy of voting and helped to reduce fraud.

Parties in Balance. As the reliance on personalities and manufactured issues suggests, presidential elections were remarkably close during these years. In both 1880 and 1884, the presidency was won by fewer than 25,000 votes in an electorate of some nine million. In 1888, as in 1876, it was won by a man who received fewer popular votes than the man who lost. Nor was there much party continuity in office. Hayes, a Republican, was followed by Garfield, a Republican; but in 1884, Cleveland, a Democrat, won, only to be followed in 1888 by Harrison, a Republican. Yet in spite of the party instability, the allegiances of the states were remarkably consistent. The shifting of the presidency back and forth between the parties during the 1880's resulted from changes in party allegiance in only five states, and not even all five changed in any one election.

This consistency of allegiance testifies to the continuing influence of the war and the absence of any real response during the 1880's and early nineties to the problems of a society passing through the Economic Revolution. The Democrats could always count on the states of the former Confederacy—the solid South—and usually on the border states. The Republicans were generally sure of most of New England, Pennsylvania, and a majority of the states of the Middle and Far West. In short, it seemed at least on the surface, even as late as the 1880's, that the parties were still divided by the memories of the Civil War and Reconstruction.

Actually, the division between the parties went back farther than that—to the 1840's and 1850's, when the Democratic party was the majority party of the nation. In the 1880's, despite the preponderance of Republican Presidents after the Civil War, the Democrats were still the majority party, having retained much of their old strength in the North. For example, in a Republican stronghold like Pennsylvania, the party's plurality in 1880 was only 37,000 out of 875,000 voters; in rock-ribbed Republican Ohio it was less than 35,000 out of a total of 715,000. At the same time, the Republicans enjoyed no such comparable strength in the Democratic South, even with Negroes voting. In Georgia in 1880, the Democratic plurality was almost 50,000 in a total electorate only one fourth the size of Ohio's.

Perhaps the most striking measure of Democratic popular strength was evidenced in the Congressional elections. In the ten Congresses elected between 1874 and 1892, the Democrats won control of the House of Representatives eight times. Moreover, the Democratic majorities averaged 47 seats as compared with an average of less than ten for the Republicans.

In substance, the Democratic party, until the 1890's, was still the majority party of the country, just as it had been before the Civil War. The essential

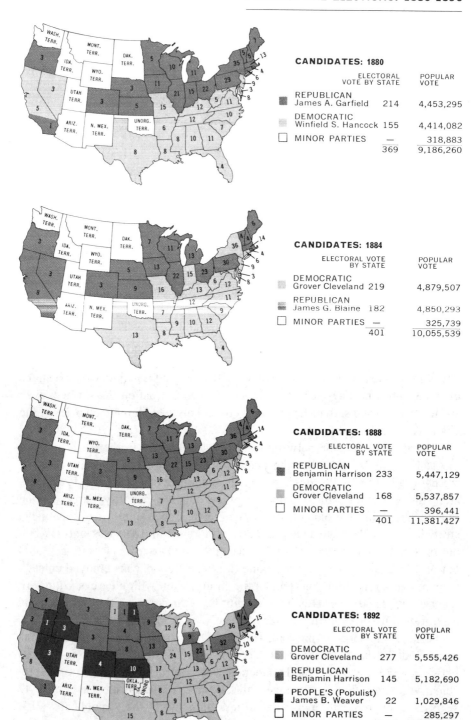

CANDIDATES: 1880

	ELECTORAL VOTE BY STATE	POPULAR VOTE
REPUBLICAN James A. Garfield	214	4,453,295
DEMOCRATIC Winfield S. Hancock	155	4,414,082
MINOR PARTIES	—	318,883
	369	9,186,260

CANDIDATES: 1884

	ELECTORAL VOTE BY STATE	POPULAR VOTE
DEMOCRATIC Grover Cleveland	219	4,879,507
REPUBLICAN James G. Blaine	182	4,850,293
MINOR PARTIES	—	325,739
	401	10,055,539

CANDIDATES: 1888

	ELECTORAL VOTE BY STATE	POPULAR VOTE
REPUBLICAN Benjamin Harrison	233	5,447,129
DEMOCRATIC Grover Cleveland	168	5,537,857
MINOR PARTIES	—	396,441
	401	11,381,427

CANDIDATES: 1892

	ELECTORAL VOTE BY STATE	POPULAR VOTE
DEMOCRATIC Grover Cleveland	277	5,555,426
REPUBLICAN Benjamin Harrison	145	5,182,690
PEOPLE'S (Populist) James B. Weaver	22	1,029,846
MINOR PARTIES	—	285,297
	444	12,053,259

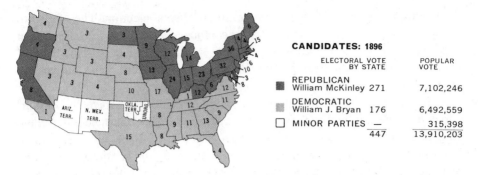

CANDIDATES: 1896

	ELECTORAL VOTE BY STATE	POPULAR VOTE
REPUBLICAN William McKinley	271	7,102,246
DEMOCRATIC William J. Bryan	176	6,492,559
MINOR PARTIES	—	315,398
	447	13,910,203

The voting pattern in presidential elections of this era remained fairly stable. The exceptions were the Populist split of 1892 and the last stand of free silver in 1896. In each case, changes of allegiance were primarily in the West and Midwest; the South remained Democratic throughout.

continuity had been obscured by the considerable but only temporary advantages that the Republicans received from the Civil War and Reconstruction.

Republicans Search for a National Base

Appeal to the South. Republican leaders were so well aware of their weakness that each Republican administration between 1877 and 1892 made some effort to extend the party's popular base. The most obvious place to begin such efforts was the South, where Republican expectations had once been bright in the knowledge that the large Negro vote was safely theirs. But ever since the failure of Reconstruction, that hope had dimmed. Indeed, the principal political lesson of Reconstruction was that the Negro vote could be a serious handicap in the South. The Republicans found that the advantage gained by obtaining the Negro vote was more than offset by the loss of white voters who were alienated by the acceptance of Negroes in the party. In those few states in which Negroes constituted a majority, white men used force or fraud to keep the party from power. The Republicans' sole hope, therefore, seemed to lie in making the southern party attractive to whites and minimizing the fact of Negro support.

Hayes adopted just this approach immediately after his inauguration. As a former Whig himself, he hoped to make the Republican party attractive to his old party associates in the South by abandoning Radicalism and by emphasizing national unity and support for economic growth. Thus in 1877, he withdrew the last federal troops from the South, named a former Confederate officer and Democrat, David M. Key, to his Cabinet, appointed other Democrats to lesser offices in the South, and supported southern demands for federal land grants to the Texas and Pacific Railroad. Much to Hayes' disappointment, however, Southerners in Congress did not carry out their side of the Compromise of 1877, which had secured Hayes' election. They failed to support a Republican for Speaker of the House. Moreover, in the South at large, very few old Whigs came over to the Republican side. In short, Hayes' efforts to build a Republican party upon appeals to southern conservatives did little to bolster the party's waning strength in the South.

Consequently, it is not surprising that Garfield, and especially Arthur, pursued a different approach when they came into office. Garfield did not live long enough to carry out any legislative program, but he was very much interested in public education as a means of uplifting the southern Negro and of building support for the Republican party. In a sense, therefore, the several attempts by Senator Henry Blair of New Hampshire during the 1880's to secure passage of an educational bill can be interpreted as an offshoot of Garfield's efforts to build a southern Republican party. The Blair bill — a major social and political issue throughout the 1880's — provided for federal aid to the states in support of the public schools, the funds to be appropriated in proportion to the degree of illiteracy. Because of the large numbers of illiterate Negroes and whites in the South, most of the ten million dollar annual appropriation (ten year total of 100 million) that was contemplated by the bill would have gone to the southern states. The measure was Republican in origin and support, and was obviously designed to clear up a major piece of unfinished national business left from the Civil War. Four times, between 1882 and 1890, the Blair bill was killed in the Democratic House after being passed as many times by the Republican Senate.

President Arthur's response to the Republican puzzle was suggested to him by the rise of independent movements in several southern states in the 1880's. These movements of dissent from the ruling Democratic party all sprang from roughly the same roots. All were protests against the social and economic policies of the "Bourbon" (conservative southern Democratic) state regimes. Although horrified by the alleged extravagance of the Radical Republican governments which they had replaced, these Bourbon governments nevertheless insisted upon paying off at face value the large debts inherited from the prewar and Reconstruction years. To meet these obligations the Bourbons exercised the most stringent economy in government and levied high taxes on land. In some states they even cut back on expenditures for public education.

In the late 1870's and early 1880's, these conservative policies aroused much political discontent in Georgia, Mississippi, North Carolina, and Virginia. Some of the new dissident Democratic leaders like former Confederate General William Mahone of Virginia advocated "readjusting" or partly repudiating the state debt in order to save the public schools and reduce land taxes. These dissidents or Independents provided a new opportunity for Republicans to crack the Democratic South. In 1881 and 1882, President Arthur turned over a large number of federal jobs to Mahone and the Independents in other southern states, hoping that such tangible support would help defeat Democrats, even if new Republicans were not immediately forthcoming. In both years, General Mahone's Readjuster party, as his dissident Democrats called themselves, won overwhelmingly in Virginia; in 1882 eight southern Independents replaced regular Democrats in Congress, presumably as a result of Arthur's cooperation with dissident southern Democrats. In 1884, the Republican presidential ticket captured more votes in the South than in the previous presidential election.

Need For the Negro Vote. If the immediate gains were substantial, the long-term ones were disappointing. In 1884, for instance, although the Republican voters in the South increased numerically, they decreased proportionately. Only in Virginia, where Mahone led his Readjusters into the Republican party, did Arthur's policy bring any significant accessions to the party. Republicans, it seemed, could no more base their party in the South upon independent or dissenter support than they could upon conservative. After trying both, it was evident that the essential strength of the party in the South still lay with the Negro, if his voting rights could be protected.

Thus in 1890 the Republicans turned once again to the policy of federal intervention in the South. President Harrison, for example, supported Congressman Henry Cabot Lodge's election bill, which would place federal registrars in the South to oversee elections and protect the Negro in his exercise of the suffrage. In substance, the bill marked a return to the hitherto repudiated Republican policy of federal intervention in the South, causing Democrats in both the North and South to stigmatize it as the "Force bill." As we have seen, though the bill passed the Republican House, it did not get through the Senate, where the Republican leadership abandoned it in return for southern support for the McKinley Tariff.

The Lodge bill of 1890 was the last effort by a Republican or Democratic administration to protect Negro voting in the South until the passage of the Civil Rights Act of 1957. Two reasons explain why no further efforts were made. The first was that in the 1890's, in the context of the Economic Revolution, the issue of the Negro ceased to dominate public attention or interest. The second was that, as a result of that revolution, the Republican party in the 1890's no longer needed the Negro or the South; during that decade, it emerged as the majority party without the help of either. But that story is properly a part of the next chapter, the history of the 1890's.

Politics and the Economic Revolution

Urban Bosses: Product of the Age. Only in the cities did politics respond appreciably to the social forces of the Economic Revolution. The urban boss, who in the early 1870's had already appeared in a great city like New York with the Tweed Ring (a group of corrupt Tammany Hall politicians led by William M. Tweed, who pilfered $200 million from the municipal treasury), flourished in many other cities by the 1880's and 1890's. Indeed, the evils of

(Continued on page 108)

The Art of Politics / Pictorial Essay

The campaign methods of the past—speeches, parades, slogans, songs, and cartoons—continued to be popular in the era of the Economic Revolution. But here, as in most other facets of American life, technological developments had their effect. The political cartoon, aided especially by advances in color lithography, became increasingly influential. To our relatively cynical and sophisticated minds, late nineteenth-century cartoons seem humorous and even gross overstatements of uninteresting issues. However, most cartoons were designed as serious representations of issues that were considered important; and they were taken seriously by an American public which continued to believe in party loyalty and the high level of personal morality preached, if not practiced, by most politicians of the age.

Concern with personal morality is illustrated in the pro-Democratic cartoon which shows Uncle Sam and a jury of Americans judging a shifty and weasel-like James G. Blaine, his pockets still bulging with ill-gotten securities from the Little Rock and Union Pacific railroads; he is depicted in sharp contrast to the erect and honest-looking figure of Grover Cleveland. This simplistic attitude

"The Political Poor Relation—an Unwelcome Guest" "Unprotected farmer (to protected monop-olists)—'Here gents, where do *I* come in?'" Puck, April 4, 1888. *Photo: Culver Pictures*

"He instituted the ordeal—can he stand it himself?" "Uncle Sam—'We have heard from you Mr. Cleveland. Now then Mr. Blaine, *you* made this issue; it is your turn to step up and —*Tell the Truth!*'" Puck. *Photo: Culver Pictures*

The statue of Washington being removed from the steps of the New York Stock Exchange and replaced by a statue of Mark Hanna. *Photo: Culver Pictures*

toward complex issues is again illustrated in a cartoon expressing the thinking of those sympathetic to the plight of the farmer. An emaciated, poorly-clothed farmer stands humbly, asking for his share, before a tableful of banqueting monopolists who are being served, to the accompaniment of music, by a servile and compliant Congress. The appeal to class consciousness that reached a high point in 1896 is evident not only in the portrayal of the ill-treated farmer, but also in the anti-Republican cartoon showing George Washington's statue, symbol of old traditions and values, being removed from the steps of the New York Stock Exchange by a group of bankers led by J. P. Morgan. On Washington's pedestal stands a statue, covered in dollar signs, of the paunchy Mark Hanna, who used his wealth to corrupt politicians.

Despite the rising popularity of the political cartoon, older campaign methods, such as oratory, continued to play an important role. Some of the most interesting and colorful political speakers of the era came to the fore through the Populist party. It attracted a new brand of grassroots leaders who, while in some cases personally bizarre, were deeply involved not only in the political and economic but also in the cultural issues of their time. Among them was the popular "Sockless Jerry" Simpson of Kansas. The name "sockless" developed because he accused his opponent in 1890 of representing

Thomas E. Watson, Populist leader from Georgia. *Photo: Culver Pictures. Below:* "Sockless Jerry" Simpson in a political debate with Chester Long at Harper, Kansas, 1892. *Photo: Kansas State Historical Society, Topeka*

the wealthy by wearing silk stockings; in return it was charged that Simpson wore none. Georgia's Populist spokesman was the red-haired and fiery-tongued Thomas Watson, vice-presidential candidate in 1896. One of the most talented Populists was Ignatius Donnelly, the party's best speaker and the author of several books, including the apocalyptic *Caesar's Column.*

Public sentiment was successfully aroused by the campaign techniques and issues of this period. These appeals to the public sometimes aggravated matters to the point of violence. A prime example was the arousal of anti-Chinese sentiment, especially in the Far West. As Chinese immigration increased rapidly (160,000 entered between 1868 and 1882) and the Panic of 1873 took its toll upon the economy, some "native" Americans blamed unemployment upon the Chinese, most of whom were willing to work for "coolie" wages. Ensuing riots—in San Francisco (1877) and Denver (1880)—helped convince Congress to pass a bill in 1882 excluding the immigration of Chinese laborers. This act did not, however, solve the economic problems that the nation had to face throughout this vital era.   *End*

An anti-Chinese riot in Denver, Colorado. *Frank Leslie's Illustrated Newspaper,* November 20, 1880. *Photo: Culver Pictures*

boss rule became more widespread than ever in the decade of the nineties. The overthrow of Boss Tweed in 1872 did not end Tammany's rule even in New York. "Honest John" Kelly in the 1880's and Richard Croker in the 1890's were as much the real powers in Democratic city politics as Tweed had been, though Kelly lacked his predecessor's personal corruption. Nor were all bosses Democrats; Philadelphia and Pittsburgh suffered under Republican rings almost as powerful as New York's Tammany Hall, and the Philadelphia Gas Ring was equally as corrupt, though on a smaller scale.

To those who believed city government should be efficient, honest, and democratic, the urban boss was one of the many problems presented by the rise of the industrial city. At the end of the 1880's one noted citizen of Minneapolis reflected this growing anxiety in a description of the rise and growth of the political boss' power in his city's government. "There has been for several years past," he wrote, "a very disreputable Ring, which has come into power by capturing the machinery of the Democratic party, through (1) diligent work in the ward caucuses; (2) by its active alliance with the liquor dealers, gamblers and so forth, . . . regardless of national political preferences; (3) by skilful and plausible championship of 'labor' and a capture of the labor vote." To the immigrants and other workers who supplied the votes, however, the boss often appeared quite different. The appeal of the boss lay in his willingness to help the immigrants and the native poor adjust to urban life. He might offer a new job, help if one of the family ran afoul of the law, or send a basket of food at Christmas or a free load of coal during a bitterly cold winter. In return, the immigrant was naturally quite willing to support the boss at the polls. It was this functional side of the urban machine, as the Progressive movement of the twentieth century was to discover, that accounted for its endurance. The prevalence of the urban boss was one of the first signs of the adjustment of politics to the social realities of the urban-industrial society created by the Economic Revolution.

Federal Inaction.   On the national level of politics in the 1880's, there was slight recognition of the new problems, though the creation of the Interstate Commerce Commission (ICC) in 1887 and the passage of the Sherman Antitrust Act in 1890 were certainly direct responses to the Economic Revolution. These two measures, however, were about the only indications that the federal government and the national parties recognized the new era.

Why didn't the Economic Revolution have a greater impact on political activity? Today, after the Progressive era, and especially after the New Deal of the 1930's, most Americans take for granted governmental intervention in the economy. It is expected that the political parties will be both the innovators and the instruments for bringing about that intervention. In the nineteenth century, however, such a concept was incompatible with the prevailing idea of how a republic ought to operate. Only socialists thought of government as a motivating force in society. While they envisioned government as the proprietor of the economy, they lacked the modern, intermediate view of government as a guiding force, correcting excesses and regulating the flow of goods and services, yet leaving the economy principally to nongovernmental forces. As we shall see later, some opponents of federal action were willing to grant a larger regulatory role to the state governments, suggesting that they were more concerned with which government should intervene rather than whether any should.

The view that government should keep its hands off the economy prevailed not only among economists, academicians, and publicists, but was also reflected in the practice of government and the political parties. For once, theory, and practice were united. Moreover, both political parties agreed on the issue. Thus, in 1874, Republican James A. Garfield maintained that it was "no part of the functions of the national government to find employment for people — and if we were to appropriate a hundred millions for this purpose, we should be taxing forty millions of people to keep a few thousand employed." Democratic President Cleveland in 1887 vetoed a small appropriation to help drought-stricken Texas farmers, on the grounds that "though the people support the Government, the Government should not support the people." In fact, of the two parties, the Democratic — in contrast with our own time — was the more committed to a concept of limited economic power for the federal government. Extreme philosophers of laissez faire, like William Graham Sumner, were Democrats, not Republicans. Moreover, it had been the Republicans during the Civil War who used the income tax and greenbacks as measures to finance the war. It was also the Republicans who provided the principal support for the Blair education bill in the 1880's. But even if the Republicans had a broader conception of governmental power in those years than the Democrats, both parties were, by twentieth century standards, extremely hostile to government intervention in the economy.

One consequence of such a restricted view of government activity was pointed out in 1884 by a writer in a popular magazine, who noted that the federal government touched the life of the average citizen "very rarely, and only at points of very little importance to him. From his rising up until his lying down, the vast aggregate of his interests and his activities are entirely beyond its scope, and there is hardly any serious interest of his life which is affected by it."

Yet it would be somewhat misleading to ignore the ways in which the federal government did influence the economy, even if its regulatory activities were limited. Both before and after the Civil War, the federal government exercised its powers to encourage economic growth through the tariff, aids to railroad construction, and currency and banking legislation. Although the federal land grants to railroads ended in 1872, other limited aids to economic growth, such as tariffs and currency reform, continued to operate, even in the so-called age of laissez faire.

Limited Steps Toward Positive Government: Currency and the Tariff. The question of currency reform arose first, stimulated by the effects of the depression of 1873. The fall in prices and the sluggishness of the economy brought demands for an increase in the money supply, especially from farmers who found money difficult to obtain. (In 1875, it will be remembered, the Resumption of Specie Act made the amount of paper currency dependent upon the Treasury's supply of silver and gold. From then on, all paper money could be redeemed in gold or silver.) By 1877 and 1878, there were insistent demands for an increase in the currency supply as a means of raising farm prices and of reducing the cost of borrowing. It was then that cheap money advocates learned about what they called the "Crime of '73," i.e., the demonetization of silver through the Coinage Act. Although free silverites and other inflationists insisted that the removal of silver dollars from the list of authorized coins of the United States was a conspiracy of the gold men, the facts seem to have been more complex than a simple conspiracy theory would recognize. In 1873, silver was overvalued; the weight of silver which went into a dollar, as defined by law, was worth more than a dollar as bullion. Hence, no silver was being presented for minting. Some congressmen may have realized that a new supply of silver might change this situation. At the time when minting of silver ceased to be legal, however, none of the metal was being presented for coinage, and the question seemed to most people an abstraction.

Within a few years, however, the situation had changed. A marked increase in silver production had driven down the price of the metal to a point where the market value of silver was again less than the value it would have had at the mint. But now the minting of silver dollars was no longer authorized by law. Consequently, the silver interests found a common cause with inflationists and Greenbackers. Both groups now joined in the cry for "the free and unlimited coinage of silver"—that is, the right to present unlimited amounts of the metal for minting without cost.

The silver question, which first arose in the Hayes administration, neatly epitomizes the limited role of government in the economy of the nineteenth century. The volume of the currency was certainly a vital question as indicated by the persistent concern with the issue until well into the twentieth century. But in the 1800's, a paper currency could not be expanded directly, because according to the prevailing theory of money, the value of a currency was derived from the precious metals; paper dollars were merely claims or receipts for bullion in the Treasury, used to avoid the inconvenience of carrying and handling heavy metal. Hence, if the volume of the currency was inadequate, the only way to increase it was to augment the amount of precious metal in the money system. Since silver was now plentiful, the inflationists reasoned that to add the yield of American silver mines to the money supply would "cheapen" money—i.e., raise prices and lower interest rates.

The issue came before the country in the silver forces' Bland-Allison Act of 1878, which required the government to purchase between two and four million dollars worth of silver each month for issuance as silver certificates

—that is, as paper money redeemable in silver or gold. President Hayes, who believed that it was dishonest to cheapen the value of the dollar in that fashion, vetoed the measure despite its support by both parties in Congress. His veto was overridden, but the number of silver dollars injected into the economy by the act was not sufficient to raise prices as its proponents had expected.

Agitation now began for the purchase of still more silver to add to the monetary system, but it was not until 1890 that the inflationists and western silver-mine owners gained their objective. In return for supporting a high tariff that year, the silverites secured the passage of the Sherman Silver Purchase Act. This act required the federal government to purchase 4.5 million ounces of silver each month, to be paid for in legal-tender notes that were redeemable in gold or silver at the Treasury. The quantity of silver to be purchased was thought to be near the total output of American mines, thereby realizing in practice the goal of unlimited coinage. But once again, the inflationists found that success eluded them. Prices did not rise and the output of American mines far exceeded 4.5 million ounces. Accordingly, the manipulation of the currency as an indirect means of governmental intervention in the economy continued to be a political issue in the 1890's; yet, only in this way did government venture to exercise responsibility for controlling the monetary system of the country.

The other indirect means of influencing economic development in these years was the tariff. The fostering of economic growth was one of the principal appeals of the Republican party in the 1870's and 1880's. Again and again in election campaigns and from the floor of Congress, party leaders proudly referred to the rapid industrialization of the country, the growth of railroad construction, and the high industrial wages as the fruits of the party's policies. "The American people," wrote a party newspaper in 1868, "owe a debt of gratitude to the Republican party for constructing a highway to the Pacific, for giving homesteads to the helpless, and freedom to the slave." By the 1880's, these particular examples of government support for economic growth were part of the past. But the party still regarded itself as the supporter of economic development through the protective tariff. Both labor's high wages and industry's high profits were attributed to it. As President Benjamin Harrison told Congress in 1892, "I believe the protective system which has now for something more than thirty years continuously prevailed in our legislation, has been a mighty instrument for the development of our national wealth and a most powerful agency in protecting the homes of our workingmen from the invasion of want. I have felt a most solicitous interest to preserve to our working people rates of wages that would not only give daily bread, but supply a comfortable margin for those home attractions and family comforts and enjoyments without which life is neither hopeful nor sweet."

The Height of Protectionism: The McKinley Tariff. By the 1880's, however, the Republican high-tariff policy was producing a formidable surplus in the Treasury. To low-tariff advocates, particularly Democrats, the surplus was a measure of the excessively high rates that the tariff exacted from consumers for the benefit of manufacturers. As a result, in 1882, a newly created Tariff Commission recommended a reduction in duties, but Congress, responding to the variety of interests that benefited from the high duties, passed a tariff that made few significant reductions. Consequently, the surplus continued to mount at the rate of $63 million a year. Indeed, in 1885, young Professor Woodrow Wilson wrote, "It has come to be infinitely more trouble to spend our enormous national income than to collect it; the chief embarrassments have arisen, not from deficits, but from surpluses."

To economy-minded men like President Grover Cleveland, the surplus seemed a great temptation to Congress to spend unwisely. As a candidate, it is true, Cleveland had shown little interest in either the surplus or the tariff that created it. Soon after taking office he confessed to Carl Schurz, the Liberal Republican who supported him in the campaign, "I am ashamed to say it, but the truth is I know nothing about the tariff. . . . Will you tell me how to go about it to learn?" Even when he learned about it, he did not become a strict free trader. Recognizing that many, if not most, Americans believed that the tariff was a protection for high wages and a spur to prosperity, Cleveland was careful not to lay himself open to charges of advocating free trade. His forceful presentation of the arguments for lower duties resulted in the Mills Tariff Bill of 1888, in which the Democratic House reduced duties; but the Republican-controlled Senate killed the measure by prolonged debate.

Since the tariff was one of the issues of the campaign of 1888, the victory of the high-tariff Republicans that year meant that upward revision was to be expected. The Republican measure, introduced by William McKinley of Ohio, constituted something of a departure from previous tariffs. While undoubtedly protective, it was also designed to reduce the revenue in order to eliminate the troublesome surplus. This result was achieved by placing certain raw materials like sugar, coffee, and tea on the free list while raising the duties on certain manufactured goods so high that none would come into the country at all. In that way protection would be high, but revenue would be low. The tariff on woolen dress goods, for example, was placed at 100 per cent, and the specific duties on a number of manufactures were scaled in such a way that the rates were almost double what they had been. For the first time, duties were also placed on farm goods, more as a sop to the farmers' discontent than as a practical remedy, since, as exporters, American farmers could not hope to benefit from a tariff.

As a means of expanding markets for American manufactures, the McKinley Tariff Act also included a reciprocity clause, which had been strongly advocated by Secretary of State James G. Blaine. The clause provided that duties on sugar, coffee, and tea, which would be removed under the act, could be restored if the countries from which such imports came placed "unreasonable" tariffs on American imports. This power was used to a limited extent in subsequent years in trade agreements with several Latin American countries.

Although the McKinley Act was one of the highest protective tariffs of the nineteenth century, it was, nevertheless, a clear indication of the limited role the nation thought government should play in the economy. A protective tariff, assuming it did protect wages and support prosperity, still was a feeble means of influencing the economic order. Almost by definition, a tariff is peripheral to the operation of a national economy; it touches only those goods involved in foreign trade and then only in a passive way. But in the late nineteenth century, even a party proud of its aid to economic growth felt it could properly go no farther.

The American Pattern Within a Broader Perspective. The practices of European industrial states during these same years demonstrate that the concept of a limited role for the national government in economic affairs was more a characteristic of the era than a uniquely American attitude. Both Germany and France in the 1880's and 1890's used the protective tariff as their principal tool for economic growth and national self-sufficiency. Neither country, it might be added, did anything to interfere with the simultaneous development of large-scale enterprise and monopoly. In fact, the Sherman Antitrust Act of the United States was unique in the western world. No other industrial nation, apparently, found big business either dangerous or undesirable.

In protecting the working class from some of the burdens of the new industrial system, it is true, European countries did more than the United States. For example, under Prince Bismarck, the "Iron Chancellor" of the recently created Empire, Germany in the 1880's provided old-age pensions and workmen's compensation for injuries sustained on the job. It is significant, however, that even the Bismarckian social legislation, which was the most advanced in Europe, lacked any minimum-wage regulations or unemployment insurance. Long before the 1880's, the British government had begun to limit the hours of work for women and children, but men remained unprotected until 1908. The first workmen's compensation act was passed in England in 1881, but only after vehement resistance. The British did not introduce a system of social legislation equivalent to that in Germany until 1908; France did not enact a comparable program of social legislation until 1910, though its first workmen's compensation act had been passed in 1898.

American progress along such lines was partly obscured by the federal character of the national government. In contrast to today, governmental power in the nineteenth century was not associated with the central government in Washington. The principal agencies of government were the states. Under the Constitution as then construed, they had broader powers, collected more taxes, spent more money, employed more officials, exercised more control, and impinged more on the everyday life of the citizen than the government in Washington. Only in the twentieth century has this division of power and authority been reversed. Hence, examples of nineteenth-century concern with the social consequences of the Economic Revolution must be sought in the policy of the individual states. Most of the industrial states, for instance, enacted factory inspection and regulatory laws in the last decades of the nineteenth century in emulation of the English factory laws. Many states also restricted the labor of women and children, especially in hazardous or heavy jobs. No state law, however, limited the hours of work or set wages for private employment on a general basis, though the workday and occasionally salaries were set by law for railroad and streetcar employees in a few states. Not a single American state in the whole nineteenth century instituted workmen's compensation laws, though many states held employers liable for injuries to their employees.

Because of the nearly unanimous belief that the federal government ought to abstain from legislating about such matters, it is therefore quite misleading to compare the social legislation of European states in these years with the total absence of it at the federal level in the United States. Nor did Europeans think the extent of governmental interference in the United States was much less than their own. Indeed, an astute observer like the Englishman Lord Bryce, who toured and studied the United States in the 1880's, thought American governmental concern with economic matters was greater than that evident in European legislatures.

In short, in order for them to have behaved like twentieth-century Progressives or New Dealers, the statesmen of the 1880's would have had to transcend the economic and constitutional assumptions of their age. It took time for the forces unleashed by the Economic Revolution to impel the political parties to reassess their basic beliefs about society, the economic order, and government. This rethinking would begin with the Populist party in the 1890's, continue with the Progressives in the following century, but not really be fully developed until the New Deal.

Issues That Could Be Settled: Civil Service and Congressional Reform. Many of the problems brought on by the Economic Revolution could not be dealt with at the national level, and since questions like the nature of the Union and the position of the Negro (once the basic topics of disagreement between the parties) were no longer active issues, less weighty concerns claimed the attention of legislators. The most notable example was the growing movement for reform of the federal civil service. Ever since Andrew Jackson had successfully argued for rotation in office, the distribution of political appointments had become a presidential headache of the first magnitude. As government bureaus grew in size, so did the headaches. When President Garfield, for instance, tried to persuade John Hay, Lincoln's former private secretary, to join his administration, Hay declined because the constant importuning by office seekers was more than he could stand. He wrote a friend that the new President was "living in a whirlwind, fighting like a baited bull against the mob, hounded down by politicians from morning till midnight."

An even more important objection to the spoils system blamed it for failing to encourage the use of trained and skilled personnel. As early as 1864, Charles Sumner had introduced a bill into the Senate requiring examinations for those seeking federal civil service positions. He pointed out even then that "the scale of business . . . and the immense interests involved will require some such system. We cannot transact our great concerns without serious loss unless we have trained men. 'Rotation in office' is proper enough in the political posts where political direction is determined, but absurd in the machinery of administration." The assumption that one citizen could fill a government job as well as another may have been valid in Jackson's day of more restricted government responsibilities, but it was no longer true in Arthur's time. By the 1870's, England, France, and Germany enjoyed the substantial benefits to be derived from an established, respected, and professional civil service.

During Reconstruction, civil service reform attracted to its banner a group of articulate, educated, and well-to-do public figures. Dissatisfied with the low level of American political life, these men hoped to purify politics and increase governmental efficiency through the elimination of the patronage system. Many of these patrician reformers, like Carl Schurz and E. L. Godkin, editor of the influential weekly, the *Nation*, had been liberal Republicans, who in 1872 and again in 1884 felt strongly enough about this issue to desert their party. In 1884, these "Mugwumps," as they came to be called by the regulars, supported Cleveland in preference to Blaine because the latter was a well-known spoilsman and the candidate of Old Guard Republicans. These Independents were relatively few in number, but their political influence was great, if only because important journals like the *New York Times* and *Harper's Weekly* shared their intense interest in improving administration through civil service reform.

Prior to the 1880's, however, neither of the principal political parties, despite the efforts of the liberal Republicans and Independents, would commit itself to civil service reform. Regular party leaders vigorously opposed reform of the civil service, which one of them contemptuously called "snivel service." It was the assassination of President Garfield in 1881 that brought new support to the cause. Since the assassin linked his insane act to his failure to receive a political appointment from the administration, a new popular concern with the iniquities of the patronage system was added to the narrowly based interest of the patrician reformers. After some debate, and in response to a recommendation from President Arthur, Congress passed the Pendleton Act in January 1883. This act laid the foundation for the modern civil service system of the United States.

The new law set up a three-man bi-partisan commission to prepare and administer the competitive tests. A very limited list of offices falling within the commission's jurisdiction was established, with the proviso that it could be extended by the President. The jobs placed under civil service regulations could be filled only by applicants who had successfully passed the examinations, thus ensuring competence. To protect appointees from political reprisals, the law provided that appointments were permanent, so long as the work was performed satisfactorily. The act forbade the levying of financial assessments upon office holders—an old device of the spoilsmen—and provided protection for those who refused to pay such political assessments. Under the original act, only about 12 per cent of all federal employees were covered, but the procedures and practices established then have since become the principles of the modern civil service.

The number of jobs covered by the system gradually increased as each outgoing President found it in his party's interest to protect incumbents by extending the system to more positions. For example, when Cleveland left office in 1889, the number of jobs under civil service regulations was double what it had been when he entered. In fact, he added almost a third of them after his defeat in 1888. Arthur had adopted the same tactic even earlier, as Harrison and others would subsequently do.

Another "housekeeping" measure that was only tangentially related to the new demands of an industrial society was the reorganization of the House of Representatives. Like the civil service prior to 1883, the House during the 1880's reflected the easygoing habits of the pre-Civil War farmers' republic. As Professor Leonard White has written, the rules of the House constituted "an unknown jungle" that no representative could penetrate. As a result of alterations and additions over the years, the rules had become so numerous and complicated that business could proceed only by suspending some of them. Since suspension required unanimous consent, the minority held enormous power. Moreover, the Speaker, though ostensibly ruling the House, was actually impotent in the face of the powerful committee chairmen and the complicated rules.

This disgraceful situation in the representative assembly of a major nation was ended in 1890 by the firm actions of Republican Speaker Thomas B. Reed, which quickly earned him the title of "czar." Reed successfully insisted that the Speaker must have the right to rule out of order any attempt by a member to obstruct proceedings or to delay a vote. If Democrats sought to prevent a quorum by refusing to answer the roll call, Reed counted them anyway; if they absented themselves, he had them brought into the chamber by force. The fact that the Democratic House in the next Congress adopted Reed's rules suggests that he was meeting the needs of a modern legislature as well as serving the interests of his party.

An Age of Whiggish Presidents

Congressional Dominance. The striking fact about the political history of these years, as contemporaries and historians alike have noted, is the weak presidential leadership. Woodrow Wilson, later an example of a quite different kind of President, wrote in 1885 that the explanation lay in the great disparity between the power and prestige of Congress and that of the President. As Wilson put it, the United States may have been a presidential form of government in theory, but functionally its form was Congressional. Tested against the administrations after the death of Lincoln, there was much truth in the assertion. Andrew Johnson, it will be recalled, had been crushed by a powerful Congress, and even a popular hero and general like Ulysses S. Grant proved incapable of resisting Congressional domination. In the years after 1877, as in the years under Grant and Johnson, all important legislation—and there was a good deal of it—originated not with the Presidents, but with Congress. The Pendleton Act, the Interstate Commerce Act, the Dawes Act, and the Sherman Antitrust Act simply received presidential assent; the impetus for their enactment came from Congress. The kind of presidential leadership that is associated with James K. Polk, Andrew Jackson, Woodrow Wilson, Theodore and Franklin Roosevelt, and Lyndon B. Johnson was absent in the years between 1865 and 1900.

Personality Factors and the Defense of Presidential Prerogative. Undoubtedly, part of this striking contrast can be accounted for by personality differences. Jackson was an irascible, self-willed man; Hayes was a quiet, gentle person. But that is certainly not the whole explanation. Several of the Presidents of the late nineteenth century showed themselves quite capable of firmly resisting legislative and other pressures. Indeed, most of them were strong rather than weak-willed men. Both Hayes and Garfield, for example, waged a vigorous and ultimately triumphant fight against Congressional control of patronage and offices.

Very early in his administration, Hayes insisted upon undisputed authority to name his own appointees to important patronage-dispensing offices even though the Senate for the preceding ten years had successfully asserted its right to be consulted on all major appointments, whether the Constitution prescribed senatorial confirmation or not. In the course of his battle with Congress over patronage, Hayes successfully overrode the opposition of even Senator Roscoe Conkling, the powerful Republican boss of New York State. Later, in 1879 and 1880, Hayes foiled attempts by the Democrats to attach "riders" to appropriation bills. Since the President could not veto a part of a bill, but had to accept all of it or nothing, a rider was a means of forcing legislation upon him. Congress assumed that the President would not dare to veto an appropriation intended to pay judges and the Army, but Hayes firmly vetoed any appropriation bill that contained riders to which he objected. After six such tussles, the House gave up and passed the money bills without the objectionable riders.

Hayes also stood resolutely against railroad presidents in the strike of 1877 when they insisted that federal troops be used to break the strike by operating the trains. Hayes permitted the soldiers to be used only to maintain order and not to move the trains. Indeed, he was a man of compassion with some true awareness of the novel forces then transforming the farmers' republic in which he had grown up. Immediately after the railroad strike, he wrote in his diary, "Can't something be done by education of the strikers, by judicious control of capitalists, by wise general policy to end or diminish the evil? The railroad strikers, as a rule, are good men, sober, intelligent and industrious." After he left the presidency in 1881, Hayes continued to be interested in the problems of labor and was greatly impressed by the social message of Henry George's *Progress and Poverty*. He also devoted a good part of his later years to working for Negro education in the South.

Although Garfield was in office only four months before his assassination, he, too, contended with Senator Conkling over appointments. At one point in his fight, Garfield exclaimed, "This brings on the contest at once and will settle the question whether the President is the registering clerk of the Senate or the Executive of the nation." Garfield's firmness won out. He finally maneuvered Conkling into abandoning his Senate seat for good. Cleveland, too, showed his determination to stand up to Congress in defense of the President's prerogatives. He compelled the repeal of the Tenure of Office Act in 1887, which a powerful Reconstruction Congress had imposed upon Johnson twenty years earlier and had used successfully against Grant.

Cleveland also courageously resisted both Congress and the powerful veterans' lobby on the matter of military pensions. In principle, the pensions program of the government was generous and, in practice, it was lenient. Nevertheless, each year the Pension Bureau rejected thousands of dubious and often fraudulent claims. Any claimant who was denied a pension by the Bureau could ask a member of Congress to present his claim as a special private act of legislation. If successful, the claimant could thus secure through Congress what the general pension laws and the Pension Bureau would not allow. Under the prodding of professional pension agents, hundreds of claimants did just that. In fact, the number of pension bills was so great that both houses of Congress regularly interrupted their normal business for specified periods simply to vote on private pension bills, which passed without debate or protest and usually with only a few members in attendance. Moreover, no President ever vetoed such legislation.

No President before Cleveland, that is. Beginning in 1886, Cleveland began to return scores of these private bills without his signature and often with messages succinctly exposing the fraudulence or inadequacy of the claims. One claimant, for instance, said that he was on his way to join his regiment when his horse fell on his ankle, thereby entitling him to a military pension. Another old soldier contended that a disease of the eyes from which he suffered was the result of a case of diarrhea he had contracted while in the Army years before. Cleveland signed the vast majority of the 2042 pension bills passed during his first administration, but he killed some 400 others with his vetoes. Furthermore, in 1887 he vetoed a general pensions bill for dependents of veterans on the ground that it was extravagant. For these actions in behalf of economy President Cleveland earned the undying enmity of the politically powerful Grand Army of the Republic, the organization of Civil War Union Army veterans.

Similarly, Cleveland's willingness to strike out against the surplus and the tariff in his message of December 1887 revealed his backbone as a President. "They told me it would hurt the party," he wrote later after his defeat in 1888, "that without it I was sure to be reëlected, but that if I sent that message to Congress it would, in all probability, defeat me. . . . The situation as it existed was, to my mind, intolerable, and immediate action was necessary. Besides I did not wish to be reëlected without having the people understand where I stood on the tariff question and then spring the question on them after my reëlection. Perhaps I made a mistake from a party standpoint: but damn it, it was right. I had at least that satisfaction. . . ."

Lack of firmness and courage in facing Congress or public opinion is not the true reason for the poor reputation of these Presidents. When it was a question of upholding the office of President against Congressional encroachment, Cleveland, Garfield, and Hayes certainly did all that could be expected of them. Indeed, it is to them that the office owes its modern independence after the ineffectiveness of Grant and Johnson. Yet there was something missing from these men, something that made a Polk, a Jackson, a Lincoln, or a Wilson a great presidential leader of party and nation.

The Whig View of the Presidency Persists. One of the missing ingredients was a vigorous conception of the office. All of the Presidents of the 1880's and early nineties, whether actually old Whigs or not, subscribed to the Whig interpretation of the presidency. After all, the Whig philosophy of presidential restraint had been a reaction against the vigorous leadership of Andrew Jackson; Hayes was, in fact, an old Whig. He firmly believed that Congress should lead in matters of legislation and the President should simply carry out its will. Even Grover Cleveland, though a member of Andrew Jackson's party, subscribed to a view that was very close to that of the old Whigs. He saw the President as the executive in the literal sense — that is, as the head of the branch of government that carried out the will of Congress and that did no more than resist unjust or extravagant measures. One valuable result of such an attitude, incidentally, was that Cleveland's administration recovered some 80 million acres of public lands, illegally acquired by railroads, cattlemen, and timber interests. It was this efficient and rigidly honest application of the laws that he must have had in mind when, in 1884, in his acceptance letter, he described the office of President as "essentially executive in nature." It was characteristic of Cleveland's approach that at the end of his first year in office, he should observe that perhaps his principal contribution as President would be to see that the separation of powers was rigorously adhered to.

Harrison, probably more than any other, fitted the Whig view of a President. In the single year of 1890 a number of important pieces of legislation passed Congress: the Sherman Antitrust Act, the Sherman Silver Purchase

Act, a new pensions bill, and the McKinley Tariff. But Harrison had no part in any of them except to sign them.

To see these Presidents as lacking a forceful conception of the presidency is but another way of saying that for all their courage in dealing with Congress, they had no cause of their own. Hayes and Cleveland seem weak compared to Lincoln or Polk, for their defenses of the presidential power were undertaken in a political vacuum. Lincoln and Jackson, who also fought for an independent executive, were concerned primarily with a larger program or policy. Hayes, on the other hand, strove simply for freedom from Congressional encroachment upon his presidential prerogatives. He was contending for an abstract, if important, constitutional principle. The same conclusion applies to Garfield and Cleveland. Indeed, in the politics of this whole period, and to a certain degree in that of the nineties as well, the presidential emphasis was on the location of power, not on its exercise. In earlier administrations, when the presidential power had been expanded, it had been as a by-product of the drive to deal with a national issue of large importance. (Cleveland's efforts to lower the tariff and end the surplus in 1887 might seem to fit that pattern, but even on that issue he lacked the backing of a united party, and the country proved to be indifferent to his reform.) The rise of the West, and the Mexican and Civil wars presented issues that had earlier forced the expansion of the presidential office.

In the years after 1877, however, the great source of national problems was neither military nor sectional, but economic. As Lord Bryce wrote in *The American Commonwealth,* "Questions of foreign policy and of domestic constitutional change are generally happily absent" in America. Moreover, even the bases of political contest common in Europe were absent in the United States. "There are no class privileges or religious inequalities to be abolished," Bryce pointed out. "Religion, so powerful a political force in Europe, is outside politics altogether." Nor were there any social questions analogous to those which agitated European politics, pushing great men and issues to the fore. The "great political issues" in America, he asserted, "have not hitherto been class issues." And in the field of economic affairs, orthodox thought decreed that government was incompetent and should, therefore, exercise little if any power.

With no issues over which to exercise power, none of the Presidents of these years, Democrat or Republican, was driven to enlarge the authority of his office. In a real sense, aside from the personalities of the incumbents, the diminished presidency of these years was yet another measure of the limited role assigned to government. It was also a manifestation of the way in which politics lagged behind the Economic Revolution, which was changing society.

In the nineties, however, even national politics would begin to feel the transforming effects of the revolution in the economic order.

SUGGESTED READING

Despite the comparatively low level of politics during the years covered by this chapter, the literature is rich. Most provocative, though bordering on the cynical, is Matthew Josephson, *The Politicos, 1865–1896** (1938, 1963). Much more favorable to the Republican party, and more recent is the general history of the party, Malcolm Moos, *The Republicans* (1956). Informed and with a broad perspective is Wilfred E. Binkley, *American Political Parties, Their Natural History* (1945). Eugene H. Roseboom, *A History of Presidential Elections* (1957) is excellent for these and other campaigns. Basic to any study of the politics of these years is the compilation of county statistics on presidential elections in W. Dean Burnham, *Presidential Ballots, 1836–1892* (1955). The essays by Burnham for the various periods are well worth examination. For a path-breaking and informative study of the way the federal government functioned see Leonard D. White, *The Republican Era: 1869–1901** (1958).

The biographical literature is large. One of the best biographies of the era is Harry Barnard, *Rutherford B. Hayes and His America* (1954), which rescues Hayes from an undeserved reputation as a nonentity. The same has not been done for Garfield; Robert Granville Caldwell, *James A. Garfield, Party Chieftain* (1931), is a critical study. Donald Barr Chidsey, *The Gentleman from New York: A Life of Roscoe Conkling* (1935), manages to make the New York boss understandable and likeable. The standard, if rather uncritical, biography of Cleveland is Allan Nevins, *Grover Cleveland, a Study in Courage* (1932). Much less favorably disposed toward his subject is Horace Samuel Merrill, *Bourbon Leader: Grover Cleveland and the Democratic Party** (1957). Merrill's *Bourbon Democracy of the Middle West, 1865–1896* (1953), fills an important gap in the history of the Democratic party during this period.

The book that has reshaped our understanding of the political relationship between Northern Republicans and the South is C. Vann Woodward, *Reunion and Reaction: The Compromise of 1877 and the End of Reconstruction* (1951).* Studies that have carried forward the story in subsequent years are Vincent P. De Santis, *Republicans Face the Southern Question: The New Departure Years, 1877–1897* (1959) and Stanley P. Hirshson, *Farewell to the Bloody Shirt: Northern Republicans and the Southern Negro, 1877–1893* (1962).

The question of the civil service has been examined from the perspective of those who pushed the reform in Ari Hoogenboom, *Outlawing the Spoils: A History of the Civil Service Reform Movement, 1865–1883* (1961), and from the standpoint of the service itself in Paul R. Van Riper, *History of the United States Civil Service* (1958). Both Josephson, *The Politicos** and White, *The Republican Era** (mentioned above) have some valuable material on this subject, too.

For the controversies over the tariff see, in addition to the biographies of Cleveland, the old, but full Edward Stanwood, *American Tariff Controversies in the Nineteenth*

---

*Available in a paperback edition.

Century, 2 vols. (1903) and Frank W. Taussig, *The Tariff History of the United States** (1931), which is authoritative, if hostile to the idea of a protective tariff.

A book that has to be used with care, but which is unfailingly interesting, is Harry Thurston Peck, *Twenty Years of the Republic, 1885–1905* (1932). Woodrow Wilson, *Congressional Government** (1885), is both incisive on the nature of American government and revealing of a future president. Enlightening the politics of the period is James Bryce, *The American Commonwealth,** which was first published in 1888, and has been reprinted in a number of editions. After De Tocqueville, Bryce is the most knowing foreign appraiser of American politics. A fresh and broad study of the Irish in America and Ireland, particularly in politics, is Thomas N. Brown, *Irish-American Nationalism, 1870–1890* (1966).

Vast numbers of people living in relatively small urban areas created congestion of all kinds. The skyscrapers on Chicago's State Street provided a solution for one type of congestion, but the crowds on the sidewalks and the traffic in the street show that city problems were then, as today, far from being solved.   Photo: Library of Congress

CHAPTER FIVE

THE NINETIES: THE FIRST DECADE OF MODERN AMERICA

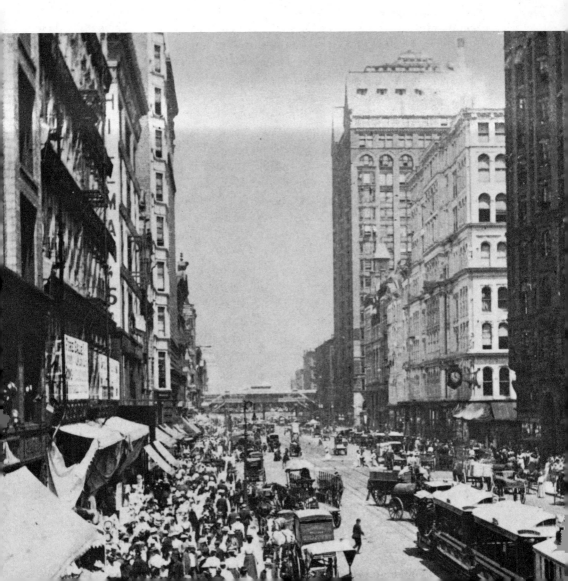

T HE YEAR WAS 1892. "We meet in the midst of a nation brought to the verge of moral, political, and material ruin," the Populist platform began. The nineties encouraged such cataclysmic pronouncements, for it was a time of widespread anxiety and social unrest. To the mounting discontent of the farmers of America, the deep and persistent depression of 1893 added strikes, violence, and other protests of the unemployed in hundreds of industrial cities. The thousands of workers who marched on Washington demanding jobs brought the country "dangerously near the conditions of things at the time of the French Revolution," announced the *Nation* in 1894. That same year the New York *Herald* justified the use of federal troops to break the Chicago railroad strike on the ground that "the nation is fighting for its own existence just as truly as in suppressing the great rebellion."

Historian Frederick Jackson Turner was not alone in 1893 when he called attention to the recent closing of the frontier. Throughout the nineties, men wondered what was in store for the nation now that its source of prosperity and its historic safety valve for social discontent were gone. Even individuals not alarmed by the effects of a closed frontier foresaw deep changes and new turnings in the offing. In 1894, Henry Adams urged his fellow historians to discover the "tendency of history" in an age of new scientific and social developments. Years later, Adams wrote that at the Chicago Exposition of 1893, men asked "for the first time whether the American people knew where they were driving." He admitted, "for one, that he did not know."

In the 1890's, otherwise sensible men talked darkly of the imminent threat of communism and anarchism. In 1893, when Illinois' governor, John Peter Altgeld, pardoned the anarchists who had been unjustly convicted of the Haymarket bombing, Theodore Roosevelt interpreted the act as a wish to start "a red government of lawlessness and dishonesty as fantastic and vicious as the Paris Commune." Supreme Court Justice Stephen J. Field, in finding a recent income tax law unconstitutional in 1895, justified his conclusion on the grounds of the dangerous times. "The present assault upon capital," he warned, "is but the beginning. It will be but the stepping-stone to others, larger and more sweeping, 'til our political contests will become a war of the poor against the rich; a war constantly growing in intensity and bitterness." The class consciousness and even class hatred that ran through the speeches and literature of the presidential campaign of 1896 came close to making Justice Field a prophet. Never had Americans so nearly approached being divided into "two nations": one of the many poor and one of the few rich.

Before the decade was out, however, the clouds would lift. Old issues like the position of the Negro may have been prematurely pushed aside and new ones like imperialism impetuously taken up, but the uncertainty and anxiety would be gone. Confidence and prosperity would dominate the opening years of the new century, but not before the Economic Revolution had transformed the political parties and helped to launch the nation upon a new life as an imperial democracy.

Portents of Change

The Intensification of Labor Violence: Homestead and Coeur d'Alene Strikes. The decade of the nineties does not really begin until 1892. The incidents of that year foreshadowed the social restlessness of the remainder of the decade. The strike of the steelworkers at the Homestead, Pennsylvania, works of the Carnegie Steel Company in July was only the first of a number of ugly clashes between capital and labor that would punctuate the decade.

The conflict at Homestead began with a dispute over wages and reached a climax in June when the company refused to deal any further with the steelworkers' union. The manager of the plant, Henry Clay Frick, endeavoring to destroy the union, announced that he would treat with the men on an individual basis only. Anticipating trouble with the union, Frick then made the initial move by temporarily closing down the Homestead works on July 1. With the shutdown of the plant, the workers prepared to resist the importation of strikebreakers. Both sides, actually, were preparing for a prolonged and, if necessary, violent confrontation; Frick had secretly engaged some 300 Pinkertons (private police) to protect the strikebreakers he intended to hire. The Pinkerton guards, in order to escape the notice of the strikers, approached the plant from the river side on a large barge. The incensed workers learned of the stratagem and, armed with guns, dynamite, rocks, and a small cannon, met the guards at the river's edge. Shots exploded and brickbats flew from both sides, but the Pinkertons could not break through the strikers' barrage. The battle lasted for 12 hours before the Pinkertons were finally permitted to surrender. Probably as many as nine strikers and seven Pinkerton men died; 40 strikers and 20 Pinkertons were shot. The arrival of the state militia the next day brought order and in time helped to end the strike in the company's favor.

That labor newspapers should vehemently upbraid the Homestead managers was to be expected, but the use of a private army by Frick alarmed many law-abiding and otherwise conservative observers. Even the general press, usually quite sympathetic to management during strikes, found this aspect of the strike hard to justify. All recognized that society itself was threatened when a labor dispute could degenerate into a small war between private armies. Yet a similar incident of armed warfare occurred later in the month between striking miners and strikebreakers at the Coeur d'Alene silver mines in Idaho. There, too, the violence reached such a pitch that troops had to be sent to the scene.

The People's Party. The very same summer that witnessed the upheaval at Homestead and the battle at Coeur d'Alene also saw the founding convention of the People's party at Omaha. Like the occurrence at Homestead, this reform party pointed a new direction for the decade. The People's party was intended to be a coalition of workers and farmers. Its principal impetus, however, was a decade of agrarian discontent. To be sure, a few urban labor leaders like Eugene V. Debs of the railroad workers and Terence V. Powderly of the Knights of Labor rallied to the support of the new party, but the platform adopted in 1892 at Omaha amply demonstrated that the interests and problems of farmers dominated. Indeed, the principal demands were concrete responses to the farmers' long-standing complaints. Thus, one plank in the platform, advocating government ownership of the nation's railroad, telegraph, and telephone networks, was intended to remedy the farmers' high cost of transporting farm products. Two others, the demand for the "free and unlimited coinage of silver" at the ratio of 16 units of silver to one unit of gold, and the increase in the currency supply until it reached at least $50 per capita, were expected to raise the farm prices by inflating the currency. The Southern Alliance's subtreasury plan (see p. 81), by which farmers could procure government loans for stored crops, was included to meet the farmers' need for cheaper credit.

The other planks of the platform were only slightly less related to agricultural problems. A graduated income tax was expected to redistribute the national income in a more equitable fashion. Finally, the platform demanded that all land held by railroads and corporations "in excess of their actual needs," and all land owned by aliens should be reclaimed by the government and "held for actual settlers only."

In a series of resolutions not included in the platform, the convention also supported such political reforms as the direct election of senators, the initiative and referendum, and a single term for President and Vice President. The only resolutions affecting urban labor in any direct fashion were demands for restriction of "undesirable immigration" and for the improvement of laws against foreign contract labor. One resolution also opposed the use of private police in labor disputes, an obvious allusion to the Homestead lockout.

To many conservatives of the times, these economic and political goals seemed radical. The Supreme Court, for example, declared the two per cent income tax unconstitutional in 1895, and government ownership of transportation and communications was thought to be straight out of the lexicons of socialism. Similarly, in the minds of many of the nation's respectable citizens, to advocate the free and unlimited coinage of silver was to threaten established property relations, for the enactment of such a policy would devalue savings and investments.

In retrospect, the Populists represented a break with conventional ideas in more than the details of their program. Their new conception of the role of government in the economy constituted the significance of the Populist movement in the nineties and later. "We believe," the platform read, "that the powers of government—in other words, of the people—should be expanded (as in the case of the postal service) as rapidly and as far as the good sense of an intelligent people and the teachings of experience shall justify, to the end that oppression, injustice, and poverty should eventually cease in the land." Notice, particularly, their goal of ending poverty. As we have seen already, few Republicans or regular Democrats believed that the federal government was anything more than a benign policeman who kept order at home and peace with foreign nations. After the Populists, government responsibility for the prosperity of the economy would be a more acceptable tenet of democratic social thought.

Prominent Populists: Emotional Reformers. The presidential candidate of the Populists in 1892 was James B. Weaver of Iowa, who had been a Republican before the Civil War because of his moral concern over slavery. Following the war, he became a Greenbacker, an allegiance that made him a link between the farmer protest movements of the 1870's and the new People's party. His running mate in 1892 was James G. Field, a former Confederate general from Virginia, whose presence symbolized the revival of the prewar alliance between southern and western farmers.

But perhaps the best-known southern Populist was Thomas E. Watson of Georgia. In the South, the Populists, as the third party, ran head-on into the race question. Negro Republicans were a natural ally for any third party in the Democratic South, but to accept them could frighten off white Democrats who might otherwise join the Populists. Watson, however, firmly grasped the nettle of race, proclaiming to whites and Negroes: "You are kept apart that you may be separately fleeced of your earnings. You are made to hate each other because upon that hatred is rested the keystone of the arch of financial despotism which enslaves you both. You are deceived and blinded that you may not see how this race antagonism perpetuates a monetary system which beggars both." At times, such an appeal to class successfully overrode the claims of race, as when 2000 white Georgia dirt farmers defied a mob of white men who threatened to lynch a Negro Populist speaker. But generally, the Populists were not prepared to challenge the orthodox southern commitment to white supremacy.

While in the South some Populists like Watson dared to challenge the iron rules of white supremacy politics, in the West other Populists defied convention by encouraging women to become involved in political affairs. Undoubtedly the best-known of the several women orators of Populism was fiery Mrs. Mary Elizabeth Lease of Kansas, who made over 150 speeches during the campaign of 1890. Like most Populists, Mrs. Lease refused to accept overproduction as a cause of the low prices farmers received for their products. How can there be overproduction, she exclaimed, "when 10,000 little children . . . starve to death every year in the United States, and over 100,000 shopgirls in New York are forced to sell their virtue for the bread their niggardly wages deny them!"

As Mrs. Lease's remarks suggest, the Populists, as a group, were emotional rather than coldly analytical reformers. Their analyses of and solutions for the farmers' problems were often crude and inadequate. The Populists were also provincial, in that they usually looked no further than the American past for their guidance. They liked to see themselves as a part of the radical tradition that, stretching back to Jefferson and Jackson, was devoted to the interests of "the people."

As self-conscious radicals, the Populists employed extreme language that frightened conservatives then and has misled historians since. It is true that the Populists tended to see issues in sharp black and white and to blame their plight upon conspiracies, such as the famous "Crime of '73" (see p. 110). Richard Hofstadter, for example, emphasizes this aspect of their thought in *The Age of Reform* and further accuses them of popularizing anti-Semitic rhetoric. However, as C. Vann Woodward has observed, in the 1890's suspicions and apocalyptic forebodings afflicted many groups, some of whom—like scholars and intellectuals—should have been able to rise above such fears more readily than the unsophisticated Populists. Occasionally, it is true, the Populists fell into the cliches of anti-Semitic rhetoric (as when they attacked the "international bankers"), but W. T. K. Nugent's researches into the Kansas Populists indicate that they gave no significant support to the rather widespread nativist agitation and anti-Semitic violence that flared up in the 1890's. In fact, the Populists supported immigrants for public office, and anti-Semitic comments were at most occasional in their literature. Moreover, Nugent's conception of the Populists as small businessmen-farmers who organized to secure better prices and more favorable marketing conditions is more convincing than Norman Pollack's portrayal of them in *The Populist Response to Industrial America* as believers in a class-conscious ideology akin to Marxism.

The Election of 1892. If the Populists in the summer of 1892 thought their party was destined to become a major party, most people in the nation did not, much as they may have been disturbed by Populist radicalism. The Republicans, as might have been predicted, nominated the incumbent, Benjamin Harrison. The name of the Democratic nominee was almost as easily foreseen as that of the Republican. By 1892, Grover Cleveland, despite his defeat in 1888, was once again prominent in his party and nation. Nor could the Democrats forget that he was their only winner in almost 40 years. Already he had forthrightly identified himself as opposed to the rising issue of free silver, having denounced in 1891 "the dangerous and reckless experiment of free, unlimited, and independent silver coinage."

It was on the issue of the tariff that the campaign was fought, since neither party was willing to take an unambiguous position on silver. Hoping to repeat their success of 1890, the Democrats again attacked the unpopular McKinley Tariff in particular and protectionism in general. At least one prominent Republican attributed his party's defeat to its defense of that tariff. Writing to President Harrison after the election, he concluded that the people "were thoroughly imbued with the feeling that the party did not do right in revising the tariff up instead of down. They beat us for it in '90 and now again."

In comparison with the close elections of the 1880's, Cleveland's margin of 350,000 votes over Harrison in 1892 was overwhelming. Moreover, solid

Republican states like Illinois, Wisconsin, and California had shifted to the Democrats; even Ohio, usually a sure thing for the Republicans, barely stayed with the party this time. Congressman William McKinley himself lost his seat in the debacle. Furthermore, the Populists captured the electoral votes of Kansas, Colorado, Idaho, and Nevada, and nationally gained over a million popular votes. It was this very good showing by a new party of dissent that foreshadowed the political developments in the rest of the decade.

But even the dissent of the substantial Populist party did not measure the full extent of the national dissatisfaction. On the surface, the victory of Cleveland seemed a triumph of conservatism. After the election, for example, Henry Clay Frick, the steel manufacturer, wrote his superior, Andrew Carnegie, "I am very sorry for President Harrison, but I cannot see that our interests are going to be affected one way or the other by the change in administration."

Yet the triumph of the undoubtedly conservative Cleveland obscured the victories of a number of radical or reform Democrats in the South and West. In South Carolina, one-eyed, coarse-spoken Benjamin Tillman, who later would threaten to "tickle old Grover's fat ribs" with his pitchfork, was reelected governor. In Illinois, John Peter Altgeld, a vehement supporter of organized labor who in the next year would pardon the Haymarket anarchists, was elected governor, while in Nebraska, young, reform-minded William Jennings Bryan won a seat in Congress. Moreover, much of Cleveland's support came in spite of his conservatism. Among his backers were urban reformers and labor leaders, who distrusted Populism and hoped to make the Democratic party the vehicle of reform. Henry George advised his followers to shun Populist candidates and to support Cleveland, while President Samuel Gompers of the American Federation of Labor told organized labor that Populism and workingmen shared no fundamental aims. In essence, Cleveland's victory resulted from an unstable coalition of conservatives and reformers that could hardly be expected to endure even in tranquil times. The depression that struck soon after Cleveland's inauguration in March 1893 provided the death blow for this shaky coalition.

The key to the history of the nineties was the depression, which dominated the thought and shaped the action of the remainder of the decade. The violence and social unrest at Homestead now became simply an introduction; the reformist politics of Populism were only a suggestion of the bigger changes to come.

And the Earth Shook

The Disease of Depression. "There has never been a time in our history," President Harrison reported in his annual message in December 1892, "when work was so abundant, or when wages were so high." But by the following February, with the sudden failure of the Philadelphia and Reading Railroad, informed observers glimpsed the first sign of financial panic. By early April, as other important firms closed their doors, the signs became clear to every-one. The slide had begun. In the middle of April, a precipitous drop in the stock market underscored the seriousness of the situation, and by summer, the reversal in the state of the economy from the previous winter was com-plete. "The month of August will long remain memorable . . . in our indus-trial history," commented the *Commercial and Financial Chronicle.* "Never before has there been such a sudden and striking cessation of industrial activity." Nor was any section of the country exempt from the paralysis. Before the year was out, some 500 banks and nearly 16,000 business firms had sunk into bankruptcy. Samuel Gompers of the American Federation of Labor estimated the number of unemployed in December 1893 at three million. The financial panic was over, but the nation now staggered under the much heavier burdens of a full-scale depression.

The depression reached bottom during 1894. Approximately 20 per cent of the labor force was without work during the winter months of 1893 – 1894; in Chicago alone, more than 100,000 men were unemployed and often with-out homes. In city after city, police stations and other public buildings had to be opened at night to the jobless so that they might have some place to sleep. Municipal and private relief agencies strained to provide even the cheapest and simplest kinds of food for the thousands who could no longer afford to buy their own. During that terrible winter, relief expenditures in New York City alone ran as high as five million dollars. For the nation as a whole, the real income of the population dropped 18 per cent between 1892 and 1894. The large numbers of unemployed wandering from city to city seeking work were novel enough sights to be frightening. Popular magazines began to print anxious articles on the problem of the "tramp." When the police raided a camp of "tramps" outside of Troy, New York, they found most of the men healthy and presumably willing to work but unable to find employment. "In nearly every case," the police reported, "a wife and children had been left in some distant city." A study of the antitramp laws and ordinances that dozens of communities hastily enacted, reported, "Nearly all the real tramp laws have a panicky look which suggests a pressing evil, real or imaginary."

For a time in 1895, there were indications that an upswing in business activity and employment was in the making, but the economy took a new tumble in early 1896. The following year, men once more spoke confidently of recovery, but not until the new century opened was the economic machinery of the United States running smoothly again.

A Policy of Inaction. Nothing illustrates better the pervasive belief in laissez faire than the character of the public action taken to offset the impact of the depression. Businessmen and statesmen alike viewed dips in the business cycle as unfortunate, inexplicable interruptions in prosperity for which there was no governmental remedy and through which the nation muddled as best it could. (Only the radical Populists suggested any departure from this attitude.) As a result, when President Cleveland called Congress into

BUSINESS ACTIVITY, 1876-1901

The era's principal economic growth occurred during the 1880's, in contrast with the generally depressed levels of the 1870's and 1890's; however, there was some fluctuation throughout. Declining wholesale prices from 1882 to 1898 coincide with the rising farm discontent.

special session, the only antidepression recommendation he proposed was repeal of the Sherman Silver Purchase Act of 1890. A temporarily compliant Congress quickly acceded to the President's request. The repeal did nothing to counter the depression, but it did much to alienate the many Democrats to whom the Sherman Silver Act was an important reform measure.

Placing the Blame. Several explanations for the panic were offered at the time. As Cleveland's request for repeal of the silver act made clear, each political party blamed the other. Labor ascribed the slump to capitalist greed. Some private citizens, like Henry Adams, attributed it to Wall Street's "dark, mysterious, crafty, wicked, rapacious and tyrannical power . . . to rob and oppress and enslave the people."

In fact, though, the explanation was at once more obvious and less immediate. The contraction had long been in the making; the bankruptcy of a few prominent companies simply acted as the trigger. One of the important causes was the inevitable decline of the railroad construction boom that had been going on since the early 1880's. The subsequent reduction in the number of orders for rails, steel, and other machinery brought about a contraction which soon spread to other industries. The chronically depressed state of agriculture offered no counterweight and may actually have aggravated the fall in demand. Moreover, European investors, hard hit by their own financial panic that started in 1890, had begun to withdraw capital from the United States. In the single year of 1892, for example, $50 million in gold left the country.

Marches of Protest: The "Industrial Armies." The depression sparked a kind of labor unrest and class antagonism that had been seen only occasionally before, as at Homestead in 1892 and in the violent railroad disputes of 1877. To contemporaries, perhaps the most convincing measure of the breadth of the discontent in the working class was the several "armies" of unemployed that marched on Washington in 1894, seeking jobs and relief. The idea apparently originated with a self-made Ohio businessman, a former Greenbacker and Populist named Jacob S. Coxey. A radical, Coxey believed that the government bore a responsibility for unemployment and should provide funds to put men to work building roads. When told that his idea could not get a hearing in Washington, he boldly responded, "We will send a petition to Washington with boots on." Coxey's little army of 100 men left his home town of Massillon, Ohio, at the end of March 1894 bound for the nation's capital. Along the way, several hundred more volunteers joined him, although the trip was certainly no lark; on crossing the Allegheny Mountains, the straggling army was engulfed in a severe snowstorm. When the 500 marchers arrived in Washington they were met by police, who were so unnerved by the spectacle that they attacked the marchers with clubs, injuring about 50 people, including some bystanders. Coxey and two other leaders were arrested for illegally carrying banners on the Capitol grounds and for walking on the grass.

The shameful attack upon Coxey's army and the inglorious ending to its march were only the beginning of the industrial army movement. Having struck a hopeful note in the midst of working-class despair, the idea spread. All told, perhaps 17 industrial armies set out in 1894 from various localities around the country to present petitions "with boots on." Two or three were considerably larger than Coxey's; one on the West Coast mobilized as many as 5000 men. The larger armies were able to commandeer trains and throw scares into the small towns through which they passed. But what the conservatives found most surprising about the armies was not the number of marchers nor even their actual behavior, reprehensible as it was thought to be. The real revelation was the evident sympathy they received along the way. "I am beginning to feel that the movement has some meaning," wrote journalist Ray Stannard Baker after following Coxey's army for a few days, "that it is a manifestation of the prevailing unrest and dissatisfaction among the labor class. When such an ugly and grotesque fungus can grow out so prominently on the body politic there must be something wrong."

The Pullman Strike. If the largely peaceful marches of the unemployed did not convince some people that "something was wrong," the violence that accompanied the industrial strikes in 1894 certainly did. Like 1886, the year 1894 witnessed a new high in the number of strikes, some of which attracted national attention. All told, some 1400 industrial strikes were called in that single year, involving over 500,000 workers—the largest number of the entire nineteenth century. Since the workers' right to strike was only reluctantly conceded in those days, violence often erupted in the course of a work stoppage. A strike of 125,000 mineworkers in Illinois, for example, lasting for what was then a relatively short length of time, only eight weeks, still required the militia to preserve order.

The strike on the railroads in 1894 aroused the nation and dramatized, as no other labor dispute of the century, the new shape and concerns of an industrial society. The strike was born of the depression. The Pullman Palace Car Company, against which the strike was first called, maintained the town of Pullman, located just outside Chicago. George Pullman, the company's founder, had built the town as a model of what workingmen's housing could be. The solid brick homes of the workers were commodious; the town itself was well planned, generously supplied with public services, and blessed with one of the lowest death rates in the nation. It represented an investment of eight million dollars by George Pullman. When the depression hit, Pullman cut the wages of employees several times in order, he claimed, to avoid the alternative of wholesale dismissals. He did not, however, reduce the rents in the town, though rents in Pullman had always been higher than in surrounding towns. Confronted by the continuing high rents, the workers formed a union to protest the wage cuts. The company refused to consider the rents as a proper matter for discussion and justified the wage cuts on the grounds of bad times. When the strike came, Pullman promptly closed his plant and waited for the workers to capitulate.

But the workers held on, despite increasing destitution and much suffering. Their plight attracted the attention of other workers' organizations in the Chicago area, including the newly formed American Railway Union (A.R.U.). Just that previous spring the A.R.U. had won a spectacular victory against J. J. Hill's formidable Great Northern Railroad in a strike lasting only 18 days. Proud of their quick and substantial victory, the leaders of the A.R.U., especially its young organizer and president, Eugene V. Debs, hoped to stay free of the Pullman strike, which could only strain their depleted treasury. But the rank and file, sympathizing with the hardpressed Pullman workers' families, voted not to handle any Pullman sleepers. The other railway companies, rather than participate in the boycott of a fellow company, promptly discharged all A.R.U. employees who took part in the boycott. The A.R.U. then, with equal alacrity, called work stoppages against all offending companies. By the end of June 1894, some 20,000 railroad men were on strike in and around Chicago. Eventually, the economic effects of the strike would be felt in 27 states.

A strike of such magnitude in the most important rail center of the nation could not fail to arouse the concern of the federal government. In fact, men high in the Cleveland administration such as Attorney General Richard Olney, were very much interested, and federal officers in Chicago were instructed to be alert for any activities which might require federal intervention. The A.R.U., for its part, well understood from experience in the Great Northern strike of a few months before, that an interruption in the movement of the mails might easily bring in the federal government. For several days, the discipline of the strikers averted any incidents; the mails moved unhampered. At the same time, the railroad companies appealed to the federal court, from which they secured an injunction against the strikers on the grounds that the strike constituted just the kind of restraint of trade that the Sherman Antitrust Act forbade. That same day, July 3, by coincidence, rioting broke out along one of the railway lines running to Chicago; cars were overturned and pushed athwart the tracks. One of the derailed trains was carrying United States mail. The federal government now had the incident it needed.

Federal Intervention. On July 4, two thousand federal soldiers arrived in Chicago to break the strike. Their arrival set off an orgy of violence, looting, burning of railway cars, and shooting. More than 20 people were killed and 2000 railway cars destroyed before order was restored. Even after quiet returned, Chicago remained an armed camp, with 14,000 state and federal troops stationed in and around the city. Debs and other A.R.U. leaders were arrested, convicted of contempt of court for violating the injunction, and sentenced to between six months and a year in jail.

The consequences of the strike were significant. The case of the convicted A.R.U. leaders, when carried to the Supreme Court of the United States in the case of *U.S.* v. *Debs* (1894), became a landmark in labor history. The high court agreed that an injunction such as was issued against the strikers was a legitimate device for the protection of interstate commerce and the mails. For the next 30 years, the court injunction remained a powerful weapon in the hands of employers threatened with a strike. "Government by injunction," friends of labor bitterly called the practice. Not until 1932 was organized labor able to induce Congress to pass the Norris-La Guardia Act, which limited the federal courts' authority to use the injunction in labor disputes.

The crushing of the strike by the federal government also meant the end of the promising American Railway Union and its experiment in industrial unionism. Moreover, the apparent cooperation between industry and government which Debs saw in the breaking of the strike was probably the most influential factor in his conversion to Socialism. For the next quarter of a century, he was the best-known Socialist leader in the United States; in 1912, as Socialist candidate for President, he received more votes than any Socialist in the history of the Republic.

Although most men who resented the antilabor action of the Cleveland administration did not become Socialists, virtually all of them now declared war on the administration. John Peter Altgeld, the governor of Illinois whom Cleveland had ignored when federal troops were sent into Chicago, was infuriated by the administration's actions. As a friend of labor, Altgeld opposed government intervention which helped the employers; as a governor, he opposed the sending of federal troops, which he had not requested, as a violation of his constitutional prerogative. Despite the fact that he was a businessman of some wealth, Altgeld now became one of the party's most vociferous and uncompromising critics of the Cleveland administration.

Revolution in Politics: Act I

In the political history of the United States, the nineties are significant because during this decade the political parties caught up with the Economic Revolution. The resulting realignment of parties and voters not only made the Republicans the majority party of the nation for the first time, but set the stage for the social and economic reforms of the twentieth century. This transformation in politics occurred in three steps. The first was the repudiation of the conservative leadership of Grover Cleveland.

The depression, climaxing a decade of mounting agrarian discontent, put the new Cleveland administration to tests that its conservative outlook could not meet. Men like Secretary of the Treasury John G. Carlisle, and Richard Olney, the Attorney General and later Secretary of State, were competent and experienced, but, like Cleveland himself, they proved unequal to the demands of the new age of cities, factories, and political dissatisfaction. It was Carlisle, for example, who encouraged the President to uphold the gold standard—that is, to redeem in gold all paper money upon demand. The principle came in for severe testing as the financial panic, first in Europe and then in the United States, caused nervous holders of United States notes to exchange them for gold, a practice that steadily depleted the Treasury's reserves. By January 1894, the gold reserve had fallen to $62 million, though $100 million had long been regarded as the lowest safe figure.

Saving the Gold Standard—At a Price. Cleveland's determination to keep the country on gold was not shared by Congress, which preferred a bimetallic standard of gold and silver. As a result, Congress would not grant the administration the necessary powers to replenish the gold reserves through long-term borrowing or by any other device suggested by the President. In February 1895, after trying several ineffective means of stopping the drain, the administration turned in desperation to the banking houses of J. P. Morgan and August Belmont, which, for a sizable profit to themselves, secured gold from abroad. Although this unprecedented measure did not immediately halt the drain, the cumulative and persistent efforts of the administration did. As public confidence in the government's paper money returned, fewer and fewer bills were presented for redemption. By January 1896, it was evident that the gold standard had been saved.

But was it worth the strenuous effort? By the middle of the twentieth century, most "nations of the first class"—to use Cleveland's term for those governments that adhered to the gold standard—had long since gone off gold without serious consequences. Although Cleveland never doubted that he had done the right thing, he could not help but recognize that it cost him the support of the majority of his party. To many Democrats and free-silver men, Cleveland's policy was nothing less than subservience to the interests of bankers, financiers, and creditors at the expense of the other classes of society. As the free-silver men pointed out, silver coin could have been used at any time to redeem United States notes, but the Treasury, intent upon adhering to the gold standard, met all demands for payment only with gold. Nor is it certain that payments in silver would have been fraught with the disastrous consequences the gold men freely predicted. After all, when the dollar was greatly devalued in the 1930's, there was almost no effect on prices or business; a similar devaluation in the 1890's — also a time of severe deflation — would probably have been no more disastrous. The real problem in the 1890's was the maintenance of both gold and silver in circulation when the former was overvalued and hence tended to be hoarded.

The policy that the administration followed was the worst possible in a depression. To preserve the gold standard, the Treasury, in effect, contracted the money supply just when the economy needed an expanding one to lift itself out of the depression. The Treasury's policy permitted domestic hoarding and exportation of gold, thus removing it from circulation. At the same time, paper money went into the Treasury, where, in order to avoid repeated redemptions, it was held as long as possible, thereby further contracting the currency supply. Finally, since gold was being hoarded and exported, bank reserves fell, thus further reducing the money available for loans and circulation. In short, in saving the gold standard, the expansion of the economy was seriously curtailed and recovery from the depression undoubtedly hampered — just as the free-silver men had predicted.

The Wilson-Gorman Tariff: A Failure in Presidential Leadership. In the gold crisis, it was triumph that hurt Cleveland; in his efforts to reduce the tariff, it was his failure that would be held against him. That he should suffer in both instances reveals once again how out of touch Cleveland and his administration were with the political developments growing out of the Economic Revolution.

During his first term, it will be recalled, Cleveland boldly proclaimed himself an advocate of tariff reduction. The subsequent disaster at the polls in 1890, which the high McKinley Tariff brought upon the Republicans, gave additional reasons for expecting that the Cleveland administration would do its best to reduce the tariff. A bill to do just that, including the addition of some raw materials to the free list, was promptly introduced on behalf of the administration by Congressman William Wilson. The Democratic House quickly and overwhelmingly passed it, though not before a modest tax on incomes had been added at the insistence of the radicals in the party. The trouble came in the Senate, where the Democratic majority was small and disunited on the issue of downward revision. Several of those who refused to support the President came from the New South (i.e., the new industrial South) which was interested in securing some protection for its infant industries. As a result, the Senate added approximately 600 amendments to the House bill, turning it into the usual tariff in which all well-organized special interests got some protection. As finally passed, the Wilson-Gorman Tariff reduced the schedules only slightly, to 41 per cent from the 49 per cent of the McKinley Act. The bill repudiated both the party's campaign pledge for reduction and the President's leadership. Cleveland, recognizing the lack of any practical alternative, let it become law without his signature.

It was evident that, in the new age of industry, not even the Democratic party could be depended upon to reduce the tariff. The chief responsibility for the high duties, after all, lay with Democratic Senator A. P. Gorman of Maryland, who had led the fight in the Senate to raise the duties and then successfully maneuvered behind the scenes to prevent the House from rejecting them.

Interestingly, the one section of the bill that emerged unscathed from the Senate's surgery was the provision for an income tax of two per cent on all incomes over $4000. Cleveland had been willing to accept the tax in order to secure the necessary votes in the House from the radicals and reformers, whose measure it was. In 1895, however, the income tax was struck down by the U.S. Supreme Court as a violation of the constitutional provision requiring that any direct tax be apportioned among the states according to population. The action of the Court was more a reflection of the anxieties of conservatives in the nineties than a result of pure constitutional principles; as recently as 1881, the very same court, in *Springer* v. *Illinois*, had upheld the constitutionality of an income tax. Moreover, during the Civil War, the Lincoln administration had used such a tax as one of its several wartime fiscal devices. Now the nation would have to wait nearly 20 years longer before a constitutional amendment would make it possible to tap the wealth being amassed by the Economic Revolution.

Revolution in Politics: Act II

Shift to the Republicans. The crowning rebuff to and the most dramatic failure of the conservative Democrats came in the Congressional elections of 1894. During the fight over the gold standard, Cleveland lost the support of a large segment of his party; in the tariff battle, he lost control of his party in Congress; and in the election of 1894, he found that he had lost the support of the nation. The transfer of seats that year from the Democratic to the Republican side of the House was the largest in history; the Republicans now gloried in an unprecedented majority of 132. Prominent Democrats like William Wilson of West Virginia, William Springer of Illinois, and Richard Bland of Missouri lost their seats. In 24 states, not a single Democrat was elected, and in each of six others, only one Democrat was returned. Without the ever-faithful and solid South, Democratic strength would have been almost wiped out. As it was, border states such as Delaware, Maryland, West Virginia, and Missouri either went Republican entirely or elected more Republicans than Democrats to the House. Old Democratic strongholds outside the South, like Indiana, Connecticut, and New Jersey, sent to Congress more Republicans than Democrats.

Impressed with the excitement of the presidential election of 1896, historians have underestimated the importance of the Congressional elections two years before. The defeat of the Democrats in 1896 comes as no surprise once the tremendous popular switch to the Republicans in 1894 is recognized. Indeed, as we shall see later, the twin Republican victories in 1894 and 1896 mark one of the great divides in American political history.

The immediate cause for Republican victory in 1894 was the depression. As usual, Americans blamed hard times on the party in power and acted accordingly. Yet it was not simply a victory by default, for the Populists, the third party in the field, did not benefit much from the Democratic losses. Although the total Populist vote increased by almost 400,000 over the 1892 returns, the party managed to send just four senators and four representatives to Congress. Only in Nebraska and North Carolina did the Populists win as much as 48 per cent of the vote, and even that degree of success was achieved solely through fusion with the Republicans. Four western states, Kansas, Colorado, North Dakota, and Idaho, all of which had been Populist in 1892, went Republican in 1894. As John Hicks, the historian of Populism, has pointed out, not a single state in 1894 could any longer be called Populist. Thus the voters, rather than accepting any available alternative, seem to have turned deliberately to the Grand Old Party. The reasons for this new support for the Republican party will be discussed later in conjunction with the election of 1896.

Cleveland and his administration by 1895 were almost bereft of support in the country. Ardent "gold bugs" and spokesmen for the old Mugwumps, such as *Harper's Weekly* and E. L. Godkin's *New York Evening Post,* still vigorously supported the President, to be sure, cherishing him as a champion of clean government and sound money. But the country at large rejected him. His mail, a biographer has noted, shrank to "less than that of an ordinary business man." In February 1895, Cleveland himself expressed his isolation to a close political friend, "Think of it! Not a man in the Senate with whom I can be on terms of absolute confidence. . . . Not one of them comes to me on public business unless sent for and then full of recrimination and doubts." Yet he continued to speak out in favor of the gold standard, the very issue provoking the mounting opposition to his party.

Free Silver· Key Issue. For Americans living in the second half of the twentieth century, it is hard to fathom the central place the issue of free coinage of silver came to occupy in the politics of the 1890's. Today, the gold standard for which Cleveland and afterwards the Republicans battled, no longer exists; it was abandoned in the course of the Great Depression of the 1930's and without any of the dire consequences predicted by the advocates of gold in the 1890's. On the other hand, it is evident that victory for free silver certainly would ·not have ushered in the millennium foreseen by the silver men. In short, both sides exaggerated the importance of the currency issue—but that is not to say it was contrived or unimportant.

On one level, the silver problem was symbolic. Western and southern reformers saw reflected in it their hopes for an improved society, based upon government concern for the welfare of the ordinary citizen. This was true even though free silver could not have achieved all that the Populists and silver Democrats wanted. But insofar as free silver did involve government interference in the economy through the manipulation of the currency, it symbolized the drive for broader reforms. Conversely, free silver represented everything abhorrent to the conservatives of the day; it threatened established ways of operating the economy; it promised to isolate the United States from the financial affairs of the principal nations of Europe; and it sought to redefine the proper role of government in the economy. Yet, important as the silver issue was as a symbol, it was also an answer to a real problem which was not clearly recognized by either side.

The issue that lay behind the demand for free silver had engaged political attention since the seventeenth century. In a new country like the United States, overflowing with natural resources and opportunities for economic gain, business expansion had required a currency supply that would grow along with it. During the colonial period and down to the Civil War, paper in the form of notes issued by banks, under more or less public regulation, had answered the need for a large and growing supply of money. The one difficulty with paper money, as the hard-money Jacksonians among others had pointed out, was that it fluctuated in value, depending on the degree to which it was "backed"—i.e., convertible into gold or silver. In order to remedy this defect of unstable value, the National Banking Act was passed during the Civil War. Under that act and others, the primary circulating medium became paper money backed by bonds of the federal government. Since the bonds were payable in gold, the act, in effect, made the currency a gold-backed one.

While this strong backing of the banknotes virtually guaranteed that there would be no depreciation, it effectively placed a limit on the quantity of currency since the volume of notes issued was now tied to the dollar value of outstanding government bonds. Hence the amount of money in circulation, instead of being responsive to the needs of the economy as it should have been, was determined by the federal government's need to borrow funds, which was quite irrelevant to the monetary needs of the economy. During part of the Civil War and immediately thereafter, this restrictive aspect of the National Banking Act was mitigated by the issuance of additional currency without any backing, the well-known greenbacks. Within four years after the Resumption of Specie Act of 1875, however, the greenbacks became both convertible into gold and fixed in amount.

By the decade of the nineties, then, the currency was inflexible in amount and unresponsive to the needs of the economy. Indeed, because the supply of currency could increase only as the amount of government bonds did, the money supply varied in reverse of the ideal. It was during good times, when business was expanding and the demand for money was the greatest, that the government would most likely retire some of its debt – that is, pay off some of its bonds. Such a retirement of the debt, however, would compel the National Banks to reduce their issues of paper money, since they had to be backed by bonds. For this reason, among others, the Populists and cheap-money men in general objected to the National Banks. Fortunately for the well-being of the economy, the constrictive effects of this inverse elasticity of the currency were offset by an increasing use of checks and bank deposits as money.

In Search of a Flexible but Stable Monetary Supply. The cheap-money men complained not only about the rigidity of the money supply, but also blamed it for the decline in prices during the 1880's and 1890's. A decline in prices, by definition, means an *appreciation* in the value of money, for as prices of goods fall, each dollar purchases more; hence, it is worth more. Free silverites blamed the fall in prices and subsequent appreciation of the dollar on the scarcity of money, arguing that money, like any other commodity, rose in value when there were not enough of it to satisfy the demand. Greenbackers, free silverites, and inflationists in general all agreed that the low prices on farm products were the result of an insufficient supply of money. (Actually, this reasoning is valid neither in theory nor in fact. An increase in the supply of agricultural commodities, for example, would cause a fall in prices regardless of whether the money supply was adequate.)

What really disturbed the inflationists was that a dollar that increased in value in this fashion was inherently as unfair as one that depreciated, though the gold men confined their expressions of horror to the latter situation. Where you stood in the credit relationship determined which you preferred, appreciation or depreciation. A farmer who borrowed – and most did – was severely hurt by an appreciating dollar. If wheat, for example, was selling at one dollar a bushel when he borrowed money and then fell to 75 cents at the time he was to repay the loan, the farmer would have to sell an additional third of a bushel for each dollar to be repaid. For this reason William Jennings Bryan referred to the gold standard as establishing a "dishonest dollar."

Despite the acuteness of the problems that the monetary policy of the United States presented to farmers and other debtors, the free coinage of silver was both an inept and inadequate remedy. For one thing, using silver as backing for paper money was little more than a tactical move by those who wanted inflation but were not prepared to go to the extreme of advocating fiat money or greenbacks. Logically, the same arguments of a limited supply that were brought against gold could be laid against silver; it was no more responsive in amount to the needs of business conditions than gold. In addition, a silver dollar (highly overvalued as it would have been at the silverites' preferred ratio of 16 to one with gold) would have driven gold into hoarding, thus reducing the money supply anyway. Finally, the underlying weakness of the free-silver position was that no one, professional economist or Populist dirt farmer, understood what is well known today – namely, that government by its own action can issue money, unrelated to its stock of gold or silver.

Yet there were aspects of the silverites' case that were eminently sound and worthy of consideration. One was their demand for a monetary supply that fluctuated in accordance with the needs of business and yet was stable. In fact, events after 1896 generally bore out the silverites' contention by bringing about just the kind of monetary system they favored. New discoveries of gold in the late 1890's increased the money supply and helped to raise prices. Even more important was the establishment of the Federal Reserve System in 1913, which introduced the kind of flexible and responsive monetary and banking system that the farmers and Populists had been demanding for so long. Nor is it an accident that after 1913 the long debate on currency and banking that ran all through previous American history finally came to an end. With the Federal Reserve System, both sides in the historical debate received recognition in law and in the nation's banking institutions: a fairly stable value for the dollar was combined with a banking system that ensured a money supply responsive to changes in business activity.

Because the nature of the money supply affected everyone, the issue of free silver swallowed up all others as the election of 1896 approached. A voter's position on a host of measures, in effect, was represented by his stand on silver. Increasingly, in the eyes of Populists and many anti-Cleveland Democrats, belief in the wonder-working properties of free silver became the test of a true reformer. But, for the success of reform, this equation turned out to be disastrous; as the election was to demonstrate, not all those who were dissatisfied with the status quo held this belief, nor, what was more important, did they think that such an equation was valid.

From both sides of the debate flowed tracts, articles, books, and speeches in an almost constant stream right down to the election. Perhaps the best known was W. H. Harvey's *Coin's Financial School* (1894), which brought the cause of silver into literally millions of homes, shops, and farmers' clubs across the country. The gold forces were able to draw upon more sophisticated sources of support, principally professional economists and bankers. But "Coin" Harvey's clever pamphlet was an effective counterargument. The exchanges between gold and silver men were usually heated, cutting, and laced with a degree of class consciousness rarely found in American political discourse. In the East, where the gold standard was orthodox, some college professors were dismissed for supporting free silver, while in the western, free-silver states, Populist legislatures took similar action against conservative professors who defended the gold standard. Even friendships and households were known to be disrupted by the money question.

Revolution in Politics: Act III

Free Silver and the Election of 1896. The way in which the silver issue enveloped all other reforms was best illustrated by the behavior of the Populist party in 1896. Populism, as the platform of 1892 made evident, stood for a reform program considerably broader than free silver, but many of the party members and leaders regarded the broad national interest in currency reform as a rare opportunity to unite all radicals and reformers in a common bid for power. Free silver was also an opportune issue that could enlist badly needed financial support from western silver-mining interests, which had a very direct stake in the restoration of silver as a part of the currency system. Hence, when the Democratic party in the summer of 1896 nominated a fervent western silverite, William Jennings Bryan, as its presidential candidate, many Populists eagerly embraced him as their own.

But not all did so. Some of the more radical or fundamentally reformist Populists, like Thomas Watson of Georgia and Henry D. Lloyd of Illinois, thought that to nominate Bryan would be to sell out the broader Populist program for a mess of silver. However, Populist leaders like Senator Marion Butler of North Carolina, who were as dedicated to reform as Lloyd or Watson, thought the party had no practical alternative. By the summer of 1896, the primary symbol of agrarian-sponsored reform was free silver; whether that was a good symbol or not did not matter. If the reform forces were to unite against the Republicans, it would have to be on free silver or nothing. And it was clear that free silver had captured the Democratic party. Certainly, a separate Populist candidate would have won no more votes than Bryan did, and there is good reason to believe that he could not have polled as many. The Populists, it is true, did make a gesture of independence by naming Thomas Watson as their vice presidential candidate while accepting the Democratic Bryan as the leader of their ticket. But with that gesture the Populist party in effect committed suicide, apparently prepared to sacrifice itself for a union of reform forces. The election was between the Republicans, who had already nominated Governor William McKinley of Ohio as their candidate, and the Democrats. Although McKinley had never been a strong gold man, under the tutelage of his campaign manager, industrialist Marcus Hanna, he espoused that cause, thus drawing the lines that shaped the campaign.

No election since 1860 had aroused the enthusiasm and passion of this one. Bryan, probably the finest orator of his day, traveled more than 18,000 miles in almost two dozen states to deliver over 600 speeches. Five million people, it was estimated, heard his powerful and apparently tireless voice, a number that would not be approached again until the advent of radio and television. McKinley, on the other hand, stayed at home in Canton, Ohio, receiving visitors and making speeches from his front porch under the careful arrangements and supervision of Hanna. The immobility of the Republican candidate was well compensated for by the whirlwind campaign of the party machine throughout the country. It kept up a constant barrage of speeches and literature on behalf of the Republican doctrines of a high tariff and a gold standard, which were alleged to be the principal sources of high wages and business prosperity. At the same time, it blamed the Democrats for the depression in 1893 and warned of an even worse disaster with free silver.

Moreover, the Republicans enjoyed an enormous campaign fund, drawn from the treasuries of businessmen fearful of a panic if Bryan was elected. Two large contributors, Standard Oil and J. P. Morgan, for example, gave $500,000 between them, more than the total campaign fund of Bryan. Before the campaign was over, Hanna was returning unneeded contributions.

By the end of October, despite Bryan's herculean speaking efforts and the enormous enthusiasm his oratory almost invariably evoked, especially in the rural districts, Mark Hanna was confident of victory. Returning a campaign contribution, he wrote, "It is all over. Reports are satisfactory just where we wanted them most." Some businessmen, however, were not so sanguine or confident. In many factories and shops, the word was passed that if Bryan were elected there would be no work the next day. It is hard to believe that these threats were either widespread or effective enough to have influenced the election results, but they do attest to the intense feelings aroused by the campaign. ("By defeating Mr. Bryan," wrote *Harper's Weekly* after the event, "the country has escaped an actual experiment in Socialism.")

The high popular interest in the campaign was also measured by the huge vote. Although Bryan lost by 600,000 votes, his total of 6.5 million was larger than that received by any candidate in any previous election. On the other hand, he ran farther behind the winner than any candidate of a major party since Grant's victory over Greeley in 1872. Bryan's energetic campaigning undoubtedly brought out voters who had never bothered to cast a ballot before, but the increase did not necessarily add to his total. The vote for Bryan was smaller than the combined vote for Cleveland and Weaver in 1892; yet in 1896, Bryan was the Populist as well as the Democratic candidate. Bryan's strength was concentrated in the South and the West, to be sure, but only in the old Populist portions. He lost California and Oregon and proved to be weak in the older agricultural states; he was defeated in Minnesota, Iowa, Wisconsin, and Illinois. In these middle-western states, agriculture was less dependent on a single crop than in the plains states; the farmers could balance an adverse world market price for their corn or wheat with dairying and hograising. In this more secure position, they were less radical than the plains farmers. As one historian has observed, "a high degree of farm ownership" in a state tended to make it Republican; farm tenancy, on the other hand, inclined a state toward Bryan. To see Bryan, then, as the spokesman of farmers everywhere is to exaggerate the social basis of his support; thousands of farmers in the older areas of the East and the West rejected Bryan in 1896 as they had rejected Populism four years before.

Triumph of the City. The really decisive reason for Bryan's defeat should have been apparent from the start: he could not capture the votes of the cities or of industrial labor. It was all very well for farmers and small businessmen to like a little inflation as a stimulus to business, but to workers, with a fixed income, free silver and inflation meant a rising cost of living. Moreover, insofar as urban white-collar and professional workers were holders of bank

(Continued on page 149)

The homes in which a people live reflect their lives and attitudes. Some of the highest architectural aspirations of an age are commonly expressed in the houses of the wealthy, a rapidly increasing group during this period when fortunes were often made virtually overnight and with comparative ease. Because there were relatively many nouveaux riches, each, as he attained his

A drawing room typical of the style found in the homes of the wealthy, ca. 1900. *Photo: Brown Brothers*

The Vanderbilt mansions, 5th Avenue at 51st Street, 1900. *Photo by William H. Jackson, Library of Congress*

A family outing,
1900. *Photo:
Brown Brothers*

A small-town,
gingerbread-Gothic
house. *Photo: Culver
Pictures*

Interior of a middle class home. *Photo: Culver Pictures*

wealth, was anxious to demonstrate precisely how financially successful he had become by building a mansion more grandiose and imposing than any other. In their attempts to outdo each other, these tycoons copied European palaces and chateaus, or had them imported in part or in toto, piling them full of exotic, gilded furniture, and adding lavish touches of their own to make them even more remarkable. Exteriors as well as interiors became ever more opulent and ostentatious, until they reached such heights of vulgarity that the reaction against such over-decorated, over-stuffed, and over-done styles has lasted until our own day.

Many in the growing middle class, insofar as their pocketbooks would allow, emulated the rich. Pleased with themselves at having achieved a better economic station in life, and proud of their taste in decoration, these burghers gave their imaginations perhaps even freer reign than the very wealthy, and enshrined their fulfilled ambitions in homes embellished with gothic towers, dormers, balconies, turrets, bay windows, and a multitude of other features from a variety of European styles. They then filled these mini-palaces to the bursting with what-nots, lamps, objets d'art, family portraits, and all the other frills and furbelows of a solidly bourgeois existence.

A family in Poverty
Gap, New York City,
ca. 1889. *Photograph
by Jacob Riis. Library
of Congress*

Inhabitants of Bax-
ter Street Alley in
Mulberry Bend, New
York City, ca.
1888–1889. *Photo-
graph by Jacob Riis.
Library of Congress*

A frontier home. *Photo: Cunningham Collection, Stillwater, Oklahoma*

In stark and tragic contrast to the cosiness and comfort of the lives of their economic betters, the many poor, whether immigrants or Negroes, Indians, or share-croppers, suffered through their existence in a variety of unpleasant settings. There was no place for decoration or ostentation when there was not even enough money to buy a bed—one that would, in all probability, have to be shared by the entire family. There was no time for building or improving or even cleaning when most, if not all, of the family had to work between ten and twelve hours a day in order to simply subsist. When time did permit, the playground for the children of the poor was most often the dingy alleys and garbage-strewn streets outside their dwellings—the Baxter's Street Alleys, Mulberry Bends, and Poverty Gaps of the nation's cities. In the two photographs on page 147, Jacob Riis has caught in the eyes of the slum dwellers something of the bafflement and resignation created by the insanity of a set of circumstances which separated their kind of poverty from the splendor of New York's 5th Avenue by only a few city blocks.

If the poor and dispossessed could escape the city or the reservation or the plantation, and stake a claim in the vastness of the West, they might, like other, more prosperous Americans who did the same, find better lives for themselves. Those building frontier homes could hardly aspire to European architectural styles, formal gardens, or wrought iron fences. But despite the primitive sod houses, despite the sickness and the death, despite the crop failures and the daily adversities, these people, unlike those in the slums of settled areas, had bought their own land and built their own houses; consequently, they had a stake in the future which made almost any hardship endurable. *End* accounts and insurance policies, they were creditors, to whom cheap money was anathema. Mark Hanna sensed the limited appeal of free silver early in the campaign. Referring to Bryan, he wrote, "He's talking silver all the time, and that's where we've got him."

And they did! The cities, where the industrial workers were concentrated, voted overwhelmingly Republican. Only 12 of the 82 cities with a population of 45,000 or more supported Bryan, and at that, seven of the 12 were in the Democratic stronghold of the South, and two more were located in the silver-producing states. For the first time, the Republicans made substantial gains in the cities of the Middle West. In the industrial East, Bryan's cause was hopeless; he did not carry a single county in all of New England and only one in New York. He even lost usually Democratic New York City. Strong evidence indicates that McKinley successfully appealed to urban immigrants, who responded to the Republican's "full dinner pail" campaign. Nor did urban voters forget that the depression had come under a Democratic regime.

Bryan, regardless of his talk about the unity of farmers and workers, was unable to make himself the spokesman of the industrial discontent that permeated the nation's working class. McKinley came closer. Both Hanna and McKinley, for example, had good labor records. Hanna had been conspicuous in urging George Pullman to arbitrate his labor dispute in 1894; McKinley as governor had supported several labor measures and had contributed to relief funds for the unemployed during the depression of 1893. In short, the Republicans, by appealing to immigrants and urban workers in general, were dealing realistically with the new America. The Democrats and Populists were not; by making their principal pleas to the rural population, they misjudged the direction in which the country was moving. By the nineties, political decisions were being made in the cities. In 1896, the decision went to the party that had frankly identified itself with the achievements of the Economic Revolution.

Actually, the shift had been under way for some time. As we have seen, in the 1880's neither party had been the favorite of the voters; hence, presidential elections had been close and without any continuity for either party. Before the depression of 1893, it appeared that the long-term popularity of the Democrats would swing the nation in the nineties behind the party of Jackson and Jefferson, leaving the Republicans permanently in the minority. The depression, however, changed that, for in 1894 a massive swing to the Republicans began, which was confirmed in 1896 with the defeat of Bryan.

Republican Mandate. The fact that makes the 1894 and 1896 victories significant is that from then on Republican victory became a habit. For the next 16 years, without interruption, the party captured the House of Representatives and the presidency. Indeed, if one looks upon the election of Woodrow Wilson and a Democratic Congress in 1912 and 1916 as exceptions, as one very well might, Republican ascendancy continued until 1932, when another revolution occurred in American politics. For this reason, the elections of 1894 and 1896 constitute a watershed. Not only had the indecisive era of American party politics ended, but a new era of Republican ascendancy had begun. The shift also was a clear sign of the political consequences of the growth of the city and the factory, for the Republican ascendancy then and later was dependent on the changes wrought by the Economic Revolution. Cities like San Francisco, Columbus, Detroit, St. Paul, and others, all regularly Democratic in the 1880's, voted Republican in 1896, and remained Republican until well into the twentieth century. On the other hand, none of the large cities that had been Republican in the 1880's and early 1890's changed party affiliation in 1896 or for many years thereafter. It is not surprising, either, that some of the earliest Progressives of the twentieth century, like Theodore Roosevelt and Robert M. La Follette, were Republicans. They epitomized the party's recognition that politics and government must come to terms with the new voters and issues raised by the Economic Revolution.

Although the Populist party never recovered from its fusion with the Democrats in 1896, it could take comfort in knowing that a large part of its program of 1892 was enacted in the next decade. In fact, the Populists helped to set the goals and the program of the Progressive movement of the early twentieth century. By 1920, the direct election of senators, the income tax, adequate railroad regulation—but not government ownership—the initiative and referendum, postal savings banks, and even a form of the subtreasury plan had all been written into law.

After the defeat of Bryan, agrarian agitation for cheap money was rarely heard again, but the reasons for the silence stemmed from economic change, not political defeat. Agricultural and other prices began to rise in 1897 and 1898, thus forestalling a revival of the farmers' demand for inflation. Several reasons probably account for the improvement in agricultural prices. The increasing urban population in the United States and Europe raised the demand for agricultural commodities. At the same time, poor wheat crops in India and Europe in 1896 and 1897 reduced the world supply. A third factor was the increase in the gold supply of the world. Discoveries of gold in the Klondike region of Alaska, in Australia, and in South Africa, as well as the introduction of the new cyanide process of extraction that permitted lower grade ores to be used, raised prices by reducing the cost of gold through an increase in its supply. In 1899, the world's annual production of gold was almost two and one half times what it had been in 1891.

Events, in short, proved both sides in the bitter and hard-fought campaign to have been poor prophets. Contrary to the forebodings of the Democratic and Populist orators, the triumph of the gold bugs did not result in ruin for the common man. Instead, farmers after 1898 actually entered upon a period of prosperity such as they had not enjoyed in two generations. But then the gold men also had their false conceptions, for events demonstrated that their favorite monetary metal could inflate the currency as readily as silver.

Removal of the Negro from Southern Politics

A final and significant measure of the degree to which the 1890's marked a new era in the life of the nation was the disenfranchisement of the Negro in the South. When President Hayes withdrew the last troops from the southern states in 1877, the conservative Democratic regimes that came to power did not insist upon the disenfranchisement of the Negroes. They were determined only to prevent the Negroes from challenging the white Democrats' control of the states. As a result, all during the 1880's and well into the 1890's, large numbers of Negroes continued to vote in most southern states. Negroes held minor political offices and sat in the state legislatures, usually representing lopsidedly black districts. A few southern states like North Carolina, Mississippi, and South Carolina even sent Negro Congressmen to Washington during these years. The last Negro Congressman from the South during this era finished his term in 1901.

This limited participation of the Negro in southern politics came to an abrupt end in the 1890's. There were at least two main reasons for the change. The rivalry between Populists and Democrats in the 1890's suddenly revived the southern whites' old fear of Negro domination. When white men fought and appealed for black votes, as occurred in the 1890's, the Negro held the balance of power. Removal of the Negro from politics, it was contended, would erase the fear of black rule and simultaneously permit white men to enjoy the benefits of a two-party system. The second reason for disenfranchisement was the wish to have white supremacy legally supported without having to resort to fraud and violence to secure it.

Circumventing the Constitution. Beginning with the constitutional convention of Mississippi in 1890, the southern states, during the next decade and a half, added to their laws devices to circumvent the Fifteenth Amendment (which forbade restricting suffrage on the basis of race). The most effective disenfranchising devices were the literacy test, supplemented by the understanding clause, and the poll tax. Because many whites were illiterate, a number of states, as an alternative to the literacy test, permitted a prospective voter to interpret a passage of the Constitution that was read to him; the assumption was that registrars would automatically pass white men and fail Negroes. Another loophole for illiterate whites was the so-called grandfather clause, which was not declared unconstitutional until 1915; it permitted any adult male to register if his father or grandfather had been a voter before 1868 — that is, prior to Negro enfranchisement.

Despite the loopholes, white men as well as Negroes were kept from the polls by the new restrictions. Many white men either could not pass the tests or were embarrassed to submit to examination. With the removal of most of the Negroes and many whites, the nineties saw the first legal reversal in a century of steady expansion of the suffrage. Moreover, the removal of the Negro from politics virtually ended the Republican party in the Deep South for the next half century. With all voters concentrated in a single party, popular participation in elections and political activity in general declined precipitously in the South. Voter apathy—always a threat to a democratic polity—settled like a pall over southern politics.

Significantly, the disenfranchisement of the Negro was accepted without serious objection in the North. As recently as the 1880's, such blatant moves to undo the results of the Civil War and Reconstruction would have been greeted with outraged protests from northern Republicans and the northern press. But in the 1890's, the protests were few and halfhearted. The great interest in Negro equality that the antislavery crusade, the war, and then Reconstruction had generated temporarily subsided; this was a new era in which economic growth and foreign expansion commanded the attention of leaders and led alike.

Equal but Separate. Even before the Supreme Court upheld the disenfranchising devices of the southern states in *Williams* v. *Mississippi* (1898), it provided a kind of sanction for them in a decision in 1896 which ruled that Negroes and whites could be compelled to accept separate facilities on trains, provided the accommodations were of equal quality. This case, *Plessy* v. *Ferguson,* concerned railroad cars, but the principle of "equal but separate" enunciated in the decision was soon applied in a host of new situations. Long before the Supreme Court decision, the principle had been practiced in schools, hotels, and trains, but it was now also applied by law to streetcars, waiting rooms, public toilets, tax offices, restaurants, and, in at least one state, telephone booths. Before the late 1890's, for example, no southern state required segregation of the races on streetcars. Soon after, however, all did.

Ironically, the sole Supreme Court dissenter in the Plessy case was the single southern justice, a former slaveholder, John Marshall Harlan of Kentucky. "The white race deems itself to be the dominant race in this country," Harlan pointed out. "And so it is, in prestige, in achievement, in education, in wealth and in power. . . . But in view of the Constitution, in the eye of the law, there is in this country no superior, ruling class of citizens. There is no caste here. Our Constitution is color blind, and neither knows nor tolerates classes among citizens."

The Great Departure

In 1936, when Samuel Flagg Bemis published his influential textbook on American diplomatic history, he referred to the acquisition of the Philippines as "the Great Aberration." The implication was that the movement of the United States into the imperialistic race for markets, sources for new investment, and colonies, which then engaged the principal European powers in Asia and Africa, was a sharp and inexplicable departure from previous American practice. In one sense it certainly was. Prior to the 1890's, with the single exception of the joint protectorate over Samoa, established only in 1889, the expansionist energies of the American people had been confined to the North American continent. The efforts of the Grant administration to acquire Santo Domingo had been completely frustrated by a continentally minded Congress, just as pre-Civil War interest in acquiring Cuba had come to nothing. Yet by the close of the nineties, the territory of the United States extended into the Caribbean and, by a series of island stepping-stones, completely across the Pacific to Asia. As President McKinley observed, "And so it has come to pass that in a few short months we have become a world power. . . ."

That the nineties witnessed a turning point in American relations with the rest of the world, there is no doubt. The question is why and how this alteration came about. The word "aberration," which Professor Bemis used, suggests an erratic outburst, without substantial roots in the past or in the broader social developments of the decade. And since the publication of Julius Pratt's *Expansionists of 1898* (1936), this view has been widely followed. As a result of Pratt's work, most historians have rejected the idea that the Spanish-American War and the colonial expansion that followed were to be explained in classic European terms—that is, as the result of businessmen's drive for markets for profitable investment. Pratt, after an examination of the business press of the nineties, showed quite conclusively that the great majority of businessmen did not want war in 1898, if only because it would disrupt trade. As an alternate explanation, Pratt pointed to the prowar feelings of the people and especially to the activities of a small group of articulate and highly active expansionists.

Voices of Expansion. Among these proponents of expansion were important political figures like Theodore Roosevelt, Henry Cabot Lodge, and John Hay; influential editors like Walter Hines Page of the *Atlantic Monthly* and Albert Shaw of the *Review of Reviews;* and prominent experts like Admiral Alfred T. Mahan, whose book, *The Influence of Sea Power Upon History* (1890), along with other writings, became almost sacred writ for the imperialists. These and other like-minded men wanted the United States to assume a larger place in world affairs, to translate America's obvious economic power into military, or more precisely, naval power. Mahan tirelessly called for a navy that would be commensurate in size and power with the continental dimensions of the United States. No nation could become great, he argued, until it became a naval power. Since a large navy required coaling stations and bases across the oceans of the world, he advocated the acquisition of territory outside the United States. "Whether they will or no," he prophesied in 1893, "Americans must now begin to look outward." Theodore Roosevelt, who was Assistant Secretary of the Navy in McKinley's first administration and destined to be a hero of the Spanish-American War, was an expansionist, an ardent booster of naval power, and an avid reader of Mahan. His close friend, John Hay, who wanted the United States to wield influence and power in Asia, had the chance to further his cause through the enunciation of the Open Door Policy in China in 1899, while he was McKinley's Secretary of State.

Yet even an influential group of men like the expansionists of 1898 cannot account for the popular will that drove the McKinley administration into war with Spain and opened the way to a new colonial empire. The expansionists were more the result of the nineties' new interest in the outside world than they were its cause. Broader forces had to prepare the ground before the spread-eagle nationalism sown by the expansionists could take root and flourish. These broader forces are to be found in the social character of the decade itself.

Nationalist Fervor and International Recognition. Americans may have been confused and even bewildered by the new industrial society they had built by the 1890's, but they did not fail to recognize the new economic power of the United States. As a result, the 1890's witnessed a high tide of nationalist fervor; Americans of all social classes swelled with a new pride of country. Even Edward Bellamy's brand of socialism took the name "Nationalism," and radical free-silverite William ("Coin") Harvey founded the "Patriots of America" society in 1895. Indeed, many more patriotic societies were founded in this single decade than in any previous one. It was then that the flag and the ritual of the flag salute were introduced into the schoolrooms of the nation. When in 1893 the United States agreed for the first time to receive and send emissaries with the "monarchical" title of Ambassador instead of the old "republican" title of Minister, President Cleveland justified the change to Congress as "fittingly" appropriate to "the position the United States holds in the family of nations." On all sides, press and pulpits rang with testimonies to American greatness. As one speaker before a group of Civil War veterans said in 1896, "The place of this nation is at the head of the column of civilization. Not that we would put other nations down. . . . Our idea has always been and is now to point to other nations the way to come up higher."

The social unrest of the decade also contributed to the drive to seek recognition among "the family of nations." Organized labor and farmers, in their dissatisfaction with the returns they had received from their efforts, were resorting to strikes and violence and were joining new political organizations like the Populist and Socialist parties. But some of their dissatisfactions were also discharged by projecting them upon outsiders such as the Spanish government, which was then trying to subdue a rebellion of its colony in Cuba. Urban labor, Populists, and Bryan Democrats, it is worth noting, were conspicuous among the supporters of the Cuban rebels and were outspoken advocates of American intervention prior to 1898.

Conservatives, too, looked to outside enemies as an answer to social turmoil in a decade beset by hard times. A country newspaper in Kansas wrote in October 1895, "While it might be putting it too strong to say that war is needed in this country now, yet who is there who does not believe, and in fact know, that such a thing would clear the atmosphere and stamp out the growth of socialism and anarchy, discontent and sectional prejudice that is gaining a foothold in this nation." In 1896, a member of Cleveland's Cabinet wrote in his diary, "The jingoism in the air is a curious thing, and unaccountable except on account of the unrest of our people, and the willingness to turn from domestic to foreign affairs." Theodore Roosevelt, who always seemed to believe in the social therapy of war, wrote to a friend in late 1897, "In strict confidence. . . I should welcome almost any war, for I think this country needs one."

The Desire for New Overseas Markets: In a more direct fashion, the Economic Revolution also helped to turn the nation's attention outward. Professor Julius Pratt's researches, it is true, effectively eliminated the business interests as an important force for war, but more recent investigations have shown that economic motives were very influential with statesmen and publicists. Their concern was not to secure colonies nor even to garner national prestige, but to open up markets for the prodigious amounts of goods that were pouring from the factories of an industrialized America.

The beginnings of this interest go back at least to James G. Blaine, Harrison's first Secretary of State. While in that office, Blaine actively promoted reciprocal trade agreements, particularly with Latin American countries, as a means of obtaining broader markets for American goods. He was acutely aware that in an age of industry the United States might well find itself with surplus production. "Under the beneficent policy of protection," he pointed out in 1890, "we have developed a volume of manufactures, which, in many departments, overruns the demands of the home market." The reciprocity clause written into the McKinley Tariff of 1890 was a further reflection of this concern. Significantly, too, in 1896 the Republican platform contained a strong reciprocity plank.

It was the depression of 1893 that convinced the leaders of both parties that the home market was insufficient to absorb American production. New foreign markets might offer a possible solution to the hard times. Both President Cleveland and Secretary of the Treasury John Carlisle, neither of whom was an imperialist in the mold of Theodore Roosevelt, talked of foreign markets as a means of halting the outflow of gold that plagued the country. When another Democrat, William L. Wilson, wanted to defend a low tariff, he called attention to its potentialities for expanding American markets. "There is not one of our leading industries," Wilson emphasized, "that can find free and healthful play within the limits of our home markets." Expand American markets abroad, he asserted, and many social problems like strikes and labor unrest would be reduced. "With all our mills running and orders ahead, labor can achieve its own emancipation and treat on equal terms for its own wages." The depression also made those outside of government conscious of the need for outlets for American goods. One prominent writer went so far as to explain the contemporary relocation of New England textile mills to the southern states as a means of getting closer to the Latin American markets! The National Association of Manufacturers was founded in 1895 as a direct result of business interest in the opening of markets in Latin America.

This emphasis on new foreign markets, it should be observed, was not the colonialist or prestige-seeking variety advocated by navalists or expansionists like Admiral Mahan or Theodore Roosevelt. But whatever the motivation behind the interest, the outward turning of American people and leaders was clear. Moreover, the distinction in motivation does help to account for the apparent contradiction between Grover Cleveland's action on the issue of Hawaiian annexation in 1893 and his stand on Venezuela two years later.

Protecting Foreign Markets. When Cleveland entered the White House for the second time in March 1893, the Senate was considering a treaty that would annex Hawaii to the United States. Annexation of the islands had been a goal of expansionists and American sugar growers on the islands for some years. In January 1893, a group of American sugar planters, with the support of the American minister in Honolulu, had overthrown the native government and had then asked the favorably disposed Harrison administration for annexation to the United States. Cleveland, however, recognized that neither the revolution nor annexation to the United States was desired by Hawaiians and promptly withdrew the treaty from Senate consideration. Later, he explained his action on the ground that "The mission of our nation is to build up and make a greater country of what we have instead of annexing islands." In the jingoist nineties, Cleveland appeared an anomaly. Two years later, however, he did not seem so out of place when he dealt with England over the boundary dispute between Venezuela and British Guiana.

When Great Britain threatened to settle the dispute militarily, Secretary of State Richard Olney, in July 1895, wrote a sharp note of protest. He invoked the Monroe Doctrine as the American justification for intervening in what appeared to be a dispute between Venezuela and Great Britain only. The language of his message was quite in keeping with the fervent nationalism of the decade. "The states of America, South as well as North, by geographical proximity, by natural sympathy, by similarity of governmental constitutions, are friends and allies, commercially and politically, of the United States," Olney wrote. "To allow the subjugation of any of them by an European power is, of course, to completely reverse that situation and signifies the loss of all the advantages incident to their natural relations to us. . . . Today the United States is practically sovereign on this continent, and its fiat is law upon the subjects to which it confines its interposition." Olney insisted that Britain submit the dispute to arbitration. The British government's cool silence of four months so irritated Cleveland that he asked Congress for money to set up a commission to decide the issue and for the authority to settle the matter by force if necessary. In short, the United States was prepared to go to war to assert a highly nationalistic interpretation of the Monroe Doctrine. Fortunately, the British government yielded.

At first glance, the chauvinism of Cleveland in 1895 seems in marked conflict with his refusal to support the annexation of Hawaii in 1893. Actually, there is less contradiction than first appears. Olney and Cleveland, for all their nationalism, were certainly not colonialists or expansionists. Both of them, for example, later opposed the acquisition of the Philippines. But anti-imperialism did not preclude a strong sense of American nationalism and power. Nor did it prevent recognizing that surplus American manufactures needed markets, especially when the country was deep in a depression. To have failed to assert vigorously the Monroe Doctrine in the Venezuelan issue of 1895 would have been to deny the new feeling of nationalism which was so characteristic of the nineties; it would also have given Britain an advantage in the commercial competition in Latin America that might well have hurt American trade. An interest in keeping foreign markets open to American goods does seem to have been an important reason behind the Cleveland administration's support of the legitimate government during the abortive Brazilian revolution of 1894–1895 (when American trade was threatened with an embargo). Several years later, Olney cited the year 1895 as the real turning point in American foreign relations. Significantly, he related that shift to the Economic Revolution. "This country was once a pioneer and is now the millionaire," he wrote. Home markets were no longer sufficient to absorb the products of "the inventive genius of the American people."

Nationalism, social unrest, and the common interest of imperialists and anti-imperialists in foreign markets all helped to explain the new American interest in the outside world. But they only provided the background for the coming of the Spanish-American War and the triumph of the imperialistic point of view. A complete explanation for that momentous step into the orbit of the great powers requires the additional and precipitating factor of Cuba.

Whipping up the War Spirit. Americans had long been casting covetous eyes upon the Spanish colony off their southern coast. In the 1850's, there had been talk of buying Cuba, and after the Civil War the Grant administration toyed with the idea of deliberately encouraging the rebellion that broke out in 1868. When a second revolt erupted in 1895 as a result of a sharp decline in sugar prices, Americans found themselves very directly involved. The rebellion, which was financed by Cuban exiles in New York, seriously interrupted the $100 million trade between the United States and Cuba and threatened to destroy the $50 million investments of Americans in Cuban sugar plantations and iron mines. The economic interests of Americans in Cuba drew the attention of the Cleveland administration, but not to any great extent.

It was the public that became exercised because of the cruelties and suffering resulting from Spain's efforts to suppress the rebellion. The *reconcentrado* policy of Spanish Governor Valeriano Weyler worked severe hardships. Under that policy Cubans who were loyal to the regime or lived in government territory were herded into camps to remove them from the threat of the guerrillas or to prevent their giving aid to the rebels. The hardship resulted not from Spanish intention, but from the lack of adequate facilities for the large number of people involved. More significant than the policy itself was its treatment by the American press, in which the Spanish governor became known as "Butcher" Weyler. The Cuban rebellion was ready-made for scare headlines. True, any war that involves guerrilla fighting, as Americans would learn in the Philippines in 1899–1901 and in Vietnam 60 years later, is sensational; it is cruel, treacherous, and frustrating when compared with conventional warfare, in which there are at least some rules and visible lines of combat. But the inherent sensationalism of the Cuban war was exploited by the New York press; a furious rivalry for circulation between William R. Hearst's *Journal* and Joseph Pulitzer's *World* set a standard for "yellow journalism" that is still unmatched. The extremism of the New York press, however, only added fuel to a fire already burning brightly.

Yellow journalism is not as important in explaining the popular outrage over the Cuban war as the new technology of the Communications Revolution which made popular indignation possible. The American people, with their heritage of colonial rebellion, needed no urging to sympathize with the rebels; they simply had to learn about the Cubans' struggle for freedom. The Communications Revolution informed them, and indeed, did more. With pictures and sensational, personal accounts by on-the-spot reporters, the news was relayed more quickly to a wider audience than ever before, making the war an experience as well as an event for millions of Americans. Democrats and Republicans, farmers and workers alike saw in the Cuban war an American and a Christian imperative to help an oppressed and valiant people. "The United States needs a war, and Spain needs a thrashing," wrote one Civil War veterans' journal in the summer of 1897. "Both wants can be supplied in Cuba. Order out the ships." In early 1898, one Bostonian wrote that he had not met a man of the upper class "who considers that we have any justifiable cause for war. Below that crust," he went on, ". . . the wish for war is *almost* universal."

The great popular interest in helping the Cubans, however, was not shared by the United States government. Neither the Cleveland nor the McKinley administrations wanted war over Cuba, though both recognized that the conflict there hurt Americans economically and endangered the peace with Spain. In this pacific attitude, both Presidents enjoyed the support of the business community, which only occasionally expressed a bellicose attitude toward Spain. But Congress and the press marched with the people. In early 1898, only one New York newspaper still opposed war.

Aggravation of the Cuban Issue. Several incidents provided opportunities for keeping up the popular pressure for war. One was the discovery and publications, in early February 1898, of an indiscreet letter from the Spanish minister in Washington, Depuy de Lôme, which described President McKinley as "weak and a bidder for the admiration of the crowd." De Lôme, of course, resigned when his words became known, and the Spanish government apologized. But popular American resentment against Spain rose, and with the departure of De Lôme, the Spanish government lost an excellent counterforce to the propaganda of the rebel junta in New York.

A more important incident was the mysterious explosion on (or next to) the United States battleship *Maine*. Late in January 1898, it had been dispatched to Havana harbor at the request of the American consul to protect the property of United States citizens. On February 15, a tremendous explosion sank the ship as it lay in the harbor, killing or drowning some 250 American sailors. The immediate assumption in the United States, given the general hostility toward Spain, was that the Spanish were responsible. A report issued on March 28 by a United States investigating commission, which concluded that the explosion was external, did nothing to scotch this belief, though no responsibility for the blast was assigned then or later. The press continued to refer to "Spanish treachery" and to preach sympathy for the Cuban rebels.

Nevertheless, as late as the end of March 1898, diplomatic conversations between the United States and Spain seemed to offer substantial hope that the war might be ended to the satisfaction of the United States. In early April, in fact, the Spanish government abandoned the objectionable *reconcentrado* policy throughout Cuba and a few days later agreed to suspend hostilities against the rebels for six months. By this time, unfortunately, American demands had jumped higher. Responding to pressure from Congress, the press, and public opinion, McKinley then asked for nothing less than complete independence for Cuba, something that no Spanish government dared agree to, though autonomy within the empire was offered. The Spanish concessions of early April, it now appears, were futile, because some time during March the McKinley administration had decided that independence was indispensable. With that decision, war became inevitable.

Unwilling himself to make the ultimate decision to go to war, McKinley, on April 11, turned the matter over to Congress. In a joint declaration on April 19, 1898, Congress declared Cuba to be free and independent and authorized the President to use the armed forces of the United States, if necessary, to compel Spain to relinquish the island. At the same time, in what came to be called the Teller Amendment, Congress declared by a unanimous vote that the United States "hereby disclaims any disposition or intention to exercise sovereignty, jurisdiction, or control over (Cuba). . . ." As a result of the joint Congressional declaration, Spain broke diplomatic relations with the United States on April 21, and on the 25th, Congress voted that a state of war existed between the two countries. Soon after war was declared, the conservative Republican, Senator John Spooner of Wisconsin, wrote to a friend, "I think . . . possibly the President could have worked the business without a war, but the current was too strong, the demagogues too numerous, and the fall elections too near."

"A Splendid Little War"

The First Encounter. Although the United States entered the war with enthusiasm, no preparations for it had been made. Even so, the powers of

Europe, which had generally sympathized with Spain, foresaw victory for the powerful republic of the New World. They were taken aback, however, by the rapidity with which 200,000 men were mobilized within a matter of months, and by the display of unity in the socially heterogeneous nation. Former Confederate officers tendered their services as eagerly as the Union men, and new immigrants and southern Negroes flocked to the colors in response to McKinley's call for 125,000 volunteers.

But even Americans were surprised to learn that the first encounter came not in Cuba, but in the western Pacific, some 10,000 miles away from the source of the conflict. Yet as early as February, Assistant Secretary of the Navy Theodore Roosevelt had begun to make plans. He alerted Admiral George Dewey, commander of the American far eastern squadron, then at Hong Kong, to be prepared to attack the Spanish fleet at Manila in, the Philippine Islands. Although this action of Roosevelt's is often cited to show how a small group of expansionists managed to transform the Cuban war into an imperialist one, the fact is that in time of war all centers of Spanish power became legitimate and necessary objects of attack. Hence, six days after the declaration of war, Dewey completely annihilated the decrepit Spanish fleet in Manila Bay, at a human cost to the American forces of only eight slightly wounded. In June, Dewey, who had by then become a national hero, was joined by units of the Army under the command of General Wesley Merrit. With the assistance of Filipino rebels, led by General Emilio Aguinaldo, the

SPANISH-AMERICAN WAR, PHILIPPINE CAMPAIGN, 1898

Spain's antiquated ships were no match for America's modern "steel navy," which swept into Manila Bay from Hong Kong and in one battle virtually ended the war with Spain in the Philippines. A show of force by the U.S. Army and Philippine rebels completed victory there.

Unlike most wars, the Spanish-American War was very limited in nature. Even with the Philippine campaign, only a few battles, involving fairly small land and sea forces, were necessary to end it. Nor was it necessary to occupy all of Cuba in order to obtain victory.

combined forces proceeded to occupy the island of Luzon against only slight resistance from the Spanish.

Strolling Into Cuba. The conquest of Cuba took longer. Incredible mismanagement and inefficiency in the United States were largely responsible for the delay, as was brought out by later investigations of the War Department. Troops did not even leave the staging area in Tampa, Florida, until mid-June. As Richard Harding Davis, one of the principal war correspondents, reported on the expedition to Cuba under General William Shafter, "It was a most happy-go-lucky expedition, run with real American optimism and readiness to take big chances, and with the spirit of a people who recklessly trust that it will come out all right in the end, and that the barely possible may not happen. . . . As one of the generals on board said, 'This is God Almighty's war, and we are only His agents.'"

The first landings at Daiquiri and Siboney on the southern shore of Cuba were so inept that only a more inept Spanish defense prevented disaster. The target of the American landings was the city of Santiago, in the harbor of which lay the Spanish fleet under Admiral Pascual Cervera. After some bloody and costly fighting at El Caney and a dramatic rush up San Juan Hill outside of Santiago, the American Army laid siege to the city. From beyond its harbor, the United States Navy watched for the Spanish fleet's inevitable break for the open sea. On July 3, Admiral Cervera elected to make his run through the tortuous harbor entrance in broad daylight only to be overwhelmed by the waiting Americans. The Spanish suffered some 450 casualties, including over 300 dead; the American losses totalled two: one killed and one wounded. It was a victory like this, rather than the stiff Spanish opposition at El Caney, that inspired John Hay to write Theodore Roosevelt, "It has been a splendid little war, carried on with magnificent intelligence and spirit, favored by that Fortune which loves the brave."

The End of One Colonial Empire, the Beginning of Another. Two weeks after the destruction of the Spanish fleet, the city of Santiago surrendered to General Shafter, just as yellow fever was ominously spreading among his men. On August 12, Spain signed a preliminary agreement ending the war. The agreement granted Cuba its freedom, ceded to the United States the island of Puerto Rico, which had been quickly conquered by General Nelson Miles' troops, and permitted the United States to occupy the Philippines, pending a final peace treaty.

The most obvious result of the war was the humiliation of Spain. "When I gave the order to fire," remembered Captain Concas of Cervera's flagship, "it was the signal that the history of four centuries of grandeur was at an end and that Spain was becoming a nation of the fourth class." The oldest and most successful colonial empire since the days of Rome was no more. For the United States, victory was not so much a sign of new power; Europeans had been well aware, long before the war began, that America was preëminent among the industrial nations of the world. It was the empire which came as a result of the war that was new.

The prospect of overseas colonies occasioned a great debate in the country, but in retrospect, the efforts of the anti-imperialists seem to have been doomed from the beginning. Even before the end of the war with Spain, President McKinley signed a joint Congressional resolution on July 7, incorporating Hawaii into the territories of the United States, thus completing the effort aborted by Cleveland five years earlier. Extending the boundaries of the United States 2000 miles into the Pacific Ocean, however, was to the imperialists only the beginning.

They wanted the Philippines, too. During much of the last half of 1898, a furious debate raged in Congress and in the press over the issue. All the hoary arguments for expansion were trotted out: the need for markets, the need for prestige in a world of colonial empires, the virtue to be gained by Christianizing heathens (even though Catholic Spain had ruled the islands for 400 years), and the necessity of helping an "immature" people, who otherwise would fall under the dominion of allegedly less-qualified rulers like Germany or Japan. Businessmen, many of whom had opposed the entrance of the United States into war with Spain, now found the possibilities of an Asian market very tempting. Mark Hanna, President McKinley's close friend and campaign manager in 1896, declared that possession of the Philippines would enable the United States "to take a large slice of the commerce of Asia. That is what we want. We are bound to share in the commerce of the Far East, and it is better to strike for it while the iron is hot."

The immediate decision to acquire the Philippines, however, was McKinley's. Although he later said that he had arrived at his decision after prolonged prayer, the record shows that the forces that shaped his action were more mundane. While the treaty was being negotiated in the fall of 1898, he carefully, and probably accurately, tested public opinion by a speaking tour. On October 26, soon after his "poll" revealed a clear popular interest in keeping the islands, he instructed the American commissioners in Madrid to insist upon the whole archipelago, not just Manila, or the island of Luzon. In the final treaty, the United States secured the Philippines, Puerto Rico, and the island of Guam in the central Pacific, in return for a payment of $20 million.

The treaty brought the debate over imperialism to a climax. The opposition was impressive. Included among the anti-imperialists were important intellectuals like William James, William Dean Howells, and Mark Twain, and labor leaders such as Samuel Gompers and Eugene V. Debs, as well as prominent Republicans like Charles Francis Adams and Carl Schurz. They were joined by Democrats on both sides of the silver fight, such as William Jennings Bryan, Grover Cleveland, and John G. Carlisle. The most powerful anti-imperialist argument was that the Filipinos did not want to substitute American for Spanish rule; they simply wanted to govern themselves. The strength of this argument was amply demonstrated by the rebellion that broke out in February 1899, under the leadership of the Filipino nationalist, Emilio Aguinaldo. Superior American military power, to be sure, quickly forced the small, ill-equipped rebel army into guerrilla tactics, but that merely made the war more brutal without shortening it. The suppression of the Filipino rebellion ultimately required four times as many American soldiers as invaded Cuba, and three years instead of the three and a half months it took to conquer the Caribbean island. The loss of American lives was triple that for the whole Spanish-American War, while the number of Filipinos killed in a military capacity alone was over 14,000 in the first year of the rebellion.

Significantly, both imperialists and anti-imperialists reflected in their arguments the widespread racism then infecting European culture. Surveying the world of 1898, white Europeans could not help but feel that they ruled supreme, for, in fact, they did, as the carving up of Africa and the commercial partition of China made evident. Instead of seeing this undoubted supremacy as temporary, growing out of a head start in technology and industrialization, Europeans and Americans chose to view it as a consequence of their racial superiority. Thus, the imperialists justified the taking of the Philippines as a duty owed "our little brown brother," who was not yet capable of self-government. The implications of the argument were not lost upon southern racists in Congress, many of whom were anti-imperialists and almost all of whom were then taking steps to deny the ballot to southern Negroes. Was this not the very argument, they slyly inquired, that southern white men had used in protesting Negro enfranchisement during Reconstruction, only to have it rejected by these same Republicans?

Nor were northern anti-imperialists free of racism in their objections to colonies. As Carl Schurz pointed out, if the Philippine Islands were acquired they might well become states on an equal footing with others. "The prospect of the consequences which would follow the admission of the Spanish creoles and the negroes of the West India islands and of the Malays and Tagals of the Philippines to participation in the conduct of our government is so alarming that you instinctively pause before taking the step." Many of the anti-imperialists doubted that American institutions could exist in such a different climate and culture. As David Starr Jordan, the president of Stanford University, observed, "Civilization is, as it were, suffocated in the tropics."

The issue of empire was settled on February 6, 1899, when the treaty was accepted in the Senate by a vote of 57 to 27 – only a single vote more than the necessary two thirds. Popular opposition to empire was probably even stronger, but William Jennings Bryan, as a leader of the anti-imperialists, dissipated its influence on the Senate when he advised acceptance of the treaty so that the issue of imperialism might be fought out in the election of 1900. As might have been anticipated, although Bryan and McKinley were the presidential candidates in 1900, imperialism was no longer a current topic, despite Bryan's valiant efforts. Once again Bryan was beaten by the issue of free silver, which the Republicans artfully made central to the 1900 campaign.

The entrance of the United States into Asia brought none of the bright consequences that expansionists had predicted and businessmen had anticipated. The Asian market proved to be an impoverished one, and the acquisition of the Philippines did nothing to develop it, though the United States proved to be a conscientious and humane, if slightly self-righteous, colonial ruler. Moreover, as early as 1907, Theodore Roosevelt, now President, was already complaining that the Philippines possessed no strategic value, and, in fact, constituted the "Achilles heel" of American security. In 1916, the United States Congress, in the Jones Act, made its first promise of eventual Filipino independence, though consummation would wait another 30 years.

The Spanish war brought the United States not only into Asia, but into the Caribbean as well. It was there, during the new century, that American imperialism would experience thorough testing and dismal failure.

Domestic Scene. The story of domestic affairs is a Republican tale. The Dingley Tariff of 1897 raised the rates above even those in the notorious McKinley Act of 1890. The party took somewhat longer to redeem its pledges on the money question. With the Gold Standard Act of 1900, the nation declared that gold was to be the only metallic base of the money supply. The act also authorized the President to float short-term loans for gold so that the Treasury would never again be caught in the vicious cycle of redemptions that had bedeviled the Cleveland administration in 1894 – 1895. The Republicans were also credited for the new boom in the economy, enjoyed by farmers as well as businessmen. The century closed, in short, with the United States as a new world power, and, for the first time in many years, riding the crest of prosperity.

SUGGESTED READING

The decade of the nineties has been surveyed fully but in a rather pedestrian manner in Harold U. Faulkner, *Politics, Reform and Expansion, 1890–1900** (1959). The two principal strikes of the decade have now been treated in detail by Almont Lindsey, *The Pullman Strike** (1942) and by Leon Wolff, *Lockout; The Story of the Homestead Strike of 1892* (1965). More favorably disposed than Wolff toward the strikers is Henry David, "Upheaval at Homestead," in *America in Crisis*, ed. by Daniel Aaron (1952). No monograph treats the depression adequately; nevertheless, the best study of it is Charles Hoffman, "The Depression of the Nineties," *Journal of Economic History*, XVI (June, 1956), 137–164. A helpful supplement to this is Samuel Rezneck, "Unemployment, Unrest, and Relief in the United States During the Depression of 1893–97," *Journal of Political Economy*, LXI (August, 1953), 324–345. The depression, as an aspect of the money question, is dealt with at some length in the technical, but important study by Milton Friedman and Anna Schwartz, *A Monetary History of the United States, 1867–1960* (1963).

The standard study on the election that opens the decade is George Harmon Knoles, *The Presidential Campaign and Election of 1892* (1942). Among the political biographies that should be added to those mentioned earlier is James A. Barnes, *John G. Carlisle* (1931); Harry Barnard, "*Eagle Forgotten*," *The Life of John Peter Altgeld** (1938), a splendid job; and Paxton Hibben, *The Peerless Leader* (1929), an overly caustic, but very readable biography of Bryan. Since then Paul W. Glad, *The Trumpet Soundeth: William Jennings Bryan and His Democracy, 1896–1912* (1960) has thoughtfully and understandably placed Bryan in the intellectual context of his time. Paolo E. Coletta, *William Jennings Bryan, 1860–1908* Vol. I (1964) is to be a full and friendly biography. Margaret Leech, *In the Days of McKinley* (1959), makes McKinley as important as he can be, and is the best study of the man. The most recent and fullest statement of McKinley as President is H. Wayne Morgan, *William McKinley and His America* (1963).

The presidential election of 1896 has itself spawned a small body of literature. Thorough on political detail, but rather weak on the social roots of politics is Stanley L. Jones, *The Presidential Election of 1896* (1964). Complementary because it does probe into social politics is J. Rogers Hollingsworth, *The Whirligig of Politics: The Democracy of Cleveland and Bryan* (1963). Robert F. Durden, *The Climax of Populism; the Election of 1896* (1965) concentrates on the South and tends to take the Populists at their own value. Of the new literature on Populism the most important is Walter T. K. Nugent, *The Tolerant Populists: Kansas, Populism and Nativism* (1963), which absolves the Populists of charges of anti-Semitism and nativism. An important article on the urban component in the election of 1896 is William Diamond, "Urban and Rural Voting in 1896," *American Historical Review*, XLVI (January, 1941), 281–305. Helpful in

*Available in a paperback edition.

understanding the election, though overly pro-Bryan, is James A. Barnes, "Myths of the Bryan Campaign," *Mississippi Valley Historical Review,* **XXXIV** (December, 1947), 367–404. The losing candidate wrote his own account in William Jennings Bryan, *The First Battle: A Story of the Campaign of 1896* (1897), which contains many of his speeches.

The disenfranchisement of the Negro is told in the two path-breaking books by C. Vann Woodward, *The Strange Career of Jim Crow** (revised ed., 1966), and *Origins of the New South* (1951).

The most provocative study on the foreign policy of the decade is Walter LeFeber, *The New Empire* (1963), which sometimes overstresses economic explanations, but always on the basis of sources. The most balanced study is Ernest R. May, *Imperial Democracy* (1961), which is distinguished by its use of archival materials of the principal countries. A short but useful examination of the coming of the war is H. Wayne Morgan, *America's Road to Empire* (1965). Walter Millis, *The Martial Spirit** (1931), set the satiric tone usually taken in regard to the Spanish-American War; the appropriateness of that attitude has been questioned by Frank Freidel, *The Splendid Little War* (1962), which is drawn largely from contemporary accounts. Two important aspects of the anti-imperialist movement are dealt with in the popular and sound Leon Wolff, *Little Brown Brother* (1961), an account of the Filipino insurrection against the Americans, and in Christopher Lasch, "The Anti-Imperialists, the Philippines, and the Inequality of Man," *Journal of Southern History,* **XXIV** (February 1958), 319–331, which detects racism among anti-imperialists.

"Be good and you will be lonesome" was Mark Twain's sardonic comment on this picture of himself. Such cynicism, Twain recognized, was both a cause and an effect of this age in which technological advance and material progress were juxtaposed with extreme poverty and human misery. *Photo:* Harper Brothers, Mark Twain Memorial

CHAPTER SIX

THE SECULARIZATION OF AMERICAN SOCIETY AND THOUGHT

N O MAN CAN AFFORD to ignore entirely either the problems or promises of living on this earth. Even during the most religious eras men have had to concern themselves with the everyday frustrations of life. Throughout most of human history the labor-saving assistance of the machine has been lacking, disease has been barely controlled, and poverty has been the lot of the vast majority. Confronted by such an existence, man has found religion a precious comfort as well as an explanation of God's purposes.

The triumph of Democracy, Science, and the Economic Revolution suggested to some in the late nineteenth century that life could be better even for the mass of men. In a democracy, all men are equal before the law and entitled to seek a good life. With universal suffrage they have the opportunity to achieve it. Moreover, an age that was scientific as well as democratic condemned pious indifference to the world on two counts. The biblical admonition that "ye have the poor always with you," men argued, ought no longer to assuage the guilt of the rich or smother the hopes of the impoverished. Science and the technology of the Economic Revolution now demonstrated that for the first time in history men possessed the means to eliminate poverty. Indeed, as we have seen, it was precisely this vision that inspired reformers like Henry George and Edward Bellamy. With such prospects, men turned eagerly to confront a world that seemed at last responsive to their efforts. Life no longer seemed hopeless, for nature now challenged man's ingenuity and power to make it an earthly paradise.

Most men, of course, did not abandon their religious interests; they simply relegated them to a more remote part of their minds while they busied themselves with the material world. One sign of the new secular interest was the decline in the influence of the Protestant ministry. Prior to the Civil War, ministers had been the recognized leaders of the intellectual community; most college presidents were ministers, for example. By the close of the century, on the other hand, men trained in worldly affairs were clearly the intellectual leaders, and the clergyman-president of the college or university was passing from the scene. Perhaps the most striking example of the secularization of society during the last decades of the nineteenth century was provided by the churches themselves, as they redefined their missions to fit the new world of cities and factories.

The Secularization of Protestantism

Probably the greatest secularizing force in the late 1800's was the Economic Revolution. By the end of the century, it had shaped the modern patterns of American religion. In his stimulating book, *Protestant, Catholic, Jew* (1955), Will Herberg points out that Americans today, despite the great number of religious denominations to which they belong, generally place themselves in one of three great religious categories. This clear recognition of Catholicism and Judaism on a par with Protestantism is very recent. For most of the nineteenth century, the American people and their culture were over-whelmingly Protestant. Only with the influx of immigrants in the second half of the century did Catholicism and Judaism begin to change the pattern, taking their places beside Protestantism as significant religions of Americans. All three broad religious groups were remolded by the forces generated in the city and the factory, but none was altered more than Protestantism.

In the 1870's, as in previous years, American Protestantism was a mélange of sects, with new ones emerging every decade. Most of the new sects, it is true, were not destined to rise above the level of influence of local congregations, but from time to time, one would assume the stature of a world religion, as in the case of the Mormons before the Civil War, or the Christian Scientists in the postwar years. The overwhelming majority of native-born Americans, however, belonged to one of the large denominations, such as the Methodists, who comprised a third of all Protestants, or the Baptists, or the Presbyterians. The Lutheran Church, strong in the upper Mississippi Valley, was the fourth largest Protestant denomination in the country in the 1870's, but its members were largely of German and Scandinavian immigrant stock. All told, there were about ten million Protestant church members in 1880; by 1900, the number would rise to almost 18 million.

Urban Life: New Challenges to the Churches. The new ways of life in the cities presented a severe challenge to Protestantism, involving it increasingly with worldly matters. Many Protestant ministers and leaders, alarmed by the crime, immorality, and disease that the cities seemed to foster, began to recognize that the urban areas were also the homes of the churchless. "The American Protestant Church, as a whole," said one minister in the 1880's, "has failed to win to itself the working class of the towns." It was true, too, that the churches did little to attract and much to alienate workingmen. Too often urban churches charged pew rent and affected an elegant decor that made working people feel uncomfortable and unwelcome. By seeming to prefer the attendance of employers, merchants, and professional men, the churches demonstrated their upper-class orientation. Samuel Gompers, the head of the American Federation of Labor, testified to this feeling in 1896 when he said that the workers "have come to look upon the church and the ministry as the apologists and defenders of the wrongs committed against the interests of the people by employers and men of wealth." Moreover, the churches often neglected or ignored the urban workers. As working-class districts filled up, the churches moved out and none came to replace them. In one area of Chicago containing 60,000 people, there was not a single Protestant church.

Social Gospel. Thus, faced with a loss of influence and genuinely concerned with the poor working and living conditions of the urban masses, some Protestant clergymen in the 1870's and 1880's began to argue that the churches had a special responsibility to interest themselves in the problems of the world. These clergymen contended that the teachings of Jesus must be applied to the conditions of the slums and the low wages of industrial workers. The Reverend Charles Loring Brace, an established leader in philanthropic work in New York, was profoundly affected by the great railroad strike of 1877. He recognized that strikes of such magnitude and violence were new in America. "They ought not to occur here. The great problem of the future is the equal distribution of wealth out of the profits of labor. . . . I believe myself that, in general, the laboring classes do not receive their fair share. Strikes are one of their means of getting more. . . ." Washington Gladden, an Ohio clergyman prominent in the working-class movement, pointed out that if the church hoped to regain its influence, it must become interested in economic and social issues. The old, narrow theology of the seminaries was no longer sufficient. The new and different world of the city demanded a fresh and broader religion.

One of the first forms this new "Social Gospel" assumed was the organization of charitable services for the urban poor and the dispossessed. Ladies of the churches brought food, clothing, and spiritual assistance to workingmen's families. Churches provided recreational facilities for young people where none had existed. Kindergartens, church schools, and youth organizations were formed in response to the secular needs of people in the industrial cities.

The most striking example of the direct response of Protestantism to the demands of the urban world was the Salvation Army. Conceived in the slums of London, this army of Christians came to the United States in the late 1870's to minister to the lowest slum dwellers, who often were beyond the interest or the assistance of the established churches. At first, the Salvation Army was roundly condemned by the conventional churches for its flamboyant practices of playing cornets, beating drums, and hymn-singing on street corners. But the dedication and helpfulness of the men and women of the Salvation Army soon won the respect of the poor and the conventionally religious alike. They set up their havens in the center of the worst slums and offered soup, bread, and a bed to all who entered, even before religious commitment was demanded. By ministering to the urban poor, these Christians showed that they had adapted themselves extremely well to the new conditions created by the city and the factory. Their belief that a hungry man had to be fed before he could be expected to pray was a realistic recognition that the spirit cannot be reached when the flesh is neglected.

Along with the adjustment of church practice to urban circumstances, there occurred a transformation of Christian teaching and doctrine. By stressing the responsibility of society for its less fortunate members, Protestant Christianity was both socialized and secularized. In the seminaries and from the pulpits, ministers taught and preached the need for understanding social problems, for working on behalf of the poor and the laboring class. In 1892, seven seminaries instituted lectureships in social ethics; two years later, three others had added similar courses to their curricula. In 1893, the students of the Union Theological Seminary in New York organized a society for the discussion of "the nature and method of sociological study and the minister's relation to the problems of the day."

The most articulate and best-known advocate of the Social Gospel was Walter Rauschenbusch, a scion of a long line of ministers. Soon after graduation from the Rochester Theological Seminary, Rauschenbusch became the pastor of a Baptist church in New York City's impoverished Hell's Kitchen, where, during the depression of 1893, he recalled later, "one could hear human virtues cracking and crumbling all around." He found that the religious principles he had learned in the seminary were becoming increasingly irrelevant in the social context of his slum parish. In 1897, he returned to the Rochester Seminary to teach, and in 1907, he published his first book, *Christianity and the Social Crisis*. "The ministry," Rauschenbusch wrote, "must apply the teaching function of the pulpit to the pressing questions of public morality," such as the problems of poverty, unemployment, low wages, poor housing and unregulated business monopoly. Secular answers would have to be sought for these secular problems; the old-time religious answers to human problems were no longer adequate. Indeed, Rauschenbusch's concern ultimately made him a socialist in political philosophy. Only a small minority of the Social Gospel leaders, however, followed him that far.

The Social Gospel reached a peak among Protestants with the formation of the Federal Council of Churches of Christ in America in 1908. Composed of 33 different Protestant denominations, the Council pledged in its statement of social principles to work for, among other things, the abolition of child labor, "a living wage in every industry, . . . the highest wage that each industry can afford," and the recognition of "the Golden Rule . . . as the supreme law of society and the sure remedy for all social ills." Now called the National Council of Churches, it remains a living symbol of Protestantism's shift in emphasis from individual salvation to the recognition of a responsibility for the secular as well as the religious condition of mankind.

Although the Social Gospel had a dramatic impact upon some Protestant denominations, others escaped the initial shock almost entirely. Churches drawing predominantly upon a rural constituency, for instance, usually felt little need to change their ways. Hence, whole denominations such as the Lutherans and the Presbyterians were conspicuously slow in responding to the new social Christianity. Even today, the Lutheran Church, especially those synods made up largely of immigrant stock, is much less concerned with social issues than the Episcopal, Baptist, or Methodist churches, which were prominent in the nineteenth-century Social Gospel movement. Insofar as these churches failed to move in a secular direction, they lost influence in a society that was becoming increasingly secular in outlook.

Urban Revivalism: A Rural Influence. Yet it would be erroneous to imply that even all urban Protestants adopted the Social Gospel. Many of these Protestants, after all, had only recently come from farms and rural towns;

they already believed in God, read their Bibles, and prayed regularly. They were not in need of missionary attention. Yet they were alienated by the urban congregations whose fashionable churches and intellectualized religion offered scant welcome and less comfort. What these recently arrived rural folk sought in the city was a religion or a church like the one they had left in the country. Many of these people found just what they sought in the urban revival meeting.

Historically, the revival was a rural phenomenon, descended from the Great Awakening of the middle years of the eighteenth century. Intellectually, the revival was a democratic repudiation of an elitist view of salvation, for, unlike the Calvinist doctrine of the elect, the central principle of the revival taught that each man could determine his own salvation, if only he would. In the cities of the 1870's, the revival meeting continued to appeal to the poor as well as to the middle class, and to speak in a socially democratic idiom.

The most successful of the urban revivalists of these years was Massachusetts-born Dwight L. Moody, who began his preaching, significantly enough, in bustling, booming Chicago. In 1875–1876, after a sensationally successful revival tour of England, Moody and his gospel singer, Ira Sankey, brought the revival to the principal cities of the United States. The crowds that filled the meeting halls numbered in the thousands and the enthusiastic converts in the hundreds.

Moody's amazing success as a preacher was the result of both his personal magnetism and his democratic, down-to-earth approach to religion. Such an approach appealed strongly to the ordinary American, who often misunderstood or resented the formal language of the trained and traditional clergy. In appearance, Moody was impressive; his massive size (he weighed 280 pounds) and full beard gave him the appearance of an outsized biblical prophet. His speech, however, was colloquial rather than grandiloquent. His homely moral lessons and his recital of stories from the Bible were couched in everyday language and images, based on the experiences of ordinary people. The story of the prodigal son thus became the tale of a boy from the country lost in the strange and threatening environment of the city. This was a boy who had been ensnared by "the billiard hall and the drinking saloons." The Christian doctrine Moody preached was simple, direct, and comforting. Scorning the entire concept of an elect, he declared salvation open to all. God, he asserted, was all-merciful; He did not restrict salvation to a special few. Jesus asked simply that all believe in Him and all would be saved. "The way to be saved," Moody exclaimed, "is not to delay, but to come and take, t-a-k-e, TAKE."

Moody was no exponent of the Social Gospel, for his emphasis was upon the individual and his soul. Nevertheless, he was clearly the product of a society of equals, in which each individual had the same chance to get to heaven. This triumph of democratic idealism embodied in the revival shows how even the more primitive kind of Christianity was being influenced by the world. Yet Moody's refusal to interest himself in the broad social problems of his time helped to account for the limited impact of his movement. During the 1830's and 1840's, revivalism had played a central role in the reform movement, particularly in the antislavery crusade. But Moody's shunning of the Social Gospel movement isolated his form of revivalism from increasingly popular issues. In short, the limited success of Moody's revivalism was also a sign of the growing secularism of the times.

Christian Science—Urban Product of a Scientific Age. If the secularization of religion is measured solely against the yardstick of the Social Gospel, Christian Science, like Moody's revivalism, appears to be indifferent to worldly affairs. Christian Scientist doctrine firmly rejected any kind of social reform or concern. For instance, the founder of the religion, Mrs. Mary Baker Eddy, prohibited her followers from introducing the innocuous strawberry festivals or Ladies Aid Societies so familiar in most other Protestant churches. But there were other ways in which Christian Science reflected the growing secularization of thought at the end of the nineteenth century.

Christian Science is the lengthened shadow of one woman, Mary Baker Eddy, a thrice-married New England farm girl. After overcoming a nervous condition with the help of a faith healer, Phineas Quimby, Mrs. Eddy began to instruct others in the art of mental healing. Since most of her first pupils were working people in the industrial cities of Lynn and Boston, it might be said that Christian Science began as a product of the city and the factory.

In 1875, with the financial assistance of some of her disciples, Mrs. Eddy published her interpretation of Christianity in a book called *Science and Health.* She claimed no originality. Her definition of Christianity, she said, was simply the rediscovery of the true doctrine, lost since the apostolic age. In her book she taught the total unreality of evil in the world. God, she asserted, was all good, and the world He created was without evil and therefore without disease or sickness. Matter did not exist; the sole reality was Spirit or Mind or Idea. Illness thus became a figment of human minds impressed with the false doctrine of the reality of material things. Christian Science, in brief, was a form of philosophical idealism.

During the early years of the twentieth century, Christian Science spread to most of the large cities of the United States and to many European countries, thereby becoming the second of the world's religions (the first being Mormonism) to originate in America, as well as one of the few to be founded by a woman. This remarkable growth was achieved in spite of bitter public hostility toward a religion whose members rejected modern medical science.

Even though Christian Science never participated in the Social Gospel movement, it reflected the interests and concerns of the late nineteenth century in at least three ways. The first and most obvious is inherent in the name of the religion: The Church of Christ, Scientist. Such a title could be acceptable only in a secular and scientific age in which a scientist's ability to probe the true nature of things was well recognized. In the second place,

Christian Science mirrored the dominant cultural and intellectual attitudes of the time in that it was founded in a city during a period of great urban growth. Indeed, it has remained the most urban-based of any Protestant church in the United States. Christian Science was at once a product of, and a contribution to, the city.

The third way in which it was typical of its age is evidenced in its pragmatism. As we shall see a little later in this chapter, the last quarter of the nineteenth century witnessed the development of philosophical pragmatism—the doctrine that truth is to be tested through works. Of all religions, Christian Science is undoubtedly the most pragmatic. Its literature and history are filled with the testimonies of those who have been healed through belief in its tenets. The fundamental appeal to potential converts is the simple assertion that Christian Science can cure the sick. "If Christian Science lacked the proof of its goodness and utility," Mrs. Eddy wrote, "it would destroy itself, for it rests alone on demonstration." Not even William James, the principal exponent of the philosophy of pragmatism, could subject religion to a more pragmatic test. In natural science, too, it should be remembered, the supreme test of truth is practice or experiment.

The Growth of Catholicism

During the years that many of the Protestant churches were passing through the transforming fires of the Social Gospel, the Roman Catholic Church in the United States was only coming of age. Catholic parishes, it is true, had existed in this country from the early part of the seventeenth century, but the American Church had always been a tiny island in a Protestant sea. Then with the influx of Irish and German Catholics after 1830, membership leaped up, only to expose Catholics to nativist fears and bigotry during the Know-Nothing agitation of the 1850's.

At the time of the Civil War, Catholics were still establishing their place and future in American society. It was not clear then that Roman Catholicism was to be a predominantly urban-based religion. Thousands of German Catholics and even some Irish Catholics took up land in the West, almost counterbalancing the tendency of Irish Catholics to settle in eastern cities such as New York, Boston, and Baltimore. In the 1880's and after, however, the arrival of hundreds of thousands of Polish, Italian, and Irish Catholics, who settled in the expanding cities, caused a remarkably rapid growth in American Catholicism and placed an unmistakably urban stamp upon the Church. In 1850, the Catholics in the United States numbered approximately 1.5 million; by 1880, the figure was over six million; at the end of the century, it had reached almost 12 million.

Though the Church grew rapidly, it still remained outside the mainstream of American life. Protestants monopolized the political, intellectual, and social leadership of the country. Catholics, if they were thought about at all by the

Protestant Establishment, were regarded as unassimilated immigrants and therefore justly without social influence. Like most immigrants, Catholics were generally poor; a Catholic middle class hardly existed. Moreover, Catholic traditions, derived mainly from the peasant cultures of Europe, lacked the Protestant middle-class ethic, which emphasized hard work, frugality, and abstemiousness, and which for so long had been accepted by native Americans. Their local churches, moreover, were clergy-controlled to a degree no Protestant thought consistent with American democratic ways. The Catholics' commitment to a carefully defined religious dogma and theology also stood in sharp contrast to Protestantism's latitudinarian conception of doctrine and its increasing tendency to confine theology to an occasional sermon and to the seminaries. Thus, both as immigrants and as non-Protestants, the Catholic minority was set apart from the native American majority. Even the hierarchy of the Church, though better educated than the laity, was largely European trained and European born. For their part, many Catholics, in the face of a hostile Protestant culture, drew even closer together, increasing their alienation from American society and offering justification for Protestant charges of "clannishness."

New World Proponents. By the decade of the 1880's, though, forces of accommodation were at work. The mere increase in the number of Catholics as well as their acquisition of wealth and position over the years eased their adjustment. Furthermore, about this time a new group of church leaders came forward, dedicated to narrowing the gulf between the Church and American culture. The most prominent of such men were Cardinal James Gibbons of Baltimore, Archbishop John Ireland of St. Paul, Minnesota, Bishop John Keane of Catholic University, and Bishop John Spalding of Peoria, Illinois. In speeches and in actions, these leaders stressed the American character of the Church and its loyalty to the historic principles of the nation. Their purpose was to help Catholics feel at home in America and to encourage other Americans to accept Catholics as fellow citizens. Both Gibbons and Ireland repeatedly called attention to the essentially favorable social climate in the United States for the growth of the Church. Ireland contrasted this to the tumultuous, often anticlerical, contemporary experience of the Church in traditionally Catholic countries such as Italy and France, and in Germany under Chancellor Otto von Bismarck. Gibbons and Ireland, in fact, were so well disposed toward American society that they were often blind to its flaws. Archbishop Ireland, for example, fulsomely praised capitalists like Andrew Carnegie and extolled the virtues of unregulated competition at the very time when reformers and even some Protestant ministers were finding good reasons for lashing out at the inequities of an industrial society.

Gibbons and Ireland also acted as mediators between a Protestant America and the Holy See in Rome. In 1887, Gibbons successfully prevented the Vatican's public condemnation of Henry George's *Progress and Poverty* and of the Knights of Labor, to which many Catholics as well as other Americans belonged. Archbishop Ireland, recognizing the conflict between the American belief in secular public schools and the Catholic commitment to religious education, worked to find an accommodation. In speeches to Catholics, he defended the secular schools as indispensable in a socially and religiously diverse nation like the United States. At the same time, he also praised the public schools before Protestant groups and suggested that if religious instruction could be included in some way, the Church would have no objection to Catholics' attending state-supported schools. A few communities actually practiced a form of Ireland's educational ideas, notably Poughkeepsie, New York, and Faribault, Minnesota, but neither the majority of Protestants nor most Catholics accepted his compromise on the school question.

Ireland made no secret of his belief that Catholics and even members of the clergy should participate in all phases of American life. He was outspoken in support of the Republican party, temperance, and American democracy. Ireland was well known in Europe for his advocacy of American Catholicism as a model for liberal Catholics, particularly in the light of the Church's remarkable success in the United States.

The Gradual Achievement of Acceptance. By the close of the century, Catholic educational, philanthropic, and social organizations testified to the improved position of Catholics and their church in American society. Another measure of accommodation was the success with which the Church withstood the attacks of the American Protective Association in the 1890's. The APA was a violently nativist organization that singled out Catholics for vicious attacks, sometimes winning political success among Protestants. But the important point is that the APA captured no support among respected Americans as the Know-Nothings had easily done in the 1850's. Both of the major parties repudiated the APA's support in the election of 1896, and leading Protestants like Theodore Roosevelt and Washington Gladden publicly and vigorously defended the loyalty of American Catholics.

Slow Response to Social Needs. Catholic response to the social influence of city and factory came more slowly than Protestant adjustment, and when it did come it was less dramatic, if only because the Catholic Church in late nineteenth-century America was a poor man's church. Indeed, one Protestant minister in 1887 said, "The Catholic Church is emphatically the workingman's church. She rears her edifices in the midst of the densest population, provides them with many seats, and has the seats well filled." This close connection between working class and church can be attributed partly to the immigrant nature of the Church; as a familiar rock in a strange, sometimes hostile world, it retained the immigrants' loyalty even in the city. Furthermore, the Church has historically concerned itself with ministering to the poor and handling the problems which the Protestant churches were only beginning to confront in the cities of America. In short, the Roman Catholic Church was already meeting at least a part of the needs of the city folk, and certainly to a greater extent than the Protestant churches of the 1880's.

The first indication that the Catholic Church, too, was responding to the new demands of an industrial society came from Europe. In 1891, Pope Leo XIII issued his important social encyclical, *Rerum Novarum,* which announced the Church's position on the problems of industrial labor, trade unions, monopoly, and class warfare. Pope Leo urged employers to recognize the "dignity of labor" and to honor their "moral obligation to pay fair wages." Despite the encyclical, the twentieth century was well advanced before the American branch of the Church acted in any obvious way to adjust its practices and outlook to the changed conditions of an urban and secularized America. In 1917, Father John A. Ryan received permission to establish the *Catholic Charities Review,* a journal of social service. Then, immediately after the First World War, the four bishops constituting the leadership of the National Catholic War Council issued a Program of Social Reconstruction, signaling a new turn in Catholic concern for social issues. Since then, the Roman Catholic Church officially and to an ever increasing degree has addressed itself to the problems of society. In the 1950's and 1960's, Catholic clergymen have been unprecedentedly prominent in protests against racial discrimination in both the North and the South.

New World Judaism

The First Wave. Like the Roman Catholics, the Jews of the United States became a significant minority only with the influx of immigrants in the nineteenth century. Some Jews, like some Catholics, had come to the colonies as early as the middle of the seventeenth century, but these Spanish and Portuguese Jewish communities were tiny in both size and influence. The great Jewish immigration of the nineteenth century came in two quite different waves. The first came principally from Germany between 1830 and 1860, while the second, which began in the 1880's and continued down to the First World War, was Russian, Romanian, Lithuanian, and Polish.

Before 1880, then, American Jews were largely German in background and constituted only a small proportion of the total population. In 1860, for example, there were no more than a quarter of a million Jews in the country. Moreover, unlike the Jews of a later America, those of the years before 1880 were not concentrated in the great cities, but were rather widely, if thinly, scattered around the country. One informed estimate is that as late as 1880, Jews constituted a larger proportion of the population in the West, than they did in the Northeast. By that date, many German Jews were already prosperous and rising in social status as businessmen, professionals, and white-collar workers. The generally high economic position of the German Jews was suggested by a government survey in 1890, which reported that almost 40 per cent of them maintained at least one domestic servant.

In the history of Judaism in America, the great contribution of this first wave of German Jews was the introduction of Reform Judaism, destined to become one of the two distinctively American forms of Judaism. Reform Judaism is both a product of the Enlightenment of the eighteenth century and a reaction against Orthodox Judaism. During the Middle Ages and into modern times, traditional or Orthodox Judaism had been relegated to the intellectual backwaters and cultural ghettoes of Europe by Christian prejudice. Thus forced back upon itself for centuries, Orthodoxy had become a mass of ancient, frequently outmoded ritual and minute details of religious law; interpretation was left to the iron authority of the rabbi or scholar.

Innovation and Renewal: Reform, Orthodox, and Conservative Judaism. Judaism emerged as a modern religion only in the last years of the eighteenth century, when the French Revolution, wielding the battering ram of the Enlightenment, broke down the physical and intellectual ghettoes in western Europe that for so long had isolated Jews from the mainstream of European civilization. In the wake of this liberation, many Jews, who later came to be called Reformers, sought to reshape their tradition-encrusted religion along the lines of the religions they saw about them, particularly Christianity; that is, in the age of the Enlightenment, they wished Judaism to be rational and respectable in the eyes of the gentile community. They removed rituals whose significance was long forgotten, delivered sermons in the vernacular language so that they would be intelligible to those who knew no Hebrew, and simplified the service and the law. Because this Reform group hoped to make its religion acceptable to Jews and non-Jews alike, it also abandoned doctrines that carried significance only for the Jewish people, such as the belief in the coming of the Messiah and the expectation of a return to the homeland in Palestine. They hoped thereby to destroy the old Christian stereotype of the "wandering Jew" by showing that the Jew as a full citizen was as much attached to the land of his birth as any Christian.

Despite its European origins, Reform Judaism became identified with America; in no other country has this variety of Judaism flourished as it has in the United States. The beginnings go back to the middle of the nineteenth century when a number of German Reform rabbis migrated to America, among whom were Isaac M. Wise, David Einhorn, and Max Lilienthal. Undoubtedly the most influential was Isaac Wise, who established Cincinnati as the center of Reform Judaism. Among many accomplishments, Rabbi Wise created an American ritual for the Reform synagogues and published *The Israelite,* a newspaper of Reform Judaism.

As Reform Judaism had been the special religious contribution of the German immigration of the 1850's and 1860's, so a resurgence of Orthodoxy was the contribution of the Jews from eastern Europe. Between 1880 and 1900 about 500,000 Russian, Polish, Lithuanian, and Romanian Jews migrated to America, more than tripling the Jewish population of 1860. An even greater number arrived during the first 15 years of the twentieth century. This influx from the eastern European ghettoes transformed American Judaism, not only religiously but socially as well. Like the Catholic immigrants who were arriving at the same time, these eastern European Jews settled in the expanding industrial centers, particularly in the Northeast and Middle West, for there on the new urban "frontier" the jobs and opportunities to make a living were to be found. Judaism, like Catholicism, became a religion of the big cities.

The tension between the Reform and Orthodox approaches to Judaism soon produced a third variety—Conservative Judaism—a sort of compromise between them. Many American Jews, while unwilling to adhere to the extremely differentiating customs and rituals of the Orthodox Jews, still could not bring themselves to follow the Reformers in abandoning so many of the traditional forms. Styling themselves Conservatives to emphasize their connection with the Orthodox past, this third branch of Judaism pragmatically abandoned some but not all of the eastern European manifestations of Judaism. In 1901, the Conservatives established a firm doctrinal base with the reactivation of the Jewish Theological Seminary in New York City.

Despite the name of this third branch of American Judaism, its willingness to reshape its theology to fit the American environment was, like Reform Judaism itself, an admission that in an increasingly worldly society religion had to adjust. Moreover, like Reform, Conservative Judaism is a distinctly American movement. One historian of Judaism even refers to it, after Mormonism and Christian Science, as the third American religion of the nineteenth century.

By the end of the second decade of the twentieth century, the Jews, like the Catholics, had assumed a place of some prominence in American religious and social life. As with the Catholics, this improvement brought upon the Jews increasing social discrimination. In the early years of the nineteenth century, when the Jewish community was tiny, there was little overt anti-Semitism. But by the 1870's, as numbers increased and some Jews with newly acquired wealth sought to move into the upper social strata, they encountered social barriers. In 1877, for instance, a prominent Jewish banking family was denied accommodations at Saratoga Springs, then a fashionable summer resort. During the 1880's, the stereotype of the Jew as an unscrupulous moneylender or an international banker appeared in some popular literature and in the private writings of a few patricians like the historian Henry Adams. But there was little organized anti-Semitism, and certainly nothing comparable to the American Protective Association's organized attacks and political campaigns against Roman Catholics. Important milestones on the road to acceptance for Jews in America were the appointment in 1906 of Oscar Straus as Secretary of Commerce and Labor, the first Jewish Cabinet member, and in 1916 of Louis D. Brandeis as the first Jewish judge to sit on the Supreme Court of the United States.

A New Position for Women

If the expansion of the city and the growth of the factory enriched the American religious experience, the effect of the city upon the family and the

AMERICAN EDUCATION 1870-1900

ILLITERACY (Percentage of the population over 10 years old)

		1870	1880	1890	1900
WHITE	Native	– –	8.7	6.2	4.6
	Foreign born	– –	12.0	13.1	12.9
	*Total	11.5	9.4	7.7	6.2
NON-WHITE		79.9	70.0	56.8	44.5
	*TOTAL	20.0	17.0	13.3	10.7

SCHOOL ENROLLMENT (Percentage of the population between 5 and 19 years old)

		1870	1880	1890	1900
MALE	White	56.0	63.5	58.5	53.4
	Non-White	9.6	34.1	31.8	29.4
	*Total	49.8	59.2	54.7	50.1
FEMALE	White	52.7	60.5	57.2	53.9
	Non-White	10.0	33.5	33.9	32.8
	*Total	46.9	56.5	53.8	50.9
MALE and	White	54.4	62.0	57.9	53.6
FEMALE	Non-White	9.9	33.8	32.9	31.1
	*Total	48.4	57.8	54.3	50.5

HIGH-SCHOOL GRADUATES (Percentage of the population over 17 years old)

1870	1880	1890	1900
2.0	2.5	3.5	6.4

INSTITUTIONS OF HIGHER EDUCATION, NUMBER AND ENROLLMENT

		1870	1880	1890	1900
NUMBER	Institutions	563	811	998	977
	Pupils	52,000	116,000	157,000	238,000
ENROLLMENT	% of pop. between 18–21	1.68	2.72	3.04	4.01

INSTITUTIONS OF HIGHER EDUCATION, DEGREES CONFERRED

		1870	1880	1890	1900
B.A. or FIRST PROFESSIONAL	Male	7,993	10,411	12,857	22,173
	Female	1,378	2,485	2,682	5,237
	Total	9,371	12,896	15,539	27,410
M.A. or SECOND PROFESSIONAL		– –	879	1,015	1,583
PH.D. or EQUIVALENT		1	54	149	382
TOTAL of ALL DEGREES		9,372	13,829	16,703	29,375

*Percentage of total population

home was quite the reverse. In a city house or flat, the work of the wife and mother differed considerably from what it had been on the farm. The size of the family shrank and the physical dimensions of the home became smaller in the city. Both of these changes made women's work lighter. Moreover, certain tasks, once entirely the responsibility of women on the farm—like raising chickens and selling eggs, making clothes, churning butter, baking bread, and canning vegetables—now were often done outside the home in factories or shops. By 1850, cheap, ready-made clothing was commonplace in the bigger cities, and by the 1870's, commercial laundries and city bakeries were available to middle-class urban householders.

Out of the Home, into the Factory and Shop. The reduction in home tasks made it possible for women to work outside the home, while increasing industrialization provided the opportunities for them to do so. All over the world, wherever the factory has taken root, female labor has been indispensable to its growth. From the beginnings of the factory system in the United States in the 1830's, women have worked outside the home. The Civil War, by draining off male labor, stimulated the employment of women—usually unmarried girls—in arsenals, factories, and in the new bureaucracy spawned by the war. Once the fighting was over, many women, finding it difficult to go back to the home-centered life of old, stayed in the factories and shops. In the 1880's and 1890's, whole new fields of women's employment opened up due to the rise of big business and the widespread use of new inventions like the typewriter and the telephone.

Work outside the home changed women, too. The Victorian stereotype of the fragile, innocent, and weak young woman could not survive the sight of thousands of working women trudging through crowded streets in the early light of dawn, working ten hours a day, six days a week, and effectively countering the advances of aggressive foremen.

New opportunities for higher education broadened women's horizons in the years after the Civil War. During the first half of the century, women could gain admission to only a few colleges, like coeducational Oberlin College in Ohio or Elmira College for women, founded in New York State in 1855. The great change came in the 1860's and 1870's, with the opening of Vassar, Smith, Wellesley, and other women's colleges. The time was more than ripe, as shown by the large number of applications Vassar received when it opened in 1865 with 350 young women students. Smith College, started in 1875, was the first American college endowed by a woman, and Wellesley, founded the same year, was the first with an all-woman faculty headed by a woman president. At the same time, as more and more state universities opened their doors to qualified women (Iowa accepted women at its opening in 1856) and as the number of private, coeducational colleges increased, it

Despite the growth of secondary and higher education during this period, the number of younger school children declined. Pressures produced by massive immigration probably displaced the white children, while the decrease of appropriations for Negro education in the South caused a decline in their schools.

became clear that the long resistance to women's pursuit of higher education was over.

As the new social forces drew more and more females out of the home, women's organizations of all kinds sprang into being. Some, like the Women's Christian Temperance Union (WCTU), were composed largely of urban, married women interested in applying their new-found leisure to some constructive purpose. Under the leadership of Frances Willard in the 1880's and 1890's, the WCTU attained a membership of 500,000, making its influence felt far beyond the liquor question. It supported women's suffrage, argued for better laws for working women, and agitated for kindergartens in the public schools. The growing importance of women's organizations was recognized by the United States Congress in 1901, when it issued a national charter to the General Federation of Women's Clubs. The local women's club in many towns was often the sole civic agency working for better parks, recreational centers, and improvement of the public schools.

Working women also organized. As early as the 1870's, women weavers in Fall River, Massachusetts organized a strike without male assistance. Women delegates attended the General Assembly of the Knights of Labor held in Richmond in 1886. By 1908, almost 65,000 working women had joined over 500 trade unions. Some of the unions, moreover, were overwhelmingly female in membership, as in the garment industry, tobacco manufacturing, and laundries.

When Lord Bryce published his *American Commonwealth* in 1888, he remarked upon the wider opportunities for employment that women in the United States enjoyed as compared with European women. Yet as late as 1900, women offered little real competition to men in the job market. Women workers filled only a narrow range of occupations; almost 40 per cent of working women in 1900, for example, were in domestic service. Nevertheless, even that figure suggests a broadening and rising place for women, when one recognizes that in 1870, almost 60 per cent of working women were household servants.

In Search of Equality. The changing economic position of women lent a new impetus to the feminist movement, which had been agitating for women's equality ever since the 1840's. Women, it is true, had secured some gains in the 1850's and 1860's, particularly in legal rights respecting the property of married women and in divorce laws. But as late as 1898, some states continued to discriminate against women. In all but seven states, for example, the father possessed primary authority over children, and six states still designated the father as the head of the family, with the wife subordinate to him. In three states the double standard was law, since adultery was a ground for divorce only when the wife was the offender. Almost nowhere in the United States in 1865 could a woman legally vote for any office or on any issue.

The enfranchisement of Negroes in 1870 brought new interest to the movement for women's suffrage; but all through the nineteenth century, progress was discouragingly slow, despite the incentive provided by the Wyoming Territory in 1869, which granted complete female suffrage. During the next 40 years, after dozens of exhausting campaigns in states throughout the Union, only the three western states of Idaho, Utah, and Colorado followed Wyoming's example. A parallel movement to obtain suffrage through an amendment to the federal Constitution also failed. It would take the shock of a world war to reduce the barriers to women's participation in the political life of the nation.

Secularizing Force of Darwinism

Charles Darwin's *On the Origin of the Species by Means of Natural Selection*, published in 1859 in London, was a strictly scientific work, but its influence extended far beyond biology. Before the century was out, Darwin's *Origin of the Species* would shake traditional religion to its foundations, bolster the ideas of laissez faire, and add a new, secular dimension to thought.

Natural Selection. Although Darwin is associated with the word "evolution," the book he wrote never mentioned it. In fact, the theory of evolution—the view that ideas and institutions change through time—was not new at all; it can be traced to the ancient Greeks. Darwin's achievement was to explain how the large number of varieties or species of animals and plants had come about. Orthodox religions explained them as acts of creation by God, but by the middle of the nineteenth century, much scientific evidence suggested that the thousands of species had evolved from a much smaller number over eons of time. Though other investigators before Darwin had tried their hand at an explanation, none was really satisfactory.

The theory of natural selection, Darwin's answer to the problem, declared that the different species had developed out of the competition of organisms to gain favorable conditions of life—access to food and water, immunity from enemies, adjustment to weather, and so forth. In his biological investigations, Darwin had noticed that every organism exhibited slight physical differences from its parents and other members of the species. Aware of the intense struggle for survival in nature, Darwin concluded that any plant or animal that managed to develop differences (for whatever reason) which would serve it better in the struggle for survival would thereby secure an advantage over its competitors. These advantages would be passed on genetically to its offspring; and gradually, over many generations, the accumulated differences would constitute a new species. Thus he spoke of the origin of the species as coming about through "natural selection."

Although some biologists found weaknesses in his explanation, many more were attracted to his theory by its remarkable simplicity on the one hand, and its breadth of scope on the other. The enormous range of animal and plant species was now explicable by the single principle of natural selection. Nothing had so effectively dramatized the power of science since Isaac

Newton's similar achievement in the seventeenth century, when he demonstrated that the same force that drew a falling apple to the earth held the planets in their vast sweeping orbits around the sun.

In many respects, the world was ready for Darwin's theory, since developments in geology and biology had already prepared the way; indeed, discussion of the mechanisms of biological evolution had been carried on for a generation. Certainly, many scientists in England, on the European continent, and in America accepted natural selection almost immediately.

Scientific and Religious Resistance and Acceptance. Yet not all scientists would be persuaded then or later. Harvard's renowned zoologist, Louis Agassiz, rejected natural selection down to his death in 1873. The most outspoken opponents, however, were church leaders. Their opposition was to be expected, for by placing man in the continuum of nature, shaped by the same forces that ruled the rest of the animal kingdom, Darwinism had challenged deeply held theological convictions. What, for example, became of the religious belief that man was superior to the brute and cast in the image of God, possessed of a soul, and destined for immortality? The doctrine of natural selection even questioned the old religious argument that the complexities of living organisms and the multiplicity of species, by their very profusion and elaborate detail, were proof of the existence of God and His awesome creative powers. Now all was said to be explained simply by the process of natural selection.

The threat that Darwinism posed to traditional religious beliefs caused many Protestant clergymen to attack it vehemently. Some, like the leaders of the fundamentalist sects, continue to oppose it today. The Roman Catholic Church also objected to the application of natural selection to man, arguing that man was a special creation, blessed with a soul and therefore not a part of the evolutionary process.

Yet after varying (but short) periods of alarm or doubt, most of the Protestant denominations and Jewish congregations accepted the tenets of Darwinism. As early as 1882, Henry Ward Beecher, minister of Plymouth Church in Brooklyn, openly defended his acceptance of Darwinism with the remark, "I would just as lief have descended from a monkey as from anything if I had descended far enough." An important sign of the rapid acceptance of Darwinism in America was a series of lectures in 1893 on evolution, given by a Scottish Darwinist at the conservative and very religious Lake Chautauqua summer school.

The spectacular achievements of science in the last half of the century caused some Americans to reject conventional religion completely. Perhaps the best-known among such agnostics or freethinkers was Colonel Robert G. Ingersoll, a prominent lawyer and Old Guard Republican. In the 1870's, Ingersoll lectured widely to enthusiastic crowds on such topics as "Why I Am Not a Christian." Referring to God, he commented, "I do not deny, I do not know, but I do not believe." In place of traditional religion, he urged his listeners to accept science as their "religion" and to forsake the supernatural entirely. Secularism could receive no stronger support.

Judaism's counterpart to Protestantism's Ingersoll was Dr. Felix Adler, who founded the Society for Ethical Culture in 1876. Like Ingersoll, Adler had had a very religious upbringing. Yet he was deeply disturbed by the wide gap between the scientific knowledge of his time and the teachings of conventional religion about the world. Unlike Ingersoll, Adler did not seek to elevate science to a religion; instead he retained the ethics of the Judeo-Christian tradition while abandoning its supernatural framework. His essentially secular religion appealed largely to Jewish and Protestant intellectuals who had lost their religious faith in an age of science.

Influence of Darwinism on Social Thought and Philosophy

Throughout the history of western civilization, governments have interfered in economic activity in one fashion or another. This generalization is as true for the Middle Ages as for the Age of Mercantilism that followed. It was even true of the United States in the first half of the nineteenth century, when both state and federal governments aided in the building of canals and railroads and encouraged infant industries through the protective tariff.

The opposite, and historically recent view that government should keep its hands off the economy as much as possible—the doctrine of laissez faire —first gained widespread support only in the 1870's and 1880's. The explanation for the change is too complex to be discussed here. But certainly one cause was the realization that the burgeoning American economy no longer needed the kinds of aids and encouragement that an earlier and less-developed society demanded from government. With industry booming and production high, laissez faire could be practiced as well as preached. And preached it was, from pulpit, classroom lectern, and editorial desk.

Social Darwinism. A misreading of Darwinism provided one of the popular justifications for laissez faire. Perhaps the foremost exponent of what later came to be called "social Darwinism" was Herbert Spencer, a widely known English advocate of evolution. In fact, as an evolutionist prior to the publication of the *Origin of the Species,* Spencer had helped to create the favorable climate of opinion that accounts for the rapid acceptance of Darwin's ideas. Unlike Darwin, Spencer did not confine his evolutionary ideas to biology, but extended them to encompass all phenomena, including thought itself. It was Spencer who coined the phrase, "the survival of the fittest," which crops up so often in the writings of social Darwinists, and which Darwin himself accepted as an apt summary of the theory of natural selection. Simply put, Spencer's social Darwinism justified the industrial millionaires and other social leaders of the time as products of natural selection. To criticize them or to seek to limit them was to contradict a law of nature, a position that was almost sinful after the acceptance of Darwin's argument.

SELECTED TRAVEL TIME AND COST 1870

Travel was preponderantly
from east to west

SELECTED TRAVEL TIME AND COST 1900

┼─┼	Railroad
▬	Wagon Trails
-----	Steamboat

PREPARED BY
UNIVERSAL MAP, INC.

Needless to say, social Darwinism was not a part of Charles Darwin's original theory of natural selection, which was intended to apply only to the field of biological evolution.

In the United States, the foremost exponent of social Darwinism was a Yale professor of sociology and economics, William Graham Sumner. Like Spencer, Sumner appealed to Darwinian biological theory to justify his belief in laissez faire, which, he repeatedly said, would permit the best to prosper and let the incompetent fall by the wayside. As an uncompromising individualist, Sumner opposed all the reform measures of his day, from free silver to the Interstate Commerce Act. He defended the leaders of big business as the natural result of a beneficent social evolution and therefore privileged to be unfettered by any government or social control. "The men who are competent to organize great enterprises and to handle great amounts of capital," he wrote, "must be found by natural selection, not by political election. . . ."

Although Sumner used social Darwinism to protect the status quo from change by the reformers, he was also tough minded and consistent enough to assail those businessmen who demanded government favors for themselves while denying them to the poor. He opposed the protective tariff as vehemently as the income tax. Moreover, unlike more smug proponents of social Darwinism, Sumner did not ignore the poverty, want, and misery that industrialism seemed to leave in its train. Such evils, he admitted, constituted the price modern society paid for its gains; forthrightly, if cold-bloodedly, he acknowledged that he, for one, was willing to pay the price.

Although probably very few businessmen read Darwin or Spencer, they sometimes managed to defend their practices in the language of both. For instance, when a member of a Congressional investigating committee asked a businessman what might be done to raise wages above 75 cents a day, the witness answered: "I don't think anything could be done. . . . The law of the 'survival of the fittest' governs that." Andrew Carnegie, the steel magnate who had risen to eminence despite his early poverty and foreign birth, also justified the status quo in the language of social Darwinism. Although the law of unrestrained competition, he admitted, "may be sometimes hard on the individual, it is best for the race, because it ensures the survival of the fittest in every department."

But William Graham Sumner's remorseless application to society of the principle of social Darwinism found few supporters even within the business community. The principal reason was that in a democratic society where ordinary citizens could influence the government through their votes, prim appeals to the self-reliant doctrine of social Darwinism were not sufficient. Andrew Carnegie, for one, recognized that something more was needed if government interference in the economy were to be avoided and large for-

Comparison of available figures shows that passenger travel time and cost decreased between 1870 and 1900, especially over routes previously without railroad transportation. Nevertheless, voyages to and from Europe continued to be less costly than travel across the United States.

tunes were to be protected from an income tax. Thus, in his essay, "Wealth" (or as it came to be called, the "Gospel of Wealth"), published in 1889, he moved away from a strict application of social Darwinism, suggesting instead that the great fortunes accumulated by individuals were actually being held in trust for society. The impartial law of competition may have put such aggregations of wealth in the hands of a few highly competent men, he conceded, but ultimately, such accumulations of money would be expended for the benefit of those not so talented or fortunate. Carnegie, along with other new millionaires of the Economic Revolution, spent millions of dollars on a variety of philanthropic enterprises, all of which, by their very assistance to the allegedly unfit, repudiated in practice the tenets of social Darwinism while serving to refurbish in part the tarnished image of the renowned robber barons.

Still Another Interpretation. Some social reformers made a use of Darwinism that was quite the opposite of the social Darwinism of Spencer and Sumner. Prince Peter Kropotkin of Russia, for instance, wrote a series of articles in the 1880's, later published as *Mutual Aid,* in which he brought together a wealth of zoological evidence to show that even in nature, ruthless competition was not the sole law. The cooperative behavior of the social insects and herd animals proved, he contended, that cooperation among human beings in society was at least as "natural" as competition. In the United States, Lester Frank Ward, often called the founder of American sociology, asserted in a number of books and popular articles that competition may be the rule in nature, but that cultivation, careful breeding, and "unnatural" surroundings produce much finer quality than uncontrolled competition. Ward's writings received very little attention in the 1880's and 1890's, but in the twentieth century, his influence on sociology was great.

Pragmatism: A Darwinian Philosophy. Darwinism, along with science in general, profoundly affected philosophical speculation in the United States. By demonstrating that apparently stable and fixed units like the natural species were actually mutable and that the world itself was continuously changing, Darwinism overturned one of man's basic suppositions about the nature of the universe. Whereas before, stability was considered the ideal state of things, now change was taken as typical of nature and hence to be equated with the good. Indeed, by showing that change was the order of the universe, Darwinism offered a new and powerful support for social reform. But if everything in the world was in a state of flux, the old search for final truth became fruitless. How could there be final truth in an evolutionary world?

When Darwinism is analyzed in this way, it is evident that the social Darwinists were not philosophical Darwinists at all. True, they talked incessantly of survival of the fittest and of the virtues of competition, but these conceptions were not peculiar to Darwinism; in fact, they were the time-worn shibboleths of classical economics and laissez faire. Moreover, insofar as the social Darwinists were defenders of the social status quo, they could hardly qualify as Darwinians in the fundamental philosophical sense of incessant change. Their use of Darwinist slogans merely reflected the impact of Darwin's ideas, not a real acceptance of them. At the end of the nineteenth century, it was fashionable to use Darwinian phraseology, even if the thrust of Darwinian ideas was completely ignored.

Some men did recognize the philosophical implications of evolutionary thought, and their development of the philosophy of pragmatism proved to be the most important American contribution to formal philosophy. Pragmatism is both a measure of the great success of contemporary science and a sign of the rejection of a theistic basis for life. In method it followed the natural sciences, emphasizing precision, clarity of thought, and reliance on the senses. It is no accident that the two men to whom pragmatism owes its formulation and popularity, Charles S. Peirce and William James, were both practicing scientists themselves. The secularism of pragmatism was equally obvious. Pragmatists paid little or no attention to the traditional concerns of religion or even of metaphysics; God, revelation, and the nature of being were beyond the senses and therefore beyond their interest. Pragmatism was the philosophy of men who believed in results, tangible objects, and this world.

Philosophically, what is pragmatism? The best-known popularizer of it, William James, defined it as "first a method; and second, a genetic theory of what is meant by truth." It was as a method that pragmatism was first presented in 1878 by Charles Peirce in a now celebrated essay, "How to Make Our Ideas Clear." Peirce was brought to formulate his new philosophy by his impatience with the vagueness, inconclusiveness, and unverifiability of such traditional philosophical abstractions as God, Truth, Beauty, and Good. Impressed by the great successes of the natural sciences, which tested truth by experimentation and measurement, he sought to apply similar tests to ideas.

The meaning of an idea, Peirce argued, was ascertainable only from its effects. "Our idea of anything," he wrote, "is our idea of its sensible effects; and if we fancy that we have any other we deceive ourselves, and mistake a mere sensation accompanying the thought for a part of the thought itself." Thus, if the same consequences, i.e., sensible effects, follow from two ideas, then there are no differences between the ideas, regardless of how different the two ideas may appear. Furthermore, as William James pointed out, if any abstract concept, no matter how remote from everyday life, "can be shown to have consequences for our life, it has meaning." Thus if a belief in God has practical consequences — if a person goes about his daily tasks taking that belief into consideration — then God is a meaningful concept for him, though not necessarily for others. In general, however, pragmatism was secular in its outlook; it gave scant support to religion, God, or the intricacies of theology.

Truth for the pragmatists lay in its usefulness, in its ability to work when tested. "Pragmatism," said Peirce, is "only an application of the sole principle of logic recommended by Jesus: 'Ye may know them by their fruits.'" If an idea "works, it will have some truth that ought to be held to," James advised. "True ideas are those that we can assimilate, validate, corroborate, and verify.

False ideas are those that we cannot." This distinction, of course, is the same as that made in the natural sciences. Pragmatists, as these remarks make clear, conceived of truth as relative, not absolute. As James phrased it, "Truth is *made,* much as health, wealth, and strength are made, in the course of experience." For the pragmatists there was no such concept as Truth; there were only truths.

As the son of a famous theologian and the brother of a great novelist, William James may appear to have had little in common with the new, often ruthless, and in some cases unlearned business leaders who gave the Gilded Age its name. Yet his life and thought were quite attuned to the robust era of the Economic Revolution. A vigorous personality who viewed the universe as unfinished and growing, James thrived on challenge and risk; he gloried in the knowledge that pragmatism demanded "toughness of mind." He was speaking for pragmatism as a philosophy as well as for himself when he said that in life "I am willing that there should be real losses and real losers, and no total preservations for all that is." An anxious quest for security and a love of quiet contemplation were no more among James' attributes than among John D. Rockefeller's or Jay Gould's. James heaped scorn upon Asian philosophies that preached the contemplative life. "The hindoo and buddhist, for this is essentially their attitude, are simply afraid—afraid of more experience, afraid of life," he contended. In another context James would refer to the "bitch goddess Success," but in pragmatism he advocated a philosophy eminently at home in the earthy, secular age of the "Great Barbecue" (as historian Vernon Parrington described the post-Civil War boom years), when what worked was often judged to be thereby good and true.

The Secularization of Culture: Realism in Literature, Art, and Architecture

In an age of Darwinism, democracy, and pragmatism, one would expect literature and art to be increasingly concerned with reality, with seeing life honestly. Probably the most profound single impact upon the contemporary literature came from Darwin's demonstration that hitherto hidden forces were the truly operative ones. Indeed, the whole history of science since the seventeenth century was studded with crucial experiments that had shown appearances to be untrustworthy when not actually wrong. Darwin's inclusion of man in the spectrum of nature and his ingenious accounting for the origin of species were only the most recent examples. This success of Darwin in uncovering the true and constant sources of change in nature encouraged some writers to seek a similar realism in their various artistic portrayals of men and society.

Realism had not always been the office of literature in America. For the popular writer the purpose had been to entertain the reader, while for the serious writer it had usually meant idealizing the past and extracting from experience lessons for the present. The principal test of cultivated writing during most of the previous century had been the ability to express in pleasing language and elevated tone the beauties of nature and the pleasures of society. Before 1870, the romance was the typical form of the novel; by the end of the century, the novel had been transformed into a mirror of the world and an instrument of social protest. The general causes of the metamorphosis were rooted in the triumphs of science and the Economic Revolution; the specific cause was a remarkable group of writers. Out of the interaction of the two issued modern American literature.

William Dean Howells: Democracy of Facts. William Dean Howells was not the first writer to champion realism in literature, but in the last half of the nineteenth century he was undoubtedly the most influential. As editor of the highly esteemed *Atlantic Monthly* between 1871 and 1881 and *Harper's Monthly* in the 1890's, Howells was in a strategic position to encourage those young writers who brought a new realism into their work. A critic's test of a novel, Howells once wrote, was to ask if it "was true to the motives, the impulses, the principles that shape the life of actual men and women." At another time, he articulated a central tenet of realism, the importance of detail and accuracy. The realistic writer, he said, "feels in every nerve the equality of things and the unity of men." To him nothing was "insignificant," and "nothing that God has made is contemptible." In such statements can be read the influence of the great contemporary European realists, Honoré de Balzac, Emile Zola, and Ivan Turgenev, from whom Howells and other American realists drew their principles. The democracy of facts that Howells advocated also neatly reflected science's own reverence for the relevant fact, no matter how humble or minute.

It would be a mistake, however, to take Howells' definition of realism literally. His own novels, for example, hardly seem realistic in our post-Freudian age; his counsel of realism did not extend to the bedroom or the bathroom. Yet the gate he pushed ajar would eventually swing wide. In 1920, the year Howells died, Sinclair Lewis' realistic novel, *Main Street*, was to head the best seller list. This coincidence marked a fitting close to the life of the man who, more than any other, had prepared the way for the popular acceptance of Lewis' novel.

Howells' most successful novel, as well as his best, is *The Rise of Silas Lapham* (1885). More than any other novel of the age, it illustrates the thought and outlook of its time. Unlike Edward Bellamy's *Looking Backward, or 2000–1887*, it is first-rate literature, and unlike *The Adventures of Huckleberry Finn*, it deals with contemporary society in an urban setting. *The Rise of Silas Lapham* is truly a social novel in that it depicts the life of a newly rich and uneducated manufacturer who is trying to make his way up the social ladder. Yet the book does not resort to muckraking, for Silas Lapham is a likable and, in some ways, even an admirable person. He is honest, if uncultivated, and in Howells' mind, it is clear, the hard work that brought Lapham

(Continued on page 196)

The photograph of garment workers in a sweat shop illustrates again that, while machines had been developed to aid men with some types of work, much tedious and time-consuming labor still had to be done by hand. In order to subsist, the majority of Americans toiled long hours for small wages, with few holidays and no fringe benefits. It is thus all the more remarkable that so many leisure-time activities were pursued. Lacking any form of mass entertainment, people eagerly created their own amusements, or participated in revival meetings and Chautauqua-type lecture groups. This sort of activity provided opportunities for entertainment, for meeting people, and for enlightenment on varied topics. The theater, despite puritanical tendencies and simple-minded fare, was immensely popular. In 1885 there were an estimated 5000 theaters scattered through 3500 American towns.

Sweatshop in a Ludlow Street tenement, ca. 1889. *Photograph by Jacob Riis. Library of Congress*

Women, becoming aware of their importance in the job market, and starting to acquire authority outside the home, began to agitate for equal status with men in all spheres. Female suffrage was first granted in the Wyoming territory in 1869, but not until 1920 was it extended nationally. Equality of men and women, it was feared (usually by men), would lead to an "Age of Brass" in which men would be dominated by women who had abandoned traditional duties and moral codes for lasciviousness and irresponsibility.

The American people, though the majority owned a copy of Shakespeare and the Bible, did most of their reading in newspapers and popular magazines such as *Godey's Lady's Book,* and *Puck.* Despite the lack of public interest and understanding, however, a few artists, using the idiom of the people, broke ground for the future. Henry James, like Mark Twain, attempted to convey speech as it was spoken and heard. Unlike Twain, who dealt with more concrete realities, James portrayed an internal world of thoughts and reactions.

An anti-feminist cartoon of the period. *Photo: Library of Congress*

THE AGE OF BRASS.

A camp meeting in Minnesota, 1875.

In order to convince the reader of the reality of his characters' emotions, James emphasized aspects of colloquial speech. For example, he stressed certain words through the use of dashes to indicate pauses, and through the use of repetition to accent and unify. This resulted in a naturalistic style, which, along with Twain's, influenced later writers.

Similarly, the two greatest American artists of the period, Thomas Eakins and Winslow Homer, were primarily concerned with realities, whether internal or

Henry James. *Photo: Culver Pictures. Below:* "D. Hayes Agnew, M.D." by Thomas Eakins. *Photo: University of Pennsylvania*

The Elite Theatre, Rands-
burg, California, ca. 1900.
*Photo: Title Insurance &
Trust Company Historical
Collection.*
Below: "The Herring Net"
by Winslow Homer.
*Photo: The Art
Institute of Chicago,
Mr. & Mrs. M. A. Ryerson
Collection*

external. Both men rejected the puerility and sentimentality which pervaded
most contemporary painting, and substituted for it a clear, direct vision of the
world as it is. Neither artist was accepted by the public of the day. Pretty pictures, such as John Singer Sargent's, reflecting prevailing sensibilities, were all
society wanted, and high society provided the only commercial outlet for paintings, since museums were virtually nonexistent and most people had little
interest and less money for art. Ignoring prevailing trends, Eakins painted
doctors with blood on their hands, patients whose naked flesh we can see being
pierced by the scalpel; while Homer exposed the primordial relationship of
man to nature. The result, in each case, was a rendering of the pain and pleasure
which life affords, in terms which remain meaningful and alive. *End*

his millions is preferable to the dilettantish indolence of the aristocratic Corey family, which represents the "old order" that Lapham and his kind were displacing.

The Minister's Charge (1887) and *A Hazard of New Fortunes* (1890) similarly exhibit Howells' social realism. Both novels portray the poor accurately and sympathetically, without being sentimental. *The Minister's Charge*, in emphasizing the responsibility of the individual for the welfare and future of society, foreshadowed Howells' later, more explicit call for reform in *A Traveler from Altruria* (1894). In that utopian novel, Howells sharply contrasted the individualistic, capitalistic society of his own America with the rational, tranquil, cooperative society of the mythical land of Altruria.

By the time Howells wrote *A Hazard of New Fortunes* and *A Traveler from Altruria*, he had been strongly influenced by his reading of Laurence Gronlund's *Cooperative Commonwealth*, a popular exposition of socialism, published in 1884. From then on, Howells' thought turned permanently in the direction of non-Marxian socialism. He was never a radical nor even a social reformer in any active sense; yet his commitment to literary realism would not let him overlook the visible paradox of progress and poverty. Despite his own considerable stake in the status quo, for example, he vigorously condemned the unfair treatment of the eight anarchists charged with the Haymarket bombing.

Henry James: Portrayer of the Sensitive Protagonist. Howells was only one of three giants of American letters in these years; the other two were Mark Twain (Samuel Langhorne Clemens), and Henry James, the brother of William James, the philosopher of pragmatism. All three authors are properly described as realists, but aside from their literary commitment, they had little in common. As men and as writers they were far apart. For instance, both Howells and Twain by the 1890's had lost much of their earlier enthusiasm for American society, but their disenchantment never caused them to abandon their native soil. James, on the other hand, found his most congenial abode in England, where he lived almost continuously after 1876. Yet the impress of his American origins remained on his work, providing one of his principal literary themes. His novels, *The American* (1877) and *The Portrait of a Lady* (1881), contrast the innocence of young America with the sophistication of old Europe. Though James clothed his realism in the form of a novel of manners, his interest clearly lay in uncovering the inner emotions and drives of his sensitive characters as they found society changing about them. Unlike Howells, he had no wish to depict social change or the lot of the poor.

Only two of James' numerous novels can be taken as an expression of his realization of social problems. *The Bostonians* (1886) was James' pronouncement on the women's movement, though he concentrated on the individuals involved, not on the reform, in which he had little interest and for which he displayed scant sympathy. Yet his realism can be seen here, too, though it is hedged, as always, with circumlocutions and indirect statement. The relationship between the two principal women characters is fraught with homosexual implications, which vaguely disturbed his conventional readers, temporarily clouding his popularity. The other novel in which he seriously touched upon a social issue was *Princess Casamassima* (1886). The social theme in the book is anarchism, then a sensational form of radical social protest in both Europe and the United States. Once again, however, James was neither sympathetic to the reform he depicted nor interested in it as such. His purpose was to probe the feelings and attitudes of his characters.

Mark Twain: Against the Genteel Tradition. Probably the greatest of the three American realists of the age was Mark Twain. Unlike Howells and James, Twain fits the popular stereotype of a realistic writer. He came from a rough-and-tumble background in rural Missouri and the mining camps of the Far West. Moreover, his successes had come as a humorous writer who deflated literary pomposities and poked fun at gentility. The greatness of Twain, however, does not lie in his western or frontier humor, but in his perceptive portrayal of human conflict and morality in *The Adventures of Huckleberry Finn* (1884), which is one of the leading works of world literature. Ostensibly the story of a boy's adventurous trip on a raft floating down the Mississippi, the book is actually a probing examination of the morality of slavery, the relation of the individual to society, and the obligations and nature of platonic love.

For our purposes, however, the importance of *Huckleberry Finn* rests in its realism, in its sharp break with the genteel tradition which had smothered both popular and serious writing in sticky conventions and ideality. The language as well as the substance of Twain's novel is realistic. Profound moral issues are clothed in everyday circumstances and settings, while the words are the uncultured, but often poetic talk of the poorly educated Huck and his slave companion, Jim. One of Twain's stock devices in his humorous writings was to mock the pompous, idealized language of the literary world of his time. Huck Finn is admirably suited to carry on this quest for reality through the ridicule of artificiality. In Huck, as Henry Nash Smith has pointed out, Twain created a figure who is freer from convention and tradition than his earlier Tom Sawyer. For despite Tom's reputation for mischief, he in fact accepts the conventions of his society as Huck does not. He stays home, he goes to school, and in the end he does mind Aunt Polly. With Huck, who deeply rebels against civility, Twain fashioned a sharper instrument for exposing moral weakness and dishonesty. Its keen edge is apparent in Twain's satirizing of the social mores of the river towns Huck and Jim visit as they drift down the Mississippi on their raft.

Besides illustrating the realism of an age of science, *Huckleberry Finn* also exhibits the influence of democracy. The deepest of moral issues is argued in the humble tongue of a runaway school boy and an escaped slave. Twain quite frankly admitted that he wrote for the common man and not for the "cultivated classes." And it was the ordinary citizen who provided an audience for his humor. Proud of his own modest origins, Twain believed fervently in the virtue and potential of the common American.

Although the influence of American democratic ideals upon Twain reveals itself in his greatest work, it is even more evident in *A Connecticut Yankee in King Arthur's Court* (1889). In fact, the book was intended to show how the improvements of technology, which much impressed Twain, had encouraged the moral improvement of man. Its plot ingeniously depicts the adventures and successes of a self-taught American miraculously transported back to early medieval England. Once there, the main character, Hank Morgan, demonstrates the superiority of American democracy and industrial society over feudalism, superstition, and an established church. The book was a paean to the practical, common-sense approach to life that Twain thought he discerned in the ordinary American. Unaffected, simple men were his ideal; he scorned the manners and affectations of the intellect as heartily as Commodore Vanderbilt did. When Howells read *A Connecticut Yankee*, he called it "an object lesson in democracy" and drew a parallel between the barons of medieval England, who overworked their serfs, and the industrial "capitalist of Mr. Harrison's day who grows rich on the labor of his underpaid wage men." Radical and reform groups also seized upon Twain's novel as a support for their opposition to big business.

Although Twain had been born and raised in a slave state, his quest for reality and honesty twice led him to a critical examination of racism. The first time was in *Huckleberry Finn;* the second was in the novel *Pudd'nhead Wilson* (1894). His second effort was less powerful and profound than the first. In *Pudd'nhead Wilson,* for example, he resorted to the time-worn literary contrivance of mistaken identity, in which two babies from different families are switched at birth. Even so, he effectively exposed the inadequacies in the racist assertion of Negro inferiority. The novel is not only an example of realistic writing, particularly in its portrayal of the Negro woman, Roxy, but also of Darwinian environmentalism. It contains Twain's retort to the racists that environment, not race or heredity, was the principal determinant of personality.

George Washington Cable: Mirror to the South. The realism of Twain, Howells, and James can also be seen in the work of a lesser figure, George Washington Cable of Louisiana. Like Twain, Cable exhibited his realism on the double levels of language and content. His painstaking, faithful reproduction of the speech of Negroes and French Creoles in New Orleans in *Old Creole Days* (1879) and *The Grandissimes* (1884) anticipated Twain's use of ordinary rural speech in *Huckleberry Finn*. His realistic content deals with the complicated, biracial society of New Orleans. In *The Grandissimes,* his finest novel, Cable frankly portrayed the enmity between the new American rulers of recently acquired Louisiana and the proud French Creoles of New Orleans. He probed the moral issues of slavery and miscegenation which had helped to shape Creole society and values. In fact, Cable's realism cut so deeply that New Orleans society soon snubbed him, despite the fact that this was the first time the fascinating life of Louisiana's Creoles had been brought to the attention of the nation.

His honesty and passion for social justice took Cable, a Southerner, into territory no other realistic writer of his time had entered. In his two collections of essays of social criticism, *The Silent South* (1885) and *The Negro Question* (1890), Cable patiently, thoroughly, and devastatingly exposed the injustice of racial segregation in the South, pleading with his fellow white Southerners to grant the Negro full equality before the law. (He never advocated social equality, though he practiced it.) His text was the national creed of equality and his goal the regeneration of the South. Despite the undeniable cogency of his arguments, his influence in the South shrank with the publication of each essay. Indeed, because of his frigid reception in the South, he moved to Massachusetts in 1885.

Stephen Crane: Beyond Realism to Naturalism. For all Cable's courage in daring to probe the race question, his literary realism was of the Howells variety—applied only within the conventional boundaries. The first to cross these limits was Stephen Crane. Indeed, literary historians speak of him more often as a naturalistic (rather than realistic) writer precisely because he went beyond realism. Realists like Howells, Twain, and Cable believed in accurate, honest reporting of the world, but only of an acceptable world; for them, certain aspects of life were simply outside a writer's legitimate concern and unsuited to appear in a book. The naturalistic writers, however, placed no such limitations on their conception of the writer's world; for them it included everything—vice as well as virtue, misery as well as happiness, poverty as well as affluence. The connection between the naturalistic writers and Darwinism is apparent. Both saw nature or the environment as harsh and amoral, and man a product of its forces; both shared a deterministic concept of the universe, in which they included man. In the world of nature there was no free will. Inexorable forces seemed to shape all individuals (and things), whether they were mountains, giant redwood trees, or men. Naturalistic writers viewed society along with nature as one of the powerful forces that determined the fate of individuals.

Stephen Crane's novella—*Maggie, A Girl of the Streets* (1893)—focuses on the then forbidden subject of prostitution, not in the usual moralistic fashion of individual responsibility and personal failure, but in the new and shocking language of social responsibility. Maggie's fall from virtue to prostitution and her tragic suicide are clearly the consequences of forces beyond her control. Since without control there is no responsibility, she could not be the author of her degradation, as many moralists insisted. When first published, *Maggie* was buried in shocked silence, only to be widely reprinted in 1896 after the success of Crane's second novel. At that date, one literary historian remarked, "modern American fiction was born." Significantly, by the end of the nineties, the environmentalist view of prostitution that Crane's

Maggie advanced was the accepted assumption in the several municipal investigations of "The Social Evil."

Crane's second novel, *The Red Badge of Courage* (1895), is not as sensational as *Maggie*, but it is equally realistic, while its prose is more economical and direct. Like *Maggie*, *The Red Badge of Courage* concerns a young person confronted by fear. In this case a young Civil War soldier is faced for the first time with the threat of death in battle. There is no sentimental glorification of war, only a stripped, taut depiction of its pressures and the anatomy of the human fear that paralyzes reason and controls the will. By its frank assertion of the inadequacy of individual will in the face of overwhelming circumstances and environment, the novel travels far beyond Howells' realism. Later, in the twentieth century, the naturalism of Crane would come to dominate American fiction in the work of Frank Norris, Theodore Dreiser, Jack London, and Upton Sinclair.

New Architecture: Skyscrapers Evolve. The drive to see life whole, without illusions or obscuring decoration, was as evident in architecture as it was in the philosophy of pragmatism or the literature of Howells, Twain, and Crane. In addition, architectural developments responded to the new social and technological changes of the 1880's and 1890's.

The tall building provides an excellent example of how an emerging, realistic philosophy of design and social and technological innovations combined to produce a new architecture. In the crowded cities of the 1880's, where urban land was increasingly precious, the tall building offered a solution. It would cut costs by using less land, yet provide additional housing and office space. The two technological innovations of the elevator and the structural steel frame made a building of more than five or six stories practical for the first time. The elevator alone was not sufficient. By introducing an elevator, for instance, architect Richard Morris Hunt was able to construct the ten-story New York Tribune Building in 1874, but such height required massive walls, which consumed precious space. In fact, the 16-story Monadnock Building, constructed in Chicago in 1891, necessitated walls 15 feet thick at its base to sustain the weight of its floors. It was only after 1884, when William LeBaron Jenney boldly introduced a steel frame into the construction of the Home Insurance Building in Chicago, that structures of ten or more stories became practical. Thereafter, architects were able to erect tall buildings with walls as thin as their aesthetics demanded and with much consequent saving of interior space.

The man who fashioned a distinct style of architecture out of the new technology and the needs of urban life was Louis H. Sullivan of Chicago. By using the steel-frame construction to great advantage in the Wainwright Building in St. Louis in 1891, Sullivan set the style for skyscrapers in the United States for the next half-century or more. The Wainwright Building is only ten stories high, but its design embodies Sullivan's forthrightness and artistic integrity. He refused to apologize for the building's height, as the standard architectural design of the time demanded. The practice had been to interrupt or obscure the long, upward-flowing lines of the tall building with embellishments or different window designs on successive floors. Sullivan broke decisively with this convention, asserting that the building's height was to be emphasized, rather than disguised. Since, in fact, it was tall, why try to make it appear to be anything else? Here and in his other architectural designs, Sullivan's governing principle was that the form of a building ought to be an honest statement of function. Form should not obscure or mislead. With Sullivan, sham, sentimentality, and romanticizing came under attack in architecture just as it was being routed in philosophy and literature.

Sullivan's passionate commitment to the wedding of form and function and to honesty of statement was carried on in the work of his student and disciple, Frank Lloyd Wright, perhaps the best-known American architect of the early 1900's. The realism and candor which Sullivan insisted upon became a central principle of architectural design in the twentieth century.

The Art of Homer and Eakins. Painting, even more than architecture, lent itself to realism. In America, Winslow Homer and Thomas Eakins were the leading exponents of a contemporary European movement that rejected the then dominant idealization in art.

Long before he became known as a painter of seascapes, Winslow Homer scorned traditional art and its falsification of feeling. "If a man wants to be an artist," he once remarked, "he should never look at pictures." The only model was the real world of nature. As an illustrator for popular magazines during the Civil War, Homer sketched army life with a fidelity that was not equalled in literature until Stephen Crane's *Red Badge of Courage.* Homer's best-known works then and now are those canvases which catch the moods of the sea. Men are often included in his pictures, but even if they fill half the canvas they are subordinated to a powerful and overwhelming sea, much as the characters in the novels of naturalistic writers are dominated by social and natural forces. Probably no artist in America or Europe has equalled Homer's skill in capturing the ocean, especially in its darker moods. Unlike the contemporary European impressionist painters, who were fascinated by bright sunlight playing on water or clouds or flesh, Homer chose to fill his canvases with somber clouds, threatening skies, and dark water, as evidenced in such well-known oils of his as "Fog Warning" (1885), "Winter Coast" (1890), and "The Gulf Stream" (1899).

Like the philosopher-pragmatists Charles Peirce and William James, Thomas Eakins maintained a healthy disdain for tradition. He painted what seemed real and meaningful in his own time and place. Eakins, one art historian has written, "was the first American artist—as distinct from craftsman or folk-artist—to make his painting out of what was there instead of relying on tradition." Much in the manner of Mark Twain, Eakins was offended by the devices and conventions of the contemporary art. He considered the artists of his time false and dishonest. His vehemence in denouncing them reminds one of Twain at his most explosive. In a letter to a friend, Eakins offered his frank opinion of the work of the seventeenth-century Dutch artist, Peter Paul Rubens, and at the same time expressed a clear statement of his own commitment to honesty of expression and fidelity to fact: "[Rubens'] modelling is always crooked and dropsical," he wrote, "and no marking is ever in the right place or anything like what he sees in nature . . . everything must be making a big noise and tumbling about, there must be monsters, too, for his men are not monstrous enough for him. His pictures put me in mind of chamber pots and I would not be sorry if they were all burnt." Even to the closing vulgarity, he sounds like the earthy Twain.

For his part, Eakins meticulously recorded on his canvas only what he saw. His many years of anatomical study at the Jefferson Medical School in Philadelphia help to account for his several paintings of medical clinics in operation. As a result of his studies, he commanded a knowledge of the structure and mechanics of the human body that few artists of his time could equal. Demanding from his students the same detailed knowledge, he urged them to "get to the character of things." The unflinching realism of his portraits and the long sittings he required of his subjects sometimes cost him clients who wanted prettier pictures and easier sittings. Even the physicians in his paintings of clinics complained of his realism, which required that they be portrayed with blood on their hands. Eakins' relentless pursuit of reality was carried through with fanatic zeal, sometimes in the face of a less committed society. In 1886, he lost his teaching post at the Philadelphia Academy of Art because of the public outcry at his stripping the loincloth from a male model to better illustrate musculature to his class of women students.

Although there is no idealization in his work, Eakins was never a slavish copier, either of other men's work or of nature's. As he said, the capstone of any work is the intuition and sensitivity that transforms a meticulously detailed reproduction of life into a work of art. His portraits, for which he was well known in his own time, reveal not only his attention to realistic detail, but also his ability to catch the emotion and inimitable character of the subject. In "William Rush Carving the Allegorical Figure of the Schuylkill River" (1877), the central figure of the young model reveals both Eakins' painstaking realism and his ability to go beyond detail to the artistic depiction of feeling. He always attempted to capture the essence of things, to penetrate appearances, just as Twain and Howells, Peirce and William James, and Bellamy and George tried to do.

Eakins recognized that even the most carefully detailed painting was different from a photograph; yet he found the new techniques of photography of great importance in his studies of motion in human beings and animals. Indeed, some of his technical innovations in photographing moving objects in the middle 1880's anticipated the later motion-picture camera. Eakins brought to his art a precision, a dedication to accurate detail, and an impersonality that clearly reflected the scientific bias of the age in which he worked. He even advocated the use of mathematics in art because of its precision and accuracy. His use of new technical advances to enrich his art, such as his experiments with photography, is reminiscent of Jenney and Sullivan, who also incorporated the new technology into their pathbreaking architectural design for the tall building.

Perhaps more than any other artist, with the possible exception of Mark Twain, Thomas Eakins summed up the spirit of the age in his work, his habits, and his outlook. Like Twain he was fascinated by tools, contrivances, and scientific machinery. He worshipped the here and the now, the practical, and the forthright; he could only ridicule idealities. His art was tough and earthy, much the same as William James' philosophy. Not many of the rising businessmen and tycoons of the age liked his frank paintings, but in their own practices in business and in their outlooks on life they were as frank, outspoken, and brutal as he was. They simply were not used to seeing their own values mirrored in art. An Eakins, a Twain, or a William James was really not far removed from a Carnegie or a Rockefeller in fundamental values. The realism of science, the materialism of an industrial society, and the social democracy of a mobile society influenced them all. By the end of the century, then, ministers and artists, tycoons and reformers were all primarily concerned with the world, either as it was or as it should be. But in either case the outlook was now secular.

SUGGESTED READING

A suitable starting point for the literature on religion is the four-volume work *Religion in American Life,* ed. by James Ward and A. Leland Jamison (1961), which includes, in addition to excellent summary articles, a two-volume bibliography. The two standard works on the Social Gospel are Charles H. Hopkins, *Rise of the Social Gospel in American Protestantism, 1865–1915* (1940), and the broader and more readable Henry F. May, *Protestant Churches and Industrial America* (1949). Herbert A. Wisbey, *Soldiers Without Swords* (1955), interestingly and authoritatively treats the Salvation Army. The story of revivalism is told with verve in Bernard A. Weisberger, *They Gathered at the River* (1958), and in the more scholarly William McLoughlin, *Modern Revivalism* (1959). Critical of the founder of Christian Science is Edwin F. Dakin, *Mrs. Eddy, the Biography of a Virginal Mind** (1929). Friendly without being sentimental is the philosophical study by Robert Peel, *Christian Science: Its Encounter with American Culture** (1958). Norman Beasley, *The Cross and the Crown: the History of Christian Science* (1952) is too uncritical to be considered good.

No excellent general history of Catholicism in this country exists, though John Tracy Ellis, *American Catholicism** (1956), is adequate. A first-rate historical work is the important Thomas T. McAvoy, *The Great Crisis in American Catholic History,*

*Available in a paperback edition.

1895–1900 (1957). Robert D. Cross, *The Emergence of Liberal Catholicism in America* (1958) does justice to the variety of views within the Church. Less well-written or convincing is Aaron I. Abell, *American Catholicism and Social Action: A Search for Social Justice, 1865–1950** (1960).

The best introduction to Judaism is Nathan Glazer, *American Judaism** (1957). Marshall Sklare, *Conservative Judaism: An American Religious Movement* (1955), is informative. On Reform Judaism in the United States the easiest introduction is Israel Knox, *Rabbi in America: the Story of Isaac M. Wise* (1957). David Philipson, *The Reform Movement of Judaism* (1907), places the movement in its European background. Concerning hostility to Jews, an important article is John Higham, "Anti-Semitism in the Gilded Age: A Reinterpretation," *Mississippi Valley Historical Review,* XLIII (March, 1957), 559–578.

The best general study of the women's movement is Eleanor Flexner, *Century of Struggle; the Women's Rights Movement in the United States* (1959). Helpful on the occupational side of the movement is Robert W. Smuts, *Women and Work in America* (1959). A valuable source on the same topic is Dorothy Richardson, *The Long Day: The True Story of a New York Working Girl, as Told by Herself* (1906).

The standard work on the defense of industrial society is Richard Hofstadter, *Social Darwinism in American Thought, 1860–1915** (1948); it needs to be qualified now by Irwin G. Wyllie, "Social Darwinism and the Businessman," *Proceedings of the American Philosophical Society,* CIII (1959), 629–635. The argument over the role of government in the economy is further elaborated in Sidney Fine, *Laissez Faire and the General-Welfare State** (1956). The best study on the author of pragmatism is Ralph Barton Perry, *The Thought and Character of William James** 2 vols. (1935).

Books on the writers of the period are numerous. Covering all the writers in authoritative and concise fashion is *Literary History of the United States,* ed. by Robert Spiller, et al. (1963). It also contains a voluminous bibliography. Among the works on individual authors only a few, selected ones can be mentioned. One of the best is Henry Nash Smith, *Mark Twain: The Development of a Writer* (1962). The most recent and perhaps the finest biography of Twain is Justin Kaplan, *Mr. Clemens and Mark Twain* (1966). Thomas Beer, *Stephen Crane* (1923) is the most thought provoking but contains factual errors; more reliable but not as well written is John Berryman, *Stephen Crane** (1950). Two complementary works on Howells are Everett Carter, *Howells and the Age of Realism* (1954), and Van Wyck Brooks, *Howells, His Life and World* (1959). The definitive study on the life of Henry James is Leon Edel, *Henry James,** 3 vols. (1953–1962), with one still being written. A good single volume piece of scholarship is F. W. Dupee, *Henry James** (1951). Arlin Turner, *George W. Cable, A Biography* (1956) is probably the finest work on that writer. Interpretative and informative is Hugh Morrison, *Louis Sullivan, Prophet of Modern Architecture** (1935). Also very good on architecture is Carl W. Condit, *The Rise of the Skyscraper* (1952). The most rewarding studies of the relevant painters are two by Lloyd Goodrich, *Winslow Homer* (1959), and *Thomas Eakins, His Life and Work* (1933); and one by Fairfield Porter, *Thomas Eakins* (1959).

CHRONOLOGICAL TABLE, 1876-1900

1876

Greenback party made its first nomination for president.
Custer defeated at Little Big Horn.
Alexander Graham Bell's Telephone patented.
Philadelphia Exposition held.
Founding of Society of Ethical Culture.
First National League baseball game played.

1877

Radical Reconstruction ended in the South.
Munn v. *Illinois* upheld Granger laws.
Thomas A. Edison invented the phonograph.
Henry James wrote *The American*.
Thomas Eakins painted "William Rush Carving the Allegorical Figure of the Schuylkill River."

1878

Bland—Allison Act passed.
Democrats won control of Congress: first time since 1858.

1879

First practical incandescent lamp made by T.A. Edison.

F.W. Woolworth opened his first successful 5-and-10 cent store.
Church of Christ Scientist founded in Boston.
Henry George published *Progress and Poverty*.

1880

U.S. Census: 50,155,783 (28.2%urban).
Salvation Army organized in the U.S.

1881

James A. Garfield, president.
National Red Cross organized.
Henry James' *Portrait of a Lady*,
Helen Hunt Jackson's *A Century of Dishonor* published.
Wharton School of Finance and Economy founded.

1881– 1885

Chester A. Arthur, president.

1882

First Chinese Exclusion Act passed by Congress.

1883

Pendleton Act (civil service reform) passed.
New York World acquired by Joseph

Pulitzer; became first important example of "yellow journalism."

1884

George Eastman discovered process of dry-plate photography on paper-backed film.
Mark Twain's *Adventures of Huckleberry Finn,*
George Washington Cable's *Grandissimes* published.

1884–1914

Skyscraper architecture introduced.

1885–1889

Grover Cleveland, president.

1885–1914

Immigration from eastern and southern Europe reached peak.

1885

William Dean Howell's *Rise of Silas Lapham,* George Washington Cable's *The Silent South* published.
Winslow Homer painted "Fog Warning."

1886

Radicals and police clashed in Haymarket Massacre.
American Federation of Labor founded.
Stanton Coit started first settlement house.
Otto Mergenthaler invented the linotype machine.
Henry James' *The Bostonians,* and *Princess Cassamassima* published.

1887

Interstate Commerce,
General Allotment (Dawes) acts passed.
William D. Howell's *The Minister's Charge* published.

1888

Louisville introduced Australian ballot to the United States.
Edward Bellamy's *Looking Backward* published.

1889

Pan-American Congress organized in Washington.
Hull–House founded in Chicago by Jane Addams.

1890

Sherman Anti-Trust and
Silver Purchase acts passed.
McKinley Tariff Bill enacted.
Alfred T. Mahan's *Influence of Sea Power Upon History,*
George Washington Cable's *The Negro Question,* and
William D. Howell's *A Hazard of New Fortunes* published.
Winslow Homer painted "Winter Coast."

1891

California Institute of Technology founded.
University of Chicago founded by John D. Rockefeller.
Louis Sullivan's Wainwright building (St. Louis) erected.

1892

Populist party founded.
Homestead Steel,
Coeur d'Alene Silver strikes.

1893

Sherman Silver Purchase Act repealed.
First international copyright law.
Frederick Jackson Turner's address, "The Significance of the Frontier in American History," delivered.
Stephen Crane's *Maggie, a Girl of the Streets* published.

1893–1897

Grover Cleveland, president.

1893–1896

Panic of 1893 resulted in failure of 491 banks and over 15,000 commercial institutions.

1894

Pullman Company strike smashed by federal troops.
Coxey's army of unemployed marched on Washington.
Wilson-Gorman Tariff Bill enacted.
Mark Twain's *Pudd'nhead Wilson,*
W. H. Harvey's *Coin's Financial School,*
William Dean Howell's *A Traveler from Altruria* published.

1895

U.S. v. *E.C. Knight* decision weakened Sherman Act.

National Association of Manufacturers first met.
Stephen Crane's *Red Badge of Courage* published.

1896

Plessy v. *Ferguson* set separate-but-equal doctrine.
Maximum Freight Rate case weakened I.C.C.
Billy Sunday began evangelical career.

1897

U.S. v. *Trans-Missouri Freight Assoc.* applied Sherman Act to railroad combinations.

1897–1901

William McKinley, president.

1898

Spanish-American War (April 21–Dec. 10).
Hawaii annexed.

1899

Open Door policy for China secured by the United States
Addystone Pipe and Steel Co. v. *U.S.:* pool among steel, iron manufacturers illegal.
John Dewey's *The School and Society,*
Thorstein Veblen's *Theory of the Leisure Class* published.
Winslow Homer painted "The Gulf Stream."

1900

First quantity production automobile factory built by Olds Company in Detroit.
Andrew Carnegie's *Wealth* published.

c. 1900

Frank Lloyd Wright introduced "prairie house."

1900–1910

"Ash Can School" of realistic painters emerged.

INDEX

A

Adams, Charles Francis, 163
Adams, Henry, 124, 131, 179
Addams, Jane, 14
Addystone Pipe and Steel Company
  v. *United States,* 49
Adler, Felix, 185
Adventures of Huckleberry Finn,
  The, 191, 197, 198
Africa, 163
Agassiz, Louis, 184
Age of Reform, The, 128
Agricultural Wheel, 81
Agriculture, and exports, 75, 78; revolution
  in, 20, 69, 75–77, 83 *See also* Farmers
Aguinaldo, Emilio, 163
Altgeld, John Peter, 12, 124, 129, 134
Aluminum Company of America, 35
American Commonwealth, The, 120, 182
American Federation of Labor, 12, 89, 91, 92,
  93, 129, 130, 169
American Protective Association, 176
American Railway Union, 133, 134
American Sugar Refining Company, 43
American, The, 196
American Tobacco Company, 44
Anaconda Copper Company, 43
Anaconda silver mine, 61
Anarchism, and anarchists, 124, 196 *See also*
  Haymarket riot
Ancient Order of Hibernians, 88
Anti-Monopoly party, 80–81
Anti-Semitism, 128, 179
Antitrust movement, 46–49 *See also* Sherman
  Antitrust Act
APA. *See* American Protective Association
Architecture, 200–201
Armour and Company, 43
Armour, Philip, 36
Arthur, Chester A., 96, 97, 102, 103, 115, 116
A.R.U. *See* American Railway Union
Atlantic Monthly, 153, 191

B

Baker, Ray Stannard, 132
Baltimore and Ohio Railroad, 24, 26
Balzac, Honoré de, 191
Banking. *See* Investment banking
Banking Act of 1863, 33
Banking Act of 1864, 33
Beard, Charles, 36
Beard, Mary, 36
Beecher, Henry Ward, 184
Bell, Alexander Graham, 2, 35
Bellamy, Edward, 14, 15, 16, 154, 168, 191, 202

Bell Telephone Company, 35
Belmont, August, 135
Bemis, Samuel Flagg, 152, 153
Bethlehem Steel Company, 36
Big business, 42–45, 80, 113, 187
Bimetallism, 135
Bismarck, Otto von, 113, 175
Blaine, James G., 96, 97, 98, 112, 115, 155
Blair Education Bill (1880's), 102, 109
Blair, Henry, 102
Bland-Allison Act (1878), 110
Bland, Richard, 137
Borden, Gail, 36
Bostonians, The, 196
Bourbons (southern conservative Democrats),
  102
Brace, Loring, 170
Brandeis, Louis B., 179
Brazil, 157
British Guiana, 156
Bryan, William Jennings, 129, 140, 143, 149,
  150, 163, 164
Bryce, James, 114, 120, 182
Buchanan, Joseph, 90
Burlington Lines, 75
Butler, Marion, 142

C

Cable, George Washington, 198–199
Calvinism, 172
Campaigns, political. *See* Political campaigns
Canada, and Indians, 68–69; and violence, 68
Carlisle, John G., 135, 155, 163
Carnegie, Andrew, 36, 41, 175, 187, 188, 203
Carnegie Steel Company, 43
Catholic Charities Review, 177
Catholicism and Catholics, 98, 174–177, 179,
  184, and racism, 177
Cattle raising, 63–66
Central Pacific Railroad, 26, 27
Century of Dishonor, A, 6, 68–69
Cervera, Pascual, 161
Chicago Exposition (1893), 124
Child labor, 15, 83–84, 86
China, commercial partition of, 163; Open
  Door policy in, 153
Chinese Exclusion Act (1882), 9 *See also*
  Immigrants, Chinese
Christian Science, 169, 173–174, 179
Cigar Makers Union, 91
Civil service, 97, 114–116
Clapham, John, 21
Clemens, Samuel Langhorne. *See* Twain,
  Mark
Cleveland, Grover, 96–97, 98, 99, 109, 112,

Tariff

Latin America, 96, 113, 155, 157 *See also* Brazil; Venezuela
Lease, Mrs. Mary Elizabeth, 127
Leo XIII, 177
Lewis, Sinclair, 191
Lilienthal, Max, 178
Lincoln, Abraham, 4, 97, 119, 120, 137
Lloyd, Henry D., 142
Lodge Bill (1890), 103
Lodge, Henry Cabot, 103, 153
Lôme, Depuy de, 158
London, Jack, 200
Looking Backward, 14, 16, 191 *See also* Bellamy, Edward

M

McCormick reaper, 76
McCoy, Joseph, 63
McKinley Tariff and Tariff Act (1890), 7, 103, 111–113, 120, 128, 136, 137, 155, 164
McKinley, William, 112, 129, 149, 153, 158, 164; and Gold standard, 142; and Spanish-American War, 159–162
Macune, Charles W., 81
Maggie, A Girl of the Streets, 199, 200
Mahan, Alfred T., 153, 156
Mahone, William, 102, 103
Maine, 159
Main Street, 191
Marxism. *See* Socialism
Maximum Freight Rate case (1896), 30
Meat-packing industry, 44
Mechanization, 34–36, 58
Mergenthaler, Ottmar, 21
Miles, Nelson, 162
Military pensions, 118
Mills Tariff Bill (1888), 112
Minister's Charge, The, 196
Molly Maguires, 88
Monroe Doctrine, 156, 157
Moody, Dwight L., 172, 173
Morgan, J. P., 36, 46, 135, 143
Mormonism and Mormons, 58, 59, 169, 173, 179
Mugwumps, 115, 138
Munn v. *Illinois,* 29, 30
Mutual Aid, 188

N

National Alliance. *See* Northern Alliance
National Association of Manufacturers, 155
National Banking Act (1864), 139
National Banking System, 81
National Biscuit Company, 44
National Catholic War Council, 177
National Farmers' Alliance, 81
"Nationalism," 154
Nationalist, The, 16
National Labor Union, 88–89
Nation, The, 115, 124
Nativism, 176

Naturalism, 199–200
Natural resources, 32
Natural selection, 183–184, 187
Negro and Negroes, 2, 7, 81, 118, 198; disenfranchisement of, 151–152, 163; and Populism, 127; and Spanish-American War, 160; and unions, 92; and voting, 7, 101, 103, 182
Negro Question, The, 199
New Deal, The, 80, 108, 114
Newton, Isaac, 183–184
New York Central Railroad, 25, 28
New York Evening Post, 138
New York Herald, 124
New York Times, 11, 115
Nickle Plate Line, 28
NLU. *See* National Labor Union
Norris, Frank, 200
Norris-LaGuardia Act (1932), 134
Northern Alliance, 81, 82
Northern Pacific Railroad, 27, 75
Nugent, W. T. K., 128

O

Old Creole Days, 198
Olney, Richard, 48, 133, 135, 156, 157
On the Origin of Species by Means of Natural Selection, 183, 185
Open Door policy, 153

P

Pacific Railway Acts (1862), (1864), 22, 26
Page, Walter Hines, 153
Panic of 1837, 88
Panic of 1857, 88
Parrington, Vernon, 190
"Patriots of America," 154
Patrons of Husbandry. *See* Grange
Peirce, Charles S., 189, 201, 202
Pendleton Act (1883), 115, 117
Pennsylvania Railroad, 24, 26
Pension Bureau, 118
People's party, 82, 125–127 *See also* Populism
Perlman, Selig, 92
Philadelphia and Reading Railroad, 129
Philadelphia Gas Ring, 108
Philadelphia Exposition (1876), 2
Philippines, 152, 157, 158, 160, 162, 163, 164
Pillsbury, John S., 36
Pinkertons, 125
Plessy v. *Ferguson,* 152
Political campaigns (1884), 98; (1892), 127 *See also* Elections, Congressional; Elections, national
Polk, James K., 117, 119, 120
Pollack, Norma, 128
Populism and Populists, 66, 82, 114, 124–129, 130, 138, 139, 140, 141-143, 149, 150, 151, 154
Populist Response to Industrial America, The, 128

2 3 4 5 6 7 8 9 10 11 12 13 14 15 16 17 18 19 20 21 22 23 24 25 SH 74 73 72 71 70 69 68